The Voyage of the *Cormorant*

Christian Beamish

The Voyage of the *Cormorant*

Patagonia Books, an imprint of Patagonia Inc., publishes a select number of titles on wilderness, wildlife, and outdoor sports that inspire and restore a connection to the natural world.

FIRST EDITION

Printed in Canada on 100% recycled paper.

Project Manager: Jennifer Sullivan, Joyce Macias
Editor: John Dutton
Illustrator: Ken Perkins
Design & Production: Good Apples

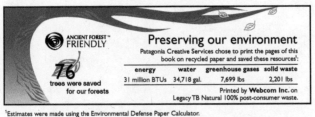

ANCIENT FOREST™ FRIENDLY

76 trees were saved for our forests

Preserving our environment

Patagonia Creative Services chose to print the pages of this book on recycled paper and saved these resources[1]:

energy	water	greenhouse gases	solid waste
31 million BTUs	34,718 gal.	7,699 lbs	2,201 lbs

Printed by **Webcom Inc.** on Legacy TB Natural 100% post-consumer waste.

[1]Estimates were made using the Environmental Defense Paper Calculator.

FSC
www.fsc.org
MIX
Paper from responsible sources
FSC® C004071

Cover illustration: Ken Perkins
Back cover inset photo: Christian Beamish Collection

Library of Congress Control Number 2012934399
ISBN 978-1-938340-03-1

Contents

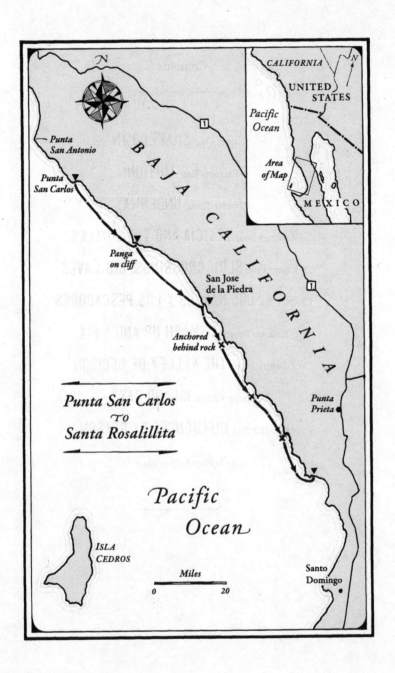

N

CALIFORNIA

UNITED STATES

N

Pacific Ocean

Area of Map

MEXICO

Punta San Antonio

Punta San Carlos

B A J A   C A L I F O R N I A

1

Panga on cliff

San Jose de la Piedra

Anchored behind rock

Punta San Carlos
TO
Santa Rosalillita

Punta Prieta

1

Pacific Ocean

ISLA CEDROS

Miles

0   20

Santo Domingo

CHAPTER 1
SHAKEDOWN

The fishermen sorted their meager catch on the beach in their workboats – the ubiquitous pangas of Baja California. There were four men, two in each boat, and they used a rusted out truck with threadbare tires to drag the vessels from the surf. I left my station wagon – also well on its way to rusting through – with my boat and trailer on the bluff and went down to where they were working.

As I approached, one of the men gestured towards my boat, her freshly painted wood and fine lines too pretty by far amid the ruined lobster traps, discarded lines, and sun-bleached husks of fish on the beach.

"You like the ocean?" he asked in English. Not waiting for a reply, he held up his hands as if to ward off the sea and said, "I don't."

The other fishermen glanced at my boat as they worked, pulling at their grimy nets and tossing out small crabs and strands of seaweed. Big surf rumbled shoreward in broad swaths of foam.

"We go out because we have to – to live," the man continued.

I nodded. "But the ocean is very beautiful here," I said.

"Not beautiful," he said. "*Peligroso.*"

"*Peligroso también,*" I agreed.

He asked what I did for work as he wrenched a foot-long sand shark from his net with a popping sound, then pitched it to the sand.

"I'm a writer, *un escritor*, for a surfing magazine," I told him.

"You better write a lot," he said, gesturing at the surf, "if you're going out there."

I built *Cormorant*, my 18-foot open boat, in 22 months – from August 2005 to June 2007 – on weekends and nights in the single-car garage of the studio apartment I rented in San Clemente, California. Working from a set of plans drawn by Iain Oughtred on the Isle of Skye in Scotland, I laminated stem and stern pieces; set up molds for the hull on a building frame; cut, bent, and secured planks; and saw a vessel steadily emerge from my efforts.

Pointed at both ends, with sleek, even curves, *Cormorant* carries more than a hint of her Viking longboat lineage. Under sail she glides through the water, with a large, trapezoidal lugsail for the main and a smaller, triangular mizzen sail, both in tanbark, which glows red in afternoon light.

I also had a set of narrow-bladed oars meant for sea work, and two spare oars as well. There would be no motor.

Modeled on traditional Shetland Islands fishing craft called sixareens – rugged, open boats that plied the North Atlantic from the Viking age until the advent of internal combustion – *Cormorant* differed from them only in her modern materials: Marine-grade plywood for the hull, secured with epoxy to timbers of Douglas fir for the keel.

A two-week supply of food, water, and gear in dry bags fit neatly in the boat, and I secured my surfboard in a padded bag over the top of my stowed equipment. My plan was to sail the sparsely populated Pacific coast of central Baja, landing in coves to camp and ride waves. This was a test run, a short getaway from work to gauge the feasibility of longer trips in the future. For now, I budgeted 10 days to sail along 100 miles of coast.

A culmination of various impulses – for time alone, for wilderness surfing, and for something I thought of as "full nature immersion" – the expedition before me also represented a living experiment. I had the notion that traveling in an ancient mode, removed from the ceaseless roar

and electronic thrum of contemporary life, I could connect to
the most basic aspect of my nature. Not so much my nature
as an individual, but my nature as a member of our species
shaped by longstanding, elemental human practices and by
the elements themselves.

I wanted to know more about what I had come to think
of as "blood memory" – a physical intimation I had of my
ancestors' knowledge. I felt it once, clearing brush under a
low forest canopy in the Santa Cruz Mountains. It had come
to me unmistakably, in the hard physical labor, that my body
had been formed by the very work that I was engaged with:
cutting limbs with a handsaw and hauling them down the
steep hillside. Even the slant of the light through the trees…
all of it was already in me and was merely activated by
repeating what my ancestors had done.

Cormorant was my way of trying to know the world as
it was before – a wilder place, where magic showed itself in
weather and animal encounters.

————————⟶

Big waves, cresting far outside the point, with 10-foot walls
of foam crashing in, prevented me from launching *Cormorant*
on the morning I first met the fishermen. I surveyed the next
point south through my binoculars and saw massive plumes
of whitewater and muscular bands of swell stretching out to
the horizon. Picturing *Cormorant* smashed to pieces in the
shorebreak, I decided to wait, make coffee on the camp stove,
and organize my gear. Later, I drove into the deserted fish

camp, the plywood shacks leaning slapdash and empty like so many forts built by slingshot-toting boys. The place was empty, without even a skinny dog around to bark a warning.

Leaving my wagon and boat, I walked into the desert and climbed the first knoll about three-quarters of a mile back on the coastal plane. Brick-red pumice stones covered the ground, and little sage plants and delicate desert flowers splashed the hillside.

I made a sketch of the camp and the headland some miles south and Punta San Carlos to the north, with the broad sweep of the bay, and including the huge mesa between the two that tops a long run of steep ravines. Below my hillside perch, the 15 shanties of camp seemed the perfect representation of man's world – ordered even in their loose conglomeration but paltry in design compared to these intricate and aromatic plants.

I was born in 1969, and I grew up in Newport Beach, California. I lived with my mother during the week and with my dad on the weekends, sleeping on a yellow vinyl pad on the floor of the room he rented from an elderly lady. In the morning, at first light, we surreptitiously put the pad back on her patio furniture, and set off for the beach.

Dad took me to surf spots all around Southern California from the time I was little, and I rode a foam surfboard he bought me, wearing a thick wetsuit with short legs and long sleeves. I loved the petroleum smell of neoprene and the pervasive smell of surf wax in the shops we visited in my yearning for a fiberglass board.

Dad would not let me get one at first, because he'd almost drowned in the '50s at Malibu when the surfer-actor, Peter Lawford, ran into him on a redwood plank and knocked Dad cold. He would have preferred if I just bodysurfed like him, particularly since he didn't like the pot-smoking surf culture of the late 1970s, being more of a Tony Bennett and Frank Sinatra man.

We stopped at liquor stores after the beach, where Dad would get a Coors in a paper sack for the road and buy me Twinkies and chocolate milk. "Let's not tell your mother about this," he said – every time.

Sometimes we slept in the car in a parking lot somewhere, and more than once a sheriff knocked on the windows with a flashlight. "Yes, sir. OK. We'll move along." And then a wearying night drive, aimless-seeming, but always southward through the coast towns. A murky, dawn surf at Windansea or Swami's would give some feeling of purpose to it all.

I got tubed one grey summer morning at Swami's for the first time – sea grass swaying in the clear water like mermaid hair, the whole section sheeting over me in silver. I knew I was on to something special then.

Jim, the neighbor across the street from my mother's house, was one of those pot-smoking '70s surfers that Dad didn't much care for. He had a bumper sticker on his VW van that read, "Happiness is sex and tube rides," and he gave me a purple 7'11" pintail semi-gun that he'd used in Hawai'i. I didn't tell Dad about the board. During the week, my best friend, Dave Misterly, and I walked to the beach most days after school – he holding the tail of the board, me on the nose – and took turns riding waves, laying the foundation for further surf travels together. By the time Dad relented and bought me my first, true high-performance board, I was already a competent surfer.

I soon got into competitive surfing, and nothing else mattered to me. I shirked my schoolwork and fell into an ongoing battle with my mother about grades and the life-ruining prospect of being a surfer. The one thing my parents seemed to agree upon was that longhaired, dope-smoking youth were not acceptable role models for me. I looked up to Tom Curren, who, before his three world titles, was still an amateur and definitely not the longhair, '70s burnout my parents feared I would become. But at 12-years-old, I could not convey the artistry of his surfing to them or how pursuing something so pure and beautiful could never be a bad thing.

It didn't matter much ultimately, since my career as a competitive surfer was underwhelming. And as my high school years wore on, it became clear to me that I had to find something to do with myself upon graduation. I had a job at a Hawaiian shave ice place at the beach but couldn't see adding a pizza delivery gig to that position and living in a shared apartment in Newport's surf ghetto. The town was awash in cocaine, and the personal tragedies of some of the trust-fund kids of my generation were already playing out. The battle with my mother over the lack of direction my life was taking continued, and the prospect of still living with her and smiling at her friends and accepting her boyfriends was no more appealing than being a pizza boy and living at a party house.

A U.S. Navy brochure arrived, and I realized that that was something I could do, something that would get me out – the Navy at least would be cut and dried, I would know exactly what was expected of me. I could just show up. I wouldn't have to win or be cool. I imagined being on watch onboard a frigate, wearing a woolen pea coat and drinking coffee from a tin mug. I thought that it was something Hemingway would do, or that I was like Jack Kerouac in the merchant marine in *Lonesome Traveler*.

So, in 1987, two weeks after graduating from Newport Harbor High School, I had a shaved head and was doing push-ups at boot camp in San Diego, urged on by my Filipino company commander whose preferred form of address was, "Motherfucker!"

I ended up with the Seabees, in construction, wearing fatigues, combat boots, and carrying an M16 rifle. I was sent to Saudi Arabia during the Gulf War in 1991, and I was at Camp Al Jubail when they unleashed hell on the Iraqis that first morning. An air raid siren wailed, and we stumbled in the dark from our tents. The spotlights on the tarmac left the camp in silhouettes and shadows: the insect-like helicopter fuselages, the scattered guard towers, the peaked tops of troop tents. Each Seabee and Marine carried his weapon; the sand stretched out in rolling dunes like an endless beach. The stars shimmered clear like diamond points in the perfectly black night sky.

Two F-18 fighter jets came streaking low, bristling with ordnance in the glow of the afterburners. One minute later the horizon erupted in flame and we felt the distant thudding of the bombs in our boot soles, and I thought how glad I was to be on "our" side. There was an evil sort of rush to the whole thing – a bloodlust for an enemy we had never seen.

Each of us – farm boy, city kid, and suburbanite alike – raised our weapons overhead and screamed a terrible, impotent war cry. It was the war cry we'd learned from the movies, and we stupidly played our parts while boys and men from mud-hut villages got incinerated, 50 miles away.

———————

"*No, no. Estoy soltero*" – a bachelor – I said when one of the other fishermen, Senor Aurelio Muñoz, asked me about my status, back at the San Carlos camp in Baja. The high surf had prevented my launch, and I was returning from my desert walk and pencil sketching when Sr. Aurelio invited me in for coffee.

He was a cherubic 50-year-old, a handsome, stout man who carried himself with straight-backed propriety. His blockhouse was the most prominent structure in the rickety little neighborhood, and it served as his kitchen, dining room, and storage area. Once inside, he put water in a pot to boil on the propane stove. The floor was smooth concrete; a calendar from 1987 hung on the wall with Jesus beckoning from the great beyond. A basket of onions, chilies, and garlic hung next to the picture. Sacks of rice and beans were stored in a glass-front cabinet adorned with pictures of family: a girl in her *quinceanera* gown, a hefty woman laughing in Aurelio's arms, two little boys on bicycles with gap-toothed smiles.

Aurelio poured hot water into a mug on the kitchen table in front of me where I sat. I stirred in a spoonful of Nescafé and a heaping spoonful of sugar and then slid the jars across to him. A band of afternoon light shone through the screen door, and flies lighted on the edges of our cups. We talked about women, and he told me about his first marriage to the heiress of a Baja general store who would never go out, or take a vacation, for fear of leaving the business, and how he left her finally and traveled all over Mexico just to have a look around.

I asked how long he thought the surf would be up, and he said two more days, adding that a *Norte* would probably start in soon – a devil wind off the high desert that we call the Santa Ana in California.

"*El Norte*," he said gravely, "*es peor que las olas grandes*." – the *Norte* is worse than the big surf.

The track into the San Carlos camp – an ill-advised drive in a Honda wagon – had been a four-hour, chassis-scraping crawl across the desert, winding down near the coast through a steep arroyo with boojum trees that seemed to mark a change in terrain to a realm of the ancient and mysterious. I hoped to arrange for someone to shuttle my station wagon and trailer 100 miles south to Santa Rosalillita, where I planned to haul out at the end of my trip.

I put the situation to Aurelio, hoping that he would be up for the job. He was not, but he suggested the other fisherman, Rudy, whom I had talked with that morning – the man who told me that he did not like the sea.

"*No te preocupes,*" Aurelio told me. "*Rudy es un amigo, un hombre muy bueno.*" They had worked together in the camp for 25 years, he said.

Aurelio then set to preparing a stew and told me about a girlfriend he had in the time between his first wife and the woman he's married to now. "*Muy guapa,*" he began, moving his hand along the imaginary curve of her body as he cut the skin from an onion. He said that although the girlfriend had been good-looking, there was a problem with her manners: "*En el restaurante, con gente respetable,*" he pointed out, emphasizing the word respetable, "*dijo ella, ¡Oye! ¡Traje las placas, cabron!*" – Hey! Bring the plates you son-of-a-bitch!

"*No es aceptable,*" he said, shaking his head.

"*No,*" I agreed.

The stew he made was subtle and rich, with urchin roe and crabmeat in risotto-like rice infused with a broth of root vegetables.

There had been no question of whether or not I would join him; it just seemed he had taken me in, in an almost fatherly way.

Later that night, after we had eaten, Rudy senior, Rudy junior, and another man whose name I never got came over to sit around the kitchen table under the single, dangling light bulb.

Rudy senior started right in. "You have to be crazy, *loco,*" he told me, "to want to go out in your little *bote.*"

"I didn't want to go today," I replied.

"That's good," he said, "because you would die."

Aurelio jumped in and told them that I had built *Cormorant*, as I had explained to him earlier in the afternoon.

"You don't have no motor?" Rudy asked me.

"*¡Sí, tengo dos!*" I exclaimed, making a show of kissing each bicep. "*¡Izquierda y derecha!*" And the men guffawed, calling out, "*¡Hijo de la chingada!*" and slapping the tabletop.

There was some discussion about which seabird is the cormorant, and I described the black shiny feathers, the long graceful neck, the sharp beak, and the webbed feet that allow my boat's namesake to swim three- or four-minutes underwater amid the crashing surf of his rocky hunting grounds. "She's a little boat," I said, "*pero muy suave en el mar...*"

Rudy senior, clearly enjoying himself, said, "*¡Si, si! ¡Es el pato!*" – it's the duck! Aurelio and the others found this hilarious, and I laughed too.

The talk turned to the latest drug violence. A police station had been attacked by *narcotraficantes* just up in San Quintín the week before. We shrugged our shoulders.

"*¿Quien sabe?*" – who knows? Where does violence like that come from?

A second block building stood in front of the one we were in and was set right on the cliff's edge with a veranda. This was Aurelio's bunkhouse. When the men went back to their places, we followed a short dirt path and went inside, where Aurelio had three bunks set up. He slept against the back wall with a radio on a bed stand playing scratchy ballads. He gave me a bunk on the opposite side by the front door, which thumped in its jamb with the wind.

I was immensely grateful to have landed here, warm in my bag in the pitch dark – even with the radio's static and Aurelio starting to snore.

———————————▶

After the Navy, and after college in Santa Cruz, I had a job as a handyman for the youth hostel at the Pigeon Point Lighthouse, 50 miles south of San Francisco. A ship captain's room came with the job, with a view of the sea all around, and from there I suited up and ran down a dirt trail to ride peeling green waves in the lee of the point.

The Coast Range rises up behind the point and runs across in a high, forested ridge, and the craggy lighthouse cove, with its waves – spinning little beauties – made it the best place I had ever lived. A vision for a boat soon came to me and left little room for other thoughts. Old photos at the lighthouse showed Portuguese whalers with their lateen-rigged, wooden craft that the men worked in and out of the cove, and the desire for that kind of life came to me like a need.

The ocean was alive at the lighthouse. A fisherman came sometimes and climbed out to a certain rock under my window. He never cast out far, preferring to let his line down and then just to stand, stock still, with his head tilted slightly as if he were trying to thread a needle with his eyes closed or to feel minute movements with a delicate instrument. Then, with a sharp, upward jerk of the rod, he would reel the line in quickly and hoist out a long and green-mottled lingcod.

When the man left the seal family returned, hauling out on their kelpy platform rocks. Cormorants stood stoic and then flew off according to their own schedules and reasons. Whales passed on their migrations in spring and fall. One evening a blue whale passed just off the farthest rocks of the point, so long that its back went on like a sidewalk until finally the little dorsal fin and the wide tail flukes slipped out of the water, hovered, and then slipped back in again.

A diver had been killed by a great white on the north side of the point 20 years before, and I could feel a presence sometimes out surfing. I found a fresh kill once in the cove on the north side, a female elephant seal, the semi-circle bite like a cliché, something from a bad movie, but real enough there.

I wrote an essay for *The Surfer's Journal* about living and surfing in the shadow of the lighthouse and shaping surfboards in an old storage room there. That established a working relationship with the magazine and, ironically, it was this ode to my favorite place that led to my leaving there. About a year after the article came out, I was offered a job as an associate editor at *The Journal* and I could not refuse – much as I loved the beachcombing and surfing lifestyle that my handyman gig allowed. The exchange involved swapping my ship captain's room at Pigeon Point for a studio apartment in San Clemente.

I knew San Clemente from trips with Dad to Trestles in my surfing youth, so, as far as wave riding was concerned, I was pretty happy. Also, the prospect of using my degree in literature as an editor – at the prestigious *Surfer's Journal* no less – was a great opportunity. The only real hitch in all of this was that I loved a young woman who was learning to farm at the sustainable agriculture program at UC Santa Cruz. For a while she still loved me, but miles and time did their work, and within six months we were over as a couple.

I realize now, seven years afterwards, that I had so idealized my relationship with the farmer woman that she ceased to exist as a real person. I was so enthralled by my vision of a cabin with her in the Coast Range, where she would tend a garden and orchard and I would build a boat and surfboards and write about the life we lived together. When she told me that she'd fallen in love with another farmer from her program and that they were moving to Vermont together, I felt the loss so keenly that I did not think I would ever completely recover. I had lost my beloved, but more than that, my beloved dream of the kind of life I would have with her.

My response to this situation was healthy in one way, not so healthy in another. I started building *Cormorant* in the garage. But I also began drinking the better part of six beers a night, with more than a few nights of whisky to fortify the buzz. I had been drinking since early high school and really perfected my approach in the Navy. But this was different. This was a creeping desire, never quite satiated, that reared its head at about three in the afternoon when I would start thinking about the coldies waiting in the fridge at home.

Aurelio got up in the dark, went to the cookhouse, and boiled water for coffee. I followed him soon after. As he predicted, *El Norte* had started at about two in the morning. A piece of tin roofing had been clanging steadily somewhere in the camp

since then, like someone kicking an empty washer. Three
other men, whom I had not met the day before, were standing
out front, and Aurelio offered them coffees. Then the Rudys,
senior and junior, and another man whose name I did not
know, arrived, and the eight of us stood sheltering from the
strong wind in front of the block building like surfers gathered
on the coast at first light.

The wind seemed to come on stronger as the orange band
of sunrise broadened in the sky to the east. We watched
rovelendos – furious blasts from the slot canyons to the south
– rip at the ocean and tear the tops off the thick swells that
still poured in, and one of the men whistled and raised his
eyebrows as if to say, "Imagine being in that!"

There would be no fishing, or voyaging, on this day, and
by the time the sun peeked over the mesa, the fishermen
who'd showed at Aurelio's were sitting three abreast in their
truck to make the long drive back up the track to the highway
and their homes in El Rosario. The Rudys walked off to their
shack, and Aurelio put a pot of oatmeal on the stove.

I went out to check on *Cormorant* and found everything
still secured, but coated in the powdery dust of camp;
runnels of dirt caked the interior. Everything inside my car
had a heavy dusting as well, since I had forgotten to put the
windows up the night before. I grabbed my jacket from the
passenger seat, and fine sand poured off it like grains through
an hourglass. A heavy gust pushed at my back like an unseen
pair of hands, and then pushed even harder. The water looked
its darkest blue, with a million ridges of whitecaps across the

bay rolling incessantly seaward. Any amount of sail up on a day like this would flip my boat right over.

I turned and walked back to Aurelio's, bent at the waist with my arms crossed and head down against the wind. He boiled another pot of water for coffee, and we sat at the kitchen table at what already felt like our respective places. The prospect of another day in camp, particularly with this wind that made doing anything outside almost impossible, weighed on me. I stood and looked out the screen door, but the ocean was the same shredded mess I had just seen.

"Maybe *mañana*," Aurelio said, making his first comment in English as he poured the water, "*es* good for you."

I nodded, and sat down and made a cup.

The wind gusted terribly then, as if the earth's atmosphere had turned inside out and sucked down onto the blockhouse. "*Mi hermano…*" Aurelio said when the gust passed, and then told me how his brother had been lost at sea, fishing from camp here. They found his body 100 miles down the coast in the waters off Santa Rosalillita, where I meant to sail.

I asked how long ago it happened.

"*Quince años*," – fifteen years before – he said. He said it so calmly, and I couldn't tell if he was simply relating an event from his own life or warning me of the forces I was preparing to encounter. Either way, he did not elaborate, and I let the silence linger.

Changing the subject, Aurelio said, "*Muchos gringos vienen aquí*," and then began to tell me about them. He told me about the gringos who had left their 30-foot sailboat untended in the

bay for months until the ground tackle finally gave way and
the boat disappeared.

In another tale, straight out of a *telenovelas*, a Mexican TV
soap opera, Aurelio had an FBI agent staying in one of the
abandoned vans behind camp, wearing only shabby clothes
and a long, unkempt beard. The agent watched the place for
six months to see if it was a transit point for drug runners;
he later returned in a helicopter, immaculately groomed and
wearing a fine black suit, to thank Aurelio for his help.

But my favorite one was about a guy who Aurelio said
looked a little like me, only with a longer beard and lighter
eyes. He'd shown up on foot, with a small knapsack, parched
and out of water. After recuperating for a few days, and
meditating in lotus position for long periods on the veranda,
the fellow started walking again, heading south on the track
for Cabo San Lucas.

I was ready to head south too, at least to check the coast
beyond the next headland.

The journeys of my forefathers, their migration from Ireland,
to New Zealand, to California, held great sway on my thoughts
– the "me" of today having been transported through time,
transported through bloodlines. Great-great-grandfather,
John Beamish, shipped out for New Zealand from Skibbereen,
County Cork, with his brother, Alleyn Beamish, in 1868,
little imagining that within the year they would be fighting
Maori warriors hand-to-hand at Turuturu-mokai, in Taranaki.

Alleyn was killed in the battle, shot in the neck by the deserter Charles Kane, who was later murdered by his adoptive tribesmen. John took a bullet from an Enfield through his shoulder, but he survived and later established a homestead in the thick forest land of Taranaki.

When I worked on a parks crew in the Coast Ranges of Northern California, cutting and hauling fallen limbs under a low canopy of oaks, I felt my great-great-grandfather's experiences on the land. Something in the slant of light and in the pulling free of branches, something in the good, steady cuts of the limb saw and the sweat across my shoulder blades, was deeply familiar. The feeling came on stronger as the work progressed. Not some misty déjà vu, but a clear, physical sense of inherited experience, very much like the work of building *Cormorant* – a blood memory.

Admittedly, I am shoe-horning my experiences in *Cormorant* into the experiences of my ancestor, straining to make a link, wrapped up in a romantic notion of something more meaningful than the endless running that day-in, day-out life seems so often to amount to. Our bodies are old – 100,000-years in their current form – contemporary experience, this digitized age, has no precedent in history.

Another admission: I am romantic, I dream-up radically impractical journeys just to try and feel or to intuit something from a past that may well have never existed – or not in the way I imagine it. Combined with this I have a tendency towards depressive states. My episodes have never been so bad that I couldn't get out of bed and face the day, but after my time at the lighthouse and losing the woman whom I thought

I loved so much, and drinking to bad effect every night, I felt
a shift come on that scared me. I wasn't ready to harm myself,
but I glimpsed a precipice in my mental state and noticed a
slide towards its edge, over which, I recognized, deep trouble
laid.

That was enough, finally, to get me to see a doctor, and
accept a prescription for anti-depressant medication. And so
I joined the millions of others who take Prozac to try and live
this life with a little less suffering.

The Rudys came back over in the afternoon as I was standing
at the screen door again, watching the frenzied sea and willing
the surf to drop for the first time in my life. I stepped aside to
let them in, and we exchanged observations about how bad
the wind was. Rudy asked me, jokingly, if I was going out
today, and I told him I thought it would be better to wait. He
agreed with Aurelio, however, that everything might calm
down tomorrow. I asked him about shuttling the Honda and
trailer down to Santa Rosalillita.

He winced and sucked air in between his teeth. *"Es muy
lejos,"* – very far – he told me. But, he added, *"Es posible."*

We agreed to talk about it more at his place and, wind-
be-damned, I put my jacket on and went out again. A flock
of gulls stood dumbly with their tails into *El Norte,* ceding
ground with a grudging waddle when I passed them on the
wet slurry of sand along the waterline. My trousers pulled at
my legs like flags wrapped around poles, and I walked with

my hood up to protect my ears; dry sand whipped across in phantom trails. Farther down the beach, I turned up a narrow canyon to the bluff top and made my way back towards the camp, thinking about what a fair price would be to shuttle the wagon and trailer.

Later, at the Rudys' place, I knocked on the plywood door, and Rudy junior, a young man of about 20, opened it for me. He had blue eyes and light brown hair, with none of the mestizo features of the other men in camp. He and Rudy senior were watching a tape on a VCR, which ran off a car battery charged by a small solar panel. Eddie Murphy, dubbed over in Spanish, hammed it up on the TV as an African prince dumbstruck by America.

I spoke in Spanish, taking care to note that I understood that driving my car and trailer to Santa Rosalillita, and their own truck there and back, would be quite an undertaking. *"¿Quatro horas por el viaje, verdad?"* – four hours for the trip? – I asked.

"Mas como cinco o sies," Rudy replied, turning off the TV. He noted that the desert track from camp to the highway would be slow going in my vehicle, a point which I conceded.

I offered 10 dollars an hour each, for a 10-hour return trip. This was not the time to try and haggle. Although I felt confident that the Rudys would do what I asked, I also felt that a willingness on my part to pay them adequately would go a long way towards maintaining good will. Besides, although I am not a rich man, 200 dollars one way or the other would not affect me terribly, and I imagined it was a pretty good day's wages here in Baja. There was also the question of gas for both vehicles, but when I counted up my cash, I only had 240 dollars.

"*Es* OK," Rudy senior said, and we shook hands on it. "My friend, Fito," Rudy told me, "you look for him in Santa Rosalillita. I will put your car there."

The wind quieted down as the sun began to set, and I organized my gear and swept out *Cormorant's* interior as well as I could. I sat at the kitchen table in Aurelio's place to write a note explaining my arrangement with the Rudys, thinking that if the Mexican police stopped them they would believe the story if for nothing else because my Spanish was so bad. Having pulled *Cormorant* off the trailer with Aurelio's help, and placed her on the beach alongside the fishermen's pangas, I walked across camp to the Rudys' place with my car keys and the note.

———————

At first light the next day, Rudy and Aurelio offered to give me a shove off. Standing knee-deep in the washing surf, each man grasped *Cormorant's* rail on opposite sides by the stern. With the next tumbling whitewater they pushed, and I leaned back into my oars, pulling deeply. *Cormorant* rose steeply up one swell then crashed down the backside almost exuberantly, as if happy to be on the water again, and I felt something of the old sea thrill I was seeking in this adventure.

The ragged swell had calmed, but there were still good, three- to five-foot waves spinning along the cliff line at the point in the blue light of dawn. I pulled farther outside to get well clear of the surf, and Rudy and Aurelio buzzed past in their pangas with the other men, and we waved farewell to one another. I watched them until they disappeared seaward, the drone of the outboards getting fainter and fainter. I zipped my jacket up and settled back to pulling on the oars over the silky water, away from the last outpost of shelter and people. The first rays of sun poured down, and the exhilaration of the open miles ahead came with the same heady sense of freedom I got walking off the Navy base for the last time, many years before.

I sailed for hours and hours, the coast trending away to the southeast until it became a blur of shapes with the desert stretching off far behind. Whitecaps appeared around mid-day, and *Cormorant* rushed along in the heave and roll – waves now higher than her rail, now well below again. The movement was mesmerizing, and I drew farther and farther from shore until the water held the deep blue of the truly open sea, the coast like a fading memory. But a whitecap rolled alongside the boat and sloshed in over the rail, soaking my trouser leg from hip to calf in shocking-cold seawater.

That snapped me into focus, and I dropped the main sail and lashed the tiller down with the rudder hard over so that *Cormorant* would turn up into the wind, driven by her mizzen alone. The swells had gotten steeper in the strengthening blow, and *Cormorant* bucked against them like a horse tied off short. Sitting on the aft-most thwart, I unfolded the waterproof chart with my free hand while holding the gunwale with the other. No single mesa or ancient volcano across the desert stood out distinctly enough to

determine with any certainty where I was on the coast, and
the headlands to the north all faded together in a hazy glare.
A run of high cliffs lay before me in the distance. There might
be a corner where they turned in and formed a cove, so I
prepared to head in and see.

Kneeling on my tightly packed dry bags, I began to shorten
sail, rolling up the bottom edge, with *Cormorant* rocking
heavily in the swell. Each time I do this I think that the term
"reefer" must have come from marijuana-smoking sailors on
the East India Company trade routes, or perhaps down in the
Caribbean. Whatever the etymology, I rolled the sail up and
tied it off in square, or "reef," knots.

Another whitecap sloshed into the boat, throwing spray in
my face.

When I was ready to raise sail again, my heart pounded
and hands shook with all this dangerous wallowing.
Cormorant made a sickeningly steep lurch when I sheeted-
in the main, and the boat shipped more gallons over the
starboard rail before she settled in to a hard heel. Bracing with
my foot against the daggerboard case, I leaned forward along
the port rail with all my weight on the driving reach to shore.
Cormorant accelerated like a surfboard when the swells lifted
the hull, and I strained at the tiller to drive her straight across
the faces, as she would easily flip if I allowed her to swing too
wildly.

The cliffs came into relief as I approached – a vertical
carapace of tannish-yellow sandstone spires, corrugated with
deeply eroded chutes. There was indeed a cove in the lee
of the cliff line. An old panga had been nudged to the edge

of the precipice overhead, its prow hovering over the wide, desolate Pacific like a totem or a funeral pyre made ready like something intended to channel spirits or to usher the dead to their final resting places. I dropped all sail, pulled the daggerboard from its case, and then lay on my belly to bring the rudder on board. All that done, I placed the oars in the locks and began working my way in.

As ragged as it had been outside, the water under the escarpments was merely textured by the wind, and a clean wave rose up and broke on a sandbar inside the cove. The next one caught me up as I nosed in and sent *Cormorant* tumbling towards the rocks in whitewater, sluicing sideways in the jumbling foam like a kayak in a rapid. I leapt overboard, clinging to the rail and dragging my heels to steer to the hard packed sand of the beach.

Any landing you can walk away from is a good landing, the saying goes, and it applies equally to airplanes and beach boats. But I now stood shivering on the wet sand in my sopping jacket and trousers, very far from any help, and the seriousness of my undertaking – the potential for real trouble – stood out more clearly than it had before. My good little ship *Cormorant* was not damaged on the landing, nor was I injured, but I still needed a moment to gather my thoughts before working my boat, bow-then-stern, up the beach. The surf was good though, and shedding my wet clothes, I changed into my wetsuit and paddled out once I had the boat secured.

Headlands with sandy coves that swept into crescent beaches formed the general character of this stretch of coast, where the waves hugged the curve of the shore in long, spiraling walls. The waves here were not monsters, but desert beauties; the joy in riding them came as much from their spangled plunging and sculpted curves, as from the sense of levitation and streaking speed.

I had brought only a 9'6" longboard with a slightly pulled-in outline, a "California gun" shaped with just these kinds of waves in mind. The board evoked freedom from the extraneous, which also resonated with *Cormorant's* clean lines. Each paddle stroke added to a reserve of forward motion so that I could pick up the wave early, while it was still an ocean swell, and then glide into a steadily steepening face.

Leaning into the initial turn, I felt like an albatross in flight as I cut a great, soaring arc over the vast and moving sea.

———————————

After surfing and with the last light of the day, I set up my tent at the base of the cliff, right next to *Cormorant* on a bed of cobblestones. I stripped my wetsuit and changed into dry pants with an army surplus sweater under a spare coat. I fired up the camp stove for a dinner of tortellini and hot ginger tea, relishing the heat and nourishment. After eating, I got in the tent with my sleeping bag and the padded surfboard cover for a bed, exhausted and satisfied by the day's efforts.

The surf crept closer on the rising tide, but I never heard it in my deep slumber, until it seemed as though a wave broke right at the vestibule of my tent, jarring me awake later in the night. I bolted up and zipped open the door to see a line of whitewater shooshing up to the very edge of the cobblestones in the beam of my headlamp. Spray pelted *Cormorant* just to the side of me, but the tide's crest came no higher than that one wave, and after a while, I lay down again until dawn.

Daybreak revealed a gray, low-tide morning, the water's edge so far down the beach that the night's encounter seemed more distant even than if I had dreamed it. I set a pot of water to boil on the camp stove and walked out to the farthest point under the cliffs. I dug a pit and thought of the latrine back at the San Carlos camp – flies in there, flies in the kitchen. I washed my hands, first in the sea, then rigorously with soap and fresh water back at my camp.

This is what it takes, I thought, to get some solitude. You travel days and days down a desert coastline and sail off by yourself. I saw not a soul, nor evidence of anybody besides the weirdly placed panga on the cliff top. And for all this effort I felt not free exactly, but at least not put-upon. There was no conversation to make, just an enveloping silence with the crash and roll of small waves to break the feeling of looking at a giant photograph. I was finally outside of the day-to-day, and perhaps outside of myself for a moment as well.

I heaved *Cormorant* around by her bow, and then by her stern in the first step of a long crabwalk to the surf. Hauling the 400-pound hull across the tide-exposed beach soon had me sweaty and frustrated, as I strained with vein-popping pulls and finally swore mightily, pissed-off and feeling stupid. Why I did not just drag *Cormorant* half way down the beach, stow my gear in her, and go surfing until the tide came up, I do not know. I must have still been on city-time – conscious that my journey had been delayed by the rough conditions back at Punta San Carlos and that my job awaited me back at the magazine. So I heaved until it felt like my arms would fall off, then lifted the water bottles in and crammed the dry bags in their places between the middle and forward thwarts until the first washes of seawater got under the hull and I could slide her into the water.

For all the strain of getting across the beach, the launching was uneventful, and I rowed out easily on the smooth, gray morning surface. *Cormorant* continued her silent momentum over the water after I laid down the oars and stood up to adjust my sweater. There was no wind. Kelp beds lay thickly here over a broad area. I sat down and dipped the oars again, and again, I pulled strongly, breathed evenly, and then pulled again, settling in to the strokes.

A harbor seal emerged behind the boat – dark chocolate in color with white flecks – then disappeared with barely a ripple. He surfaced 30 yards farther down, peering at me with globular, sea-goggle eyes. I said good morning softly, and he slipped back into his lair, and then came up again, tailing me at 20 yards for the next mile or so. With no daggerboard or rudder out, *Cormorant* slid over the dense kelp, and the effect was of rowing across a forest at treetop height.

It was migration time for the grey whales, and I would have thought that I would be seeing a lot of them en route to the lagoons just south of here. But the wild seas of the previous days had made it too rough to spot the whales' spouts or the round, glistening shapes of their backs. But later on this second day out, the sun began to burn off the marine layer, and I saw two of them no more than 100 feet off the starboard rail. A light breeze was starting in, and I raised the main to catch it, but the whales were gone from sight as quickly as they had appeared.

The day was long for the light wind, and I ambled along with my sails barely filled, almost thinking of nothing; there was nowhere to go, and no means of getting there any faster. The desert spread out in rolling hills here, with a broader run of beach than the previous day's high mesas and more prominent headlands. By sunset I had traveled 20 miles and lay about a mile seaward of the rock island at San Jose de La Piedra, where the chart showed (and where, Sr. Aurelio assured me, there exists) a light-tower.

And there it was, a faint illumination in the deepening evening.

The wind fell off, and I went to oars again, facing forward to keep a lookout for shoaling reefs as another line of sea cliffs lay ahead. The surf crashed into the steep walls and sea caves, and the moon at my back cast a faint glow. Still, I could see the next point in silhouette, darker against the night sky, and I pushed on, fairly sure now of where I was. Coming around the headland, I saw a campfire in the corner of the cove with a couple of trucks and tents set up. These would be surfers who drove out across the remote tracks for the waves and the solitude as well, and I was happy to see them, if only to have witnesses to my adventure. It was well and truly dark now, and I came in closer under oars. A big wave swept silently past lifting *Cormorant* but not catching her, and I turned and rowed for deeper water then threw the hook.

The moon and stars sparkled on the inky water. I leaned
against the aft thwart snuggled down in my sleeping bag,
wearing a wool cap and eating chocolate. Soft exhalations
came out of the darkness. I heard the breaths again and
propped myself on an elbow and there, six feet out, were five
dolphin floating side-by-side, the smooth domes of their heads
reflecting the night sky, their beaks glistening just on the
surface.

$$\longrightarrow$$

I surfed for a few hours with the campers in the cove the
next morning, after a strange night of dolphin dreams on the
boat. Later, I pulled anchor and put *Cormorant* on a broad
reach seaward until I lined up with the most prominent point
in the distance, perhaps 10 miles south. I had a beautiful,
intoxicating sail on the steady wind, making unbelievable time
surfing down the gentle swells with surges to seven knots.

The point came into view more clearly a few hours on, and I
began to think that I was farther south than I had anticipated.
I had passed a tallish, lighter colored headland with a big bay
swooping around inside to the southeast and then out again
to the more desolate place I was now off from. The wind was
coming on harder so I tied in all three reefs, and *Cormorant*
heeled over to starboard as I reached in to get closer to shore.
All tightened down, she was handling well despite the blow; I
was learning what a capable boat *Cormorant* is. The wind was
not relenting as the sun dipped towards the horizon. I had run
too long and squandered all my daylight; now I needed to find
a place to land or to anchor. I tacked and sailed in to a cove,

but the beach was too steep, with an ugly four-foot shore dump exploding on the sand. I knew better than to try to land there.

My remaining option seemed to be to try and take what cover I could behind a 30-foot high rock island where cormorants and pelicans were posted up for the night. A three-quarter moon shone down in the deepening dusk, and I threw the hook and dug out my warmest clothes: arctic army pants, wool socks and down booties, a woolen sweatshirt, army sweater, waterproof jacket over the top with a wool hat – wool gloves too. Working through worst-case scenarios, I considered the possibility of a horrible *Norte*, and having to swim in with flippers and a dry bag with clothes and food and water, but realized the best thing to do was to stay in the boat.

After eating a little, I stretched the rain fly over my head and tried to sleep. But sure enough, the wind pulled around to the north and started gusting to 30 knots. The anchor did its work beautifully, but I'd swung adjacent a reef with breaking surf and whitewater coming right across to *Cormorant*'s stern. I had to move. I retrieved the anchor (which fortunately worked free easily) and made my way across the cove under oars to the inside, northwest corner and re-set the anchor.

I slept for a while there, but heard and felt some surf nearby, with one wave in particular coming close enough for me to bolt upright to see what was happening. Once again, I'd swung in too close and if a bigger set had come through... well, I didn't want to think about it. So I pulled the hook once more and reset further off, then lit the candle lantern and hung it under the aft thwart for a little glowing calm in this night of tearing wind. I stretched out in my sleeping bag

finally, with my feet under the midships
thwart, and then slept pretty well in the
midst of the fray.

After such a precarious night, the day
dawned clear and calm. *Cormorant* had
remained snug at anchor through all the
turbulence of wind and swell, but as I
attempted to hang the rudder to sail, I
discovered that the brass screw that holds
the upper gudgeon for the rudder-pin had
sheared off in the previous days' workings.
Fortunately, I had a well-stocked tool- and
repair-kit in a paint bucket, and I used a
heavy stainless screw to replace the broken
brass one.

The light morning air moved us along
slowly as two fishermen motored up. The pilot
gestured like the younger Mexicans do these days,
as if to say, "What's up? What the hell are you doing?"
And not in a way you would greet your mother. I asked if we
were at the point with the extinct volcano, as the crumbling
mountain here did seem vaguely cone-shaped. "*Si*," came the
reply. Then I asked if they knew if any more fierce winds were
coming. The pilot (now more friendly after his testy greeting)
said no, nothing bad, and asked me where I was going.

They soon motored off to the north and I continued on
my slow tack seaward, hoping to catch the Northwesterly
when it came up. There were lots of dolphins all around in
the clear, blue water with shafts of light penetrating to the

depths. Some of them swam near the boat, but none took any noticeable interest. They seemed to group themselves by ages – the older, bigger dolphins leaping in a pack, the smaller ones mimicking, and each pod on its own course.

Cormorant lies so close to the water that you can reach over and drag a hand. She moves in virtual silence, with perhaps the merest creaking of a line or of the leather collar on the yard across the mast top, but nothing jarring, nothing to clang and startle the sea life. So ghosting along a couple of miles offshore on a fine day with light winds, the boat might

compel the birds to swim off a few extra yards, but you see
them close up: the small phalaropes with the clucking motion
of their heads as they paddle; the sooty shearwaters in their
hundreds like smoke-colored gulls coursing just inches above
the surface; the terns, white like painted spirits, hovering then
diving; and the black coots chopping away with stiff wing
beats in asymmetrical formations.

I set a course for the next headland a mile or two down,
and stretched across the aft thwart with my feet propped on
my board and head resting on a life preserver on the mizzen
partner beam. One, two, three, my lids shuttered with the soft,
lapping sound of the water. I awoke some time later to find
Cormorant perfectly on course, the next headland significantly
closer, and myself warm and rested in the morning sun. I
celebrated with crackers and a tin of sardines. Within an hour,
I rounded the northern-most point of a broad bay that reached
many miles across and was punctuated by small points and
coves all along into the distance. Once *Cormorant* came inside
the point, the wind jumped up, and *Cormorant* got lively,
coming on to a heel and cutting confidently.

The outermost cove had an interesting little sand point,
but the second one inside was unbelievable: the waves only
two feet, but peeling absolutely flawlessly like moving water
sculptures. I rounded up and set the anchor. Cactus and
agaves lined the point and the hills behind, with the wave
curling right along the shore. Mussels the size of little loaves
of bread covered the rocks at tide line, and it looked as though
no human had ever walked the beach. I suited up, pulled the
longboard from its case, and jumped in – the water so clear

that it made the waves transparent as they stood to break and fizzed into bright whitewater, which cast a shadow on the sand bottom. I paddled into the waves diagonally, the surf spilling across so quickly that I had to freefall on a sliver of a rail to make it.

I rode many, many waves over the next couple of hours. As the swells poured around the tip of the point they stood up ahead, and with the speed they afforded, I could walk right to the tip of the board and hang there, levitating over the contoured face. The waves slowed a little in places, allowing a swooping turn downward until they stood again and made a reeling run across, a few of them going for 300 yards, all the way down the point to the center of a white sand beach.

At the end of each ride I came ashore and walked back to the point along the curve of the beach. And later, I laid my surfboard on the sand and went up an arroyo, thinking it might be a good place to camp. But I saw fresh lion tracks in the crust of the sandy draw – no claw marks, just big, distinct, kitty paw prints. I chose to stay onboard and began to realize that instead of hassling with hauling out and getting waterborne again, it was easier to just stay on the boat at anchor. I had learned that I could trust the hook, and now my thoughts turned to ways of making staying aboard more comfortable.

———————➤

Another night gave way to dawn with the surf much diminished, and I decided to sail onward after a leisurely breakfast of oatmeal and coffee. From my cove anchorage, I would cut the corner of the bay straight across, a distance of roughly five miles, and then sail close inshore, no more than a half-mile out, once I regained the coast. Having lingered in the cove, enjoying the pristine desert shore, and making a late start and then sailing at a slow-but-steady pace throughout the day, it was not until late afternoon that the next significant headland came slanting up out of the sea.

The water in the lee of the steep face was oily smooth, and hundreds upon hundreds of cormorants swam outside a wide kelp bed like an armada of jet black little ships, slipping under in rows as I sailed upon them. There were two surfers in the lineup, a guy and a girl, and I got my suit on and made a quick paddle to the beach to collect mussels for dinner and then joined them, happy for the company, chattering away about the many miles I had sailed.

We rode waves through the last light of day, and when the two surfers paddled in, I paddled out to *Cormorant* to pull anchor and row ashore. The guy met me on the beach as I landed and helped drag the boat above the high tide line, while two ospreys regarded us with fierce gazes from gnarled nests of driftwood atop separate rock spires on either side of the small cove.

I offered to share the mussels I had harvested and he invited me up to their camp. The woman said she would cook pasta, and I set to sautéing the mussels in oil with lots of chopped garlic. They were traveling in a 4x4 van with an old lab named Doogan. Once the pasta was ready, I divvied up the mussels, and we sat to eat together by the warmth of their fire. We talked about ourselves and found we even knew some of the same people in Santa Cruz, where they lived. They felt like dear friends in that vast desert night by the light of the fire.

I slept down in the dunes overlooking *Cormorant*, grateful to have met such good people. The woman brought me coffee in the morning, and with the high tide the surf was not working, so the three of us walked out to the point where the thousand cormorants from the previous evening now stood shoulder-to-shoulder next to several hundred pelicans. A Stellar sea lion with his thick, woolly mane sat majestically, his back arched and head held high, California sea lions like courtiers at his flanks.

When the tide dropped later in the day, we grabbed our boards and walked to the point, wading out before jumping in to paddle. The surf undulated off the headland, warbling with the backwash off the cliff face when it first broke, and then found the sand bank, cupped to it, and ran along perfectly – providing, like so many of these coves, a finely tuned wall to ride.

The rest of the day proceeded as before, the three of us surfing together until just before dark, and then dinner, a camp fire, and blessed, exhausted, sleep. First light saw me prepping *Cormorant* for travel, and again the woman brought me coffee. With the high tide it was an easy launch, and I rowed out over the smooth water, set my sails, and stood up to wave goodbye to my new friends who stood watching me from the headland.

I made slow progress south-southeast in a dropping two-knot breeze and went to the starboard oar while handling the tiller with my left hand, stroking slowly in the soft wind to give just a little more push. I crept past a point where a wrecked sailboat lay on its side, dead on the rocks, and then passed another run of smaller, somewhat jagged points and cliffy headlands. I ran on, wing-and-wing the main sail out to the port side, and the mizzen open to starboard when the wind finally came up in the afternoon.

Making good progress, I kept about a mile offshore. As I sailed along, sunlight sparkled the water through cold gray clouds. I felt immense gratitude as I continued down the coast, happy to have come so far and seen so much. I also proved to myself that my little craft was a capable camp cruiser – a true "sea-boat," as the Irish sailor, Conor O'Brien, called such craft. His essential book, *Sea-boats, Oars and Sails*, written in the early 20th century, defines a sea-boat as "a means of transport as well as something to go sailing in; one that will bring her owner to whatever place he wishes on any day when boats of the same size are out fishing."

The outer point of Santa Rosalillita, the last headland of the trip, passed one hundred yards off my port side, followed by a quarter-mile run of cliffs to the inner point, and then a broad reach across the bay for an easy beach landing just before dark. A van came speeding across the hard sand, the driver flashing the headlights on-and-off, and a man about 50-years-old pulled up and told me that he was a friend of Rudy's friend Fito and that he had been waiting for me to arrive all afternoon, and drove me back to my car where the Rudys had left it.

Not only had they found and reattached the trailer's license plate that I'd lost on the track into camp the week before, they also had washed the car, as it had gotten covered in thick mud from my drive in. How could I return the favor or repay the kindness Rudy and his son and Senor Aurelio had shown me?

A boy on a quadrunner helped me drag *Cormorant* by her bow line across the beach to my trailer. I drove the whole way home that night under a full moon illuminating the Valle de Los Cerrios nature preserve, through the two military check points with friendly banter among the soldiers, (*"No señores, no marihuana, ni armas..."*), and then inched along for three hours through the border traffic at dawn the next day.

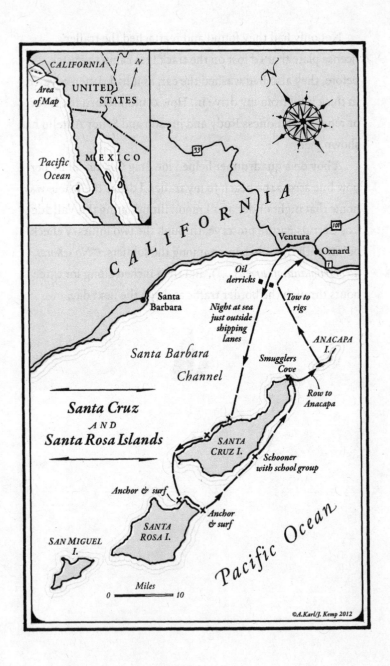

CHAPTER TWO

TUITION

Plank by plank, *Cormorant* had come together in the single car garage of my studio apartment on Avenida Monterey, a shabby street of rental units and small houses a few blocks up from the pier in San Clemente. I worked every night and weekend in solitude, under the shop lights I had installed, much of the time sitting on a crate thinking out the next step. When I finished the hull, about six months into the project, I sketched *Cormorant* upside down on her building frame and made copies on postcards as invitations to about 30 people:

A party for the christening of

Cormorant

Saturday, March 18th 2006 at the home of

Christian Beamish

234 Monterey, San Clemente, CA 92672

Come inspect the hull, enjoy refreshments

and light fare, and be merry!

RSVP not required.

I dragged *Cormorant* into the driveway on her building stand and then fixed posts at each corner from which I strung white Christmas lights and black and white streamers of crepe paper. I filled the bathtub with ice and beers, bought many bottles of wine, made a huge pot of chili with cornbread, and put a fire pit on the front lawn.

We got roaring drunk. Dad's old cronies stood around in sports coats, and a few buddies of mine from my Newport days came with lady friends who stood resplendent by the light of the fire. My mom's brother and his wife came down from Laguna Beach, and my cousin and his fiancée came from Dana Point. I also invited the crazy neighbor girl and her jazznik boyfriend from Michigan City, Indiana; he knew some kids who had a band and arranged for them to play. A friend from up north showed up clad in a lavender headdress and a shawl of eucalyptus boughs. One of my female friends came to me, upset and scandalized, about the guy who was having boisterous sex with his girlfriend in the bathroom behind the thin, sliding door, but I couldn't be bothered by trivialities – the party was a great success.

A rain shower broke overhead, soaking the hull, and we cheered the omen and poured beer and whisky on the wetted planks. The drunker guests let the rain soak them to the skin. Mickey Muñoz, one of the great California surfers from the 1950s and 1960s was there – an old friend of Dad's who I had reconnected with via the magazine – and through my bleary gaze I recognized that I did indeed have people in my life and that, goddamnit, I was fortunate. Dad is a classic himself, with a bit of Frank Sinatra in his always trimmed and neatly combed (if not perfectly washed) hair. My friends from Newport seemed to appreciate his cardigan, even if it was greased with chili. His generation pioneered the life so many of us now pursue: He was a ski patrolman in Aspen, Colorado, in his youth in the early 1950s, and an L.A. County Lifeguard in the summer.

With the rock-and-roll kids playing acoustically in the garage, and a friend in tree-man regalia dancing around the fire, the gathering had found its own momentum. When a sheriff's cruiser came by, he slowed, regarded the scene, and kept on cruising – perhaps unwilling to break up a party where 70-year-old men in blazers shared the space with young women at the height of beauty and career.

<hr>

About a year-and-a-half later I wheeled *Cormorant*, just completed, scuff-free and freshly painted, across the sand on a jet ski cart to launch for the first time. The lifeguards questioned the presence of an 18-foot boat on the beach, but

I would not be deterred. I had checked the law, and with no motor on board I was permitted to launch from any beach as long as there were no swimmers near. This I relayed in an even-but-insistent tone, adding that I had the situation well in hand and that I was "a trained professional."

Academically at least, I knew how *Cormorant* was meant to work, but in truth I had only ever sailed in a dinghy once or twice before, 25-years earlier. I had never rowed a boat either, so launching through the surf on my first outing may not have been the best idea. But June 4, 2007, was a gentle, warm day with little waves, and I wanted to establish my right to access the ocean just down the street from my house.

At the water's edge I pulled *Cormorant* off the expensive, balloon-tire cart I had bought. A small surge lifted the hull, and I shoved off and leapt aboard and took up the oars. My stroke missed completely, which sent me sprawling off the midships thwart, wriggling on my back like a sand crab on the floorboards. The next little breaker caught the boat sideways and jostled her back to shore. "*A trained professional…*"

I quickly regrouped and pushed off again, the oar blades biting in this time, and I pulled forward, up one row of jumbling foam then over a small, cresting swell and soon across the smooth water beyond the surfline. Here I had the chance to pause and acknowledge the fact that I was actually floating. *Cormorant* was a functioning boat, a true vessel – a means of moving through the world. There was the curve of the gunwale, the stout mast with the halyard run through the top and coiled at its base, the rich color of the tanbark sail. A few more strokes, and I went forward to hoist the main.

Hoist the main! On my own boat!

The breeze puffed just lightly, the sail billowed out as if by magic. *Cormorant* coursed forward, a miracle.

The sea was like pewter under a high ceiling of clouds. *Cormorant* reached northwest passed the end of the pier, the breeze picking up a little once I cleared the rock stack of West Reef. The ocean stretched before me, Catalina Island a distant shape on the horizon, and I wanted to sail onward for days and days. I came about and ran back in to the pier, then put out to sea again, farther this time. The bluffs of San Clemente became small off the stern, the houses on the hills impressionistic dabs of white. The sea lit up gold on its scalloped edges when the sun dipped away late in the evening.

Night fell as I ran in again, but I did not want this dream to end. "Bound is boatless man," goes the Viking proverb, and I hadn't known how true that was until now. I passed the pier well off the end and decided to come about again and sail out to sea once more, my eyes adjusting to the dark.

One week later, running down-channel in the afternoon with a strong breeze dead aft in Dana Point Harbor, *Cormorant* broached and went over before I could interpret what was happening. Capsized, with my gear scattered and adrift, *Cormorant's* rails were just even with the surface once I righted her, making bailing futile. A passing yachtsman threw me a line and towed me into the beach on the inside of the harbor where I could bail out the boat.

I realized that I had not built in sufficient buoyancy. I had also incorrectly rigged the mainsheet, which controls the mainsail – having tied off the line rather than jamming it in its cleat where it could be snapped free in an emergency. I had the daggerboard down as well, which gave the boat a fulcrum to "trip over" as the wind forced us into a sharp turn.

"Tuition," I told myself and mounted four docking fenders – two under the fore-most thwart and two under the aft – for additional buoyancy to supplement the foam blocks that I had epoxied in place beneath the side benches during construction. The following weekend I rowed out in the harbor to test the newly added buoyancy, standing on the starboard gunwale while gripping the opposite side and rocking back and forth until *Cormorant* went over again. This time, despite being swamped, the extra buoyancy gave a foot of freeboard above the waterline once I righted her – enough to bail the boat and get under way again.

A capsize in cold water and heavy swell was one of my worst-case scenarios – sloshing about fully clothed in an indifferent and powerful sea, driven towards a cliff or a reef while trying to right my vessel. I realized, with a thought as unoriginal as it was practical, that prevention is key. I planned to sail reefed down in rough conditions and wear a wetsuit if a passage looked challenging.

Most important, I told myself, I needed to acquiesce to the days that were beyond my capabilities. But of course, disasters tend to catch one off guard.

These sails were practice runs for the initial Baja run I made, when I met Aurelio and the Rudys. After that trip, I was keen to see where else *Cormorant* might take me. I made a couple of upwind journeys to the hallowed surfing grounds near Point Conception, and with these sails and a portion of the Pacific coast of Baja safely under the hull, I wanted to sail next to the Channel Islands , which lay 27 miles across the Santa Barbara Channel.

———————————→

I could see the juvenile elephant seal quite clearly in the early light, 10 feet down off the bow, rolling onto his side underwater, trying to gauge what the bright yellow parachute of my sea anchor might be. He swam under the hull and surfaced alongside, his face two feet from mine where I sat on the floorboards, still in my sleeping bag up to my waist. We stared at each other for a moment, one bristly-faced mammal to another, until I said, "Hi little guy," which startled him, and he vanished with an abrupt splash.

Adrift, I'd slept in the boat 10 miles out from Ventura, approaching the line of oil derricks. Beyond lay the shipping lanes with regular incoming and outgoing traffic – enormous, industrial craft stacked high on the decks with steel containers overseen by a superstructure aft, which suggests massive computer banks more than any keen-eyed sailor on watch.

Evening had come down in a great calm, the water turning orange with the sunset. A high line of pelicans flew shoreward, and dolphins broke the surface lazily in the far distance. It had been a slow day of light and shifting air, my island destination obscured by summer haze. As the sun slipped away I faced the prospect of rowing all night if I was to reach land either in retreat or in pressing on. But the little voice had come to me a week before, quiet and sure in its insistence: *Get a sea anchor.*

Deciding not to think about the deep-keeled work boats that plow out and back from the derricks at all hours, or the tugs that tow barges along this stretch of sea, often at night, I posted a light on the bow, deployed the drogue, wriggled into my sleeping bag under the thwarts, and slept the exhausted sleep of a man alone in an open boat.

Morning broke to reveal a marine layer of high fog and a reasonable six-knot breeze out of the south, which we typically get in the early hours in summer in Southern California. After my seal encounter I ate a handful of trail mix, slugged back some water, and scrambled my gear together to take advantage of the wind that I knew would soon enough fall away. I could see the island faintly, 12 miles off, and with *Cormorant* gliding along in the gentle wind on the big water, I thought about how this moment had come into being through equal parts physical work and mental visualization: "When all is lashed down and the rigging pulled taut, the boat on her course slipping through the water," I had written in my journal, "the work is then culminated, coalesced into wholeness. Only the essential remains."

The fog lifted and the wind laid down completely. Again, the ocean stretched out flat, deep blue, and perfectly still. Santa Cruz Island slept on curled legs like a dog, its knobby spine all descents and inclines, miles and miles long. I went to

oars, closing the remaining few miles stroke by steady stoke.
A massive breath broke the silence like an air-compressor
releasing, and I saw the long, long back of an enormous blue
whale pass just 50 feet off my stern.

Jagged coves along the rocky coast backed into steep
arroyos running a couple hundred feet up, oaks and
manzanita growing on the slopes and in the small meadows
on the headlands with the buckwheat, coffeeberry, and white
sage of the native coastal scrub. I anchored in a narrow cut
and stern-tied to an outcrop on a ledge. Next, I arranged a
swatch of marine canvas I had for a boat tent, running a line
between the main mast and mizzen and using the spare oars
for poles. It had been 24 hours since I left Ventura, and I was
finally here, safe on the island. Soon after dark and after a
quick pouch meal of beans and rice on the camp stove, I slept.

The next morning was gray again with summer fog, and
I swam ashore to scout the coves before continuing on for
the day. Climbing up the steep draw and looking down on
Cormorant at anchor gave me the feeling of having really
traveled. Marine layer obscured the mainland coast, and there
was only the sound of birds in the scrub and a faint breeze.

Back on board I rolled and stowed the canvas, undid
the stern tie, pulled and stowed the anchor, and set out
under oars. The rowing was gorgeous just under the high
sea cliffs, tucked in so close that the port oar blade swept
just inches from the rock face. I worked up the inside coast
of the island, following indentations in the sheer cliffs that
formed protected, kelp-laden grottos. Eight or ten harbor seals
watched me, each of them dipping under and then surfacing

again, curious, watchful. They shadowed me, pausing when I paused, their little seal faces bunched together like a choir before slipping under one-by-one.

There were lots of birds too, guillemots, gulls, cormorants, and pelicans, and the ocean had an almost purple quality with the depth of an apparently immediate drop off. The sun broke through around midday, and with it a rising northwesterly breeze. I kept rowing, but the swell and the wind kept pushing the bow off to the side until I was using as much energy to keep head-on into the flow as to make forward progress. I pulled a good 200 yards off to get free of the rock coast, and then raised the mast like the marines with the flag on Iwo Jima, as I balanced in the rocking boat. Then I went aft to hang the rudder, leaning off the stern on the mizzen partner beam, barely able to breathe with my weight on my diaphragm, dunking in the cold seawater up to my elbows with the heave of the swell. All this with glances at the island as the wind drove us in. Finally, I unfurled the mizzen sail, running its sheet through the block on the rudder head and securing it to the base of the mast, and then after moving forward to hoist the main and back again to sheet it in, both sails snapped full and pulled us away.

Cormorant sailed beautifully, clawing to windward with tacks of less than a mile right across the teeth of the blow – fully reefed, spray flying. I think I even growled a little in fighting glee. Gaining distance toward the corner of the island over the course of a couple of hours, I saw an urchin boat anchored under a cliff that even from a short distance seaward did not look to be any sort of cove. But seeing the divers on deck I thought I would sail in and round up to ask them how far to the northwestern-most corner.

"Ahoy!" one of the men called out as I brought the sail down, pleased that I had done the job smartly. I returned his greeting, and he asked if I would like to tie-off from the stern of his boat.

What had looked like a straight run of cliffs from 200 yards seaward was in fact another kelp grotto in a deep recess that led back to a massive cave with a broad area of perfectly sheltered water. Numerous harbor seals and sea lion pups frolicked while an equal number slept on rock slabs around the entrance. I drifted down to the divers' boat, and the fellow who had called out threw me a line, which I ran through an eye in the stem and he then tied off.

He reached over and gave me a hand up as I stepped across to the deck of his vessel, a commercial boat out of Santa Barbara. We introduced ourselves; the captain, Rick, and his mate, Jerome, both told me how good *Cormorant* had looked on her reach into the cove.

The talk was first of what I was doing out there. The men were not surprised at my voyaging in such a small craft or at my two surfboards strapped in place along the port rail. As the conversation progressed it became obvious that these two – grizzled and salty as they were, with the Vietnam War and six decades of life each behind them – had broader interests than their rough looks would suggest.

Although the corner of the island was only another mile onward, the captain said that I was welcome to anchor in the cove with them that night as it was already late in the

afternoon, and they were done working for the day. The swell
I was here for was not forecast to arrive for two more days,
and with such an interesting place to tuck into and these
fellows to talk with, I accepted the invitation.

Sitting on upturned buckets, we drank warm Dr Pepper
as Rick and Jerome filleted their catch of sea cucumbers, Rick
telling me that they were not too proud to augment their
urchin take, unlike some of the other divers.

They had worked together out on the islands for 30 years.
As they coiled their hoses and poured the discarded parts of
the cucumbers overboard, they talked in an unhurried flow,
one man sometimes taking up the line of thought from the
other. Jerome, with his thick glasses, burly trunk and arms,
and missing teeth, was as craggy as the cliff wall and seemed
shaped by his years on these weather-lashed islands. When a
seal swam by the boat, he barked a greeting with a croaking
echo from down in his throat that was so realistic, the sea
lions on the rocks answered back. And when *Cormorant* came
untied and was drifting towards the cliff wall, Jerome leapt
in, swimming powerfully with the line in his teeth to retrieve
her. Rick and I pulled him and my boat back in, and Jerome
lolled onto his back bellowing his seal bark through a gap-
toothed smile. Rick smiled through his short, silver beard.

Dinner was as awful as the company was good. The
captain ladled out gobs of canned chili heated on the stove,
and when we got that down, he served out heaping portions of
baked beans – all of which we were obliged to finish because
there was no refrigeration onboard the little, low slung work
boat. The thought of the farts to come as we drank another Dr

Pepper – the two divers on their adjacent bunks in the boat's cuddy – made me decide to sleep with my own gasses under the canvas on *Cormorant*.

We had coffee in the morning, and Rick brought out his charts of the islands, both he and Jerome pointing out good anchorages and places where spring water comes out of the rocks. With a couple of cups in us, the talk went to the state of the fisheries and the surveillance the fishermen were under – the hidden cameras on the islands and fly-overs with small planes, checking that they did not stray into closed areas.

"I know why they're doing it," Rick said, "but it's a little over the top. They think we want to take everything – fish it out 'till it's gone.'"

These men knew their islands and loved them. They spoke with reverence about the creatures they worked amongst. Jerome told me that if I stayed out here long enough, I would be able to make friends and hang around with the harbor seals. He also said that just two weeks previous, around the corner at another cove, in about 20- or 30-feet of water, a big white shark cruised passed. "She was just beautiful," Jerome said, "with a silver back that faded perfectly to white on her belly."

They had an entire lifetime of experience between them in the islands, and the details sloshed over the edges of their conversation. They mentioned the treasure from a Spanish galleon that likely lay off a particular shelf on the backside of San Miguel, but the ocean out there is too awful in its predator-to-prey ratio to retrieve it. They talked of how two of their friends lost their boat off the north coast of Santa Rosa and made it ashore only to have to hobble 10 miles

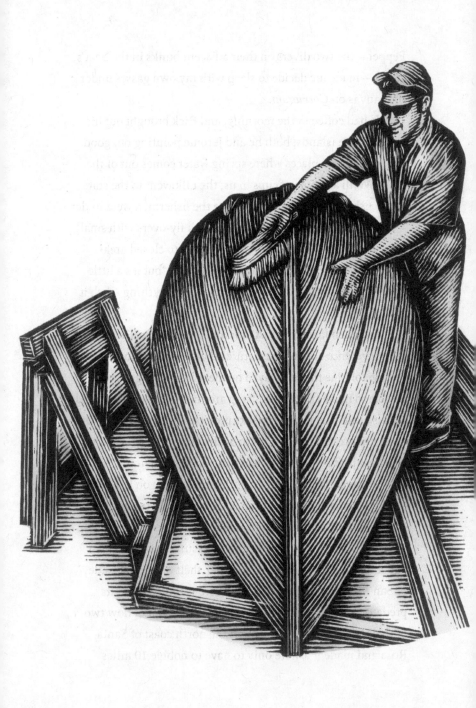

barefoot and naked to the ranch on the other side of the island – having shed their wetsuits after being rubbed raw on their inner thighs. Rick also told about the island fox that trotted right past him every time he walked a particular trail in the evening near one of their anchorages, and he told of the time he found a human femur out in the sand dunes.

The men got a late start because of all their talking, and it was midmorning before I moved on, sailing well seaward again to find the line that would bring me past the northwest corner of the island. Drifting fog obscured the tops of volcanic-looking spires that stood from the sea like fortress walls. Deep swells surging up and draining back heavily even on this day of relative calm gave an ominous aspect to this end of the island. I came across just clear of the spires, and it felt as though the giant was away, that I had snuck by his lair on tiptoe. The very edge of the world is what it looked like.

Santa Rosa Island lay seven miles off, and I came up a few points closer to the freshening wind to start across the channel. I was well into my third day of traveling for a swell that I hoped would arrive and that I hoped would translate into good waves. Out here I was far removed from help. This was the real ocean. I rounded up twice to tie-in extra reefs as the wind increased, and even so I had to hike out off the starboard gunwale, grasping at a loop of line I had secured at the oarlock. I always wear a lifejacket in open water and tie one end of a line to my belt and the other end to the boat in the thought that if I did go over, it would be easy to catch a blow to the head.

The wind gusted harder over the ridges of Santa Rosa, and I struggled to keep on our close reach into the corner of the bay across the channel. She's light, it's true, but *Cormorant* has a stiff backbone that lets her smash headlong into a steep sea when she needs to, then shake the water from her wings and charge on. The ranch buildings came into focus as I got nearer to the bay, and I knew that the wind I was coming through, stiff though it had become, barely registered on the scale of what can blow on the outer Channel Islands. As I rounded up in the little bay, I thought of investing in a second, heavier duty mainsail with an extra set of reef points sewn in.

I threw the hook in the transparent water of the bay, just inside an arm of rocks that reached about 150 feet off the beach and rose into a small pinnacle at the end. The hard wind cut at the surface and shoved at *Cormorant's* bow. But the anchor held securely with a long scope of line run out in good, sandy bottom, and I rigged up the tent, wrapped my sleeping bag around me, and settled into an afternoon of reading.

The weather forecast on my hand-held VHF radio called for high winds and a small craft warning for the following three days. Suddenly, the 35 miles I had put between myself and the mainland felt even farther. I ate cheese and crackers and sardines, drank water, and slept soon after it got dark. The next morning, a golden dawn over Santa Rosa, I boiled up a nice pot of blessed hot, black, and sweet tea. I had not slept well in the heavy roll from the previous day's blow, so I took the morning slowly with a breakfast of granola.

After putting all of my gear in its place, I pulled the anchor and fit it into the chocks I'd built in the bow area, and set off under oars towards what I anticipated might be the first day of surfing on this trip. Rounding the bend south of the anchorage brought a surf setup into view, which consisted of a reef off a point with a broad white sand beach.

I edged in, watching thick shoulders of swells heave up and throw wide open, blasting out spray from their hollows. The current drew towards the surf zone, and I backed away 150 yards before dropping the anchor in the inky blue of the deep channel. The boat pulled to the set, and I turned my attention back to the waves, noting how the bottom fell away on each one, and how you would have to put yourself well in front of the gathering swell to have any hope of negotiating the intensity that followed. Some movement off towards Santa Cruz Island caught my eye, and I brought my binoculars up to see a boat fast approaching with surfboards lashed to the console roof.

These are sensitive times: A Byzantine system of pedigree, skill, and sometimes the willingness for violence determine who can surf unmolested at a particular spot. Guessing that I had 10 minutes before the boat would arrive, and having no way of knowing what the surfers' attitude would be, I hurried into my wetsuit, grabbed my shorter board, leapt over, and paddled to the lineup to establish whatever priority being the first one out might give me.

The surfers motored into position and watched for 20 minutes or so. Perhaps seeing me flung airborne over the reef on two consecutive waves, the lip detonating squarely on my body and dragging me shoreward underwater for 30 yards, made the surf seem unrewarding. Whatever the reason, they soon left.

Paddling across from *Cormorant* to the empty lineup before the surfers in the boat got there had been a bit unnerving, with the water really deep just off the reef and Jerome's story about the white shark still fresh in my mind. I was riding a shorter surfboard as well, so I sat lower in the water. I was using a 6'7" of my own design – a single fin with two cuts, called wings, which stepped the outline into a narrower tail section. This was another in a long line of surfboards I shaped that only sometimes achieved what I hoped for on a wave.

On this particular board, although the width in the forward section allowed for good paddling momentum relative to the length, the single fin was an ineffective rudder at maximum speed. I think the rocker (the curvature of the bottom of the board from nose to tail) was too flat as well and did not contribute to a smooth traverse of steep contours. Still, I had one ride – a good bottom turn and a rocketing line across the top part of the wave, silver spray flying all around – that satisfied my efforts.

------------➤------------

With the midday breeze coming up, I paddled back to the boat and stowed my equipment to move on to another part of the island. The reef was a challenging surfing situation but not good enough for me to want to stay. Also, the bay I anchored in the previous night was too choppy for my liking, and it would have been a chore to beat back against the rising wind. The opposite direction was an easy glide, the sugary sand beach and grassy knolls off the starboard rail scrolling past slowly once I pulled anchor and set sail.

After perhaps 45 minutes of this gentle sailing, I rounded up and set anchor in a kelp forest in the middle of an open cove, off a nice run of beach. A low bluff, no more than six-feet high, ran along the length of the white sand, perhaps 30 feet back from the edge of the water, with a wide meadow behind that led upwards to a rocky knoll. The beach on either side gave way to low rock walls, each one forming a point that jutted into deeper water where the surf rolled in.

I set up the tent and sat contentedly out of the sun, feeling much like I had as a boy in forts my neighbor friends and I built in the shrubby trees down the street. But this was so much better – the water clear blue and sparkling in the sun, green blades of kelp reaching up from the depths, and the island like one that might have been drawn from imagination. Four days gone now and all I wanted was more of this. There were still days ahead to savor, but I was greedy for the very thing that I was experiencing. *Cormorant* had proved herself a tough little voyager, and I was fully acclimated to the mode of travel.

Back in Baja the previous winter, as I rowed ashore at Santa Rosalillita, tired but by no means spent at the end of the final day of my trial expedition, I realized that ending my

journey there was completely arbitrary. I had sufficient water
and many days' stores of food, and I remembered thinking
how much easier it would have been just to camp for the night
and travel on in the morning, than to have to drive back home
to the routine. All the work I had put into building *Cormorant*
felt, if not wasted exactly, then certainly under-realized in
only one two-week cruise and the odd weekend overnighter.
After all, she does not sail at the pace of contemporary life,
and 10 days or two weeks is what it takes merely to settle into
the rhythm of boat life.

The logical run from Southern California would be south
again during winter with northwest swells lighting up the
points in the upper portion of Baja. The journey, ideally,
would extend into the spring season once past the halfway
mark of Punta Eugenia, coinciding with the early south swells
on the points and reefs on down to Cabo San Lucas. All of
that open desert coast, the sea life and the waves, the solitude
and simplicity of *Cormorant* – it was too wonderful not to
attempt.

But I didn't just have "a job," I worked for the finest surfing
publication in the world. Leaving meant uncertainty. Staying,
however, meant letting this perfect vision dissolve into a
memory of something I thought of once but never pursued.

———————◆———————

Towards evening I paddled ashore with a dry bag, and set
up a lean-to at the base of the little bluff, using driftwood
and the rain fly from my tent. I planned to enjoy a good, if

sandy, night's sleep on solid ground. I walked out to the point at the very corner of the island, the Pacific open before me all the way to Tahiti, and then turned to climb the lichen-covered rock knoll. The Chumash had lived here for more than 10,000 years, and it was not a stretch to think of feeling a remnant vibration of their presence. I squatted down and placed my palms on the rock, simultaneously absorbed by, and absorbing, the silence.

Cormorant lay at anchor below, the amber light of evening falling over everything.

I heated soup on my stove and ate as darkness enveloped the island. It wouldn't have been right to make a campfire here, so untouched it seemed, so I fixed up the food by the light of my headlamp and then ate as a night shadow myself. I stood up and felt dizzy – not just from fatigue, or from standing up too fast, but from a sense of the domed curvature of earth in space, and by the enormity of the cosmos. Deeper in the night, after I had slept awhile and then got up to pee down at the water's edge, the sky held an astounding number of stars, the Milky Way like a fissure between the orbs of the great brain of the universe. I thought of Dad with a pang – such a gentle soul, truly a gentleman – and of mother and of my creation under this very sky.

Morning held fog, the ocean gray and oily smooth. The next point over held a silky wave that broke cleanly in silvered whitewater all the way across. I crawled out of my damp but warm bag, and pulled on my wet, cold, and sandy wetsuit. The other board I had brought was an 8'2" that I had shaped and named *El Californio*, as it was designed for just such essentially Californian surf: three- to five-feet high and flawlessly shaped. Like a longboard, the 8'2" holds a long, straight curve in its outline with a lot of volume in the center of the surfboard, which helps it pick up waves easily. The deck tapers to thin rails that slice the water, and the underside is convex and matches the taper on the topside. These features make the board cut along one line, high in the curving lip of the wave, and the surfer rides in a tuck, simply letting the elements conspire. On this wave, it was a smooth drop and a high glide across, an easy race down again and another tight trim up high – the water surface pulled taut and still, like a held breath.

———————

I planned to cross back to Santa Cruz and sail down the backside of the island, camp and surf for another two days before the big crossing back to the coast. An infamous stretch of rough water called the Potato Patch lies off the southwest corner of Santa Cruz Island, and from the southeast corner of Santa Rosa, I was obliged to sail right through it.

The next day the wind rose cold and earlier than normal, the morning fog only lifting to a high gray pallor, and I could already see whitecaps a mile or two distant in the channel. I reefed down before setting out, wrapped up in a sweater under my jacket, with a scarf and wool hat. With the wind on her port side, and a little aft of midships, *Cormorant* skipped over the water swiftly, and I kept a sharp eye all around – ducking to peek under the sail for vessels off to starboard and glancing up-channel to try and gauge the strength of the wind coming down.

At this point I thought only of clearing Gull Island, a rock table standing up from the sea a half-mile off the corner of Santa Cruz. First, a mere white-fringed spot far off, Gull Island then rose more distinctly, although its high flat mesa was obscured from time to time by spray from heavy surf breaking. Approaching, the wind drove us harder, and although my instinct was to sail for shore inside the rock island, I knew I was safer far outside, and so I fell off a point or two and let the wind and current take us seaward. And seaward I was – big ocean swells heaving us up and *Cormorant* speeding down the backsides – and well clear of the island and its surrounding kelp beds.

A look back to Santa Rosa showed only a low ridge on the horizon now, with hills rolling back behind. Ahead, down the coast of Santa Cruz, high rock promontories plunged into the sea, fading in the distance, more formidable than gentle Santa Rosa. Mostly running before the breeze, I put the bow in line with the farthest headland and shaped a long diagonal course that would close the mile-and-a-half of distance between *Cormorant* and the shore, five miles farther down. The wind eased as I got closer in, until I ran out again in the hope of sailing farther on the wind, but the breeze continued to lighten throughout the afternoon. I wallowed and crept shoreward once again, the mainsail held open with an oar braced under the opposite gunwale.

What I first thought were massive antennae turned out to be the yardarms of a great schooner anchored in a picturesque bay. Pushing along under oars, facing forward with the sails hanging limp like laundry on a line, I moved at the pace of a slow walk, and watched as the crew on deck of the schooner swung off lines in the rigging and plunged into the ocean, then climbed back on board with a rope ladder off the side.

They were schoolkids on a summer program; their young instructors evaluated *Cormorant* from behind sunglasses. One of the schoolgirls, standing in a gaggle of her friends, asked where I had come from, and I told them that I'd sailed down from Santa Rosa. The instructors invited me for lunch, and I threw a line to a woman on deck, and she tied *Cormorant* off with a bowline in about two seconds and then reached out her hand to help pull me up on board.

The kids – there were about 20 of them – all gathered and asked questions about the boat and about what I was doing out here all by myself. The instructors told them to clear off and get lunch and then invited me below to the wardroom where they ate, separate from their charges. From having slept under the swirling heavens the night before, making the big channel crossing, and being in a solitary meditation in recent days, the company of the young men and women was both welcome and slightly challenging.

But the food was glorious – as glorious as only plain hot dogs with ketchup, mustard, and relish can be when you're really hungry. The ship was heavily planked, with a deck that was as spartan as the cabin. It had been overhauled to meet Coast Guard regulations for school programs at sea and so had a touch too much steel and auxiliary equipment, but the instructors taught the kids how to raise the sails and work the ship. The young men told me about the spread of canvas and how the ship came alive in a blow with a deep vibration all the way through her timbers, and we enjoyed our mutual appreciation for such things.

It was nice, once I got used to using my voice again, to find myself in such good company. The men and women were just out of university with degrees in subjects like biology and environmental science. They wore knives in leather sheaths on their belts, and stiff Carhartt trousers, and they were attractive in a sun kissed and hearty sort of way. They knew a lot about this old ship and the islands throughout the Channel group, and what's more, they had surfed on each one of them.

In the evening, the instructors called the kids aft to sit around the quarterdeck for sea shanties. With a group of 20 high school students I was prepared for grumbling and a general dismissal of something so unhip as a group sing-a-long. But the kids sung out with full and gorgeous voices, and they were genuinely kind and supportive of one another. I had never seen anything like it – adolescents actually appreciating the differences in their group – the kids who were smaller, or shy, were encouraged and applauded for being their secret little selves. It was as if the students loved each other in the way their parents must have loved them.

The instructors put me up for the night with a thick cushion on the deck of the tall ship, *Cormorant* set off with a long trailing tie from the stern, and the only strange note of my visit came with the first mate's admonition that I not "engage in any nudity," as he helped me arrange my sleep spot. I said that I would not, and felt suddenly like a stranger when I had been a friend. But I pushed that thought from my mind and told myself that he was only being watchful of the youth in his care.

Morning was again cloudy with high overcast and I set off under oars after coffee and cereal, the whole lot of my fellow sailors seeing me off from the rail of their ship and me singing to them "Sailing Onward to Mangalay," from the last night's round of shanties. It was a real boon in the world that those kids had their three weeks at sea on such a noble vessel, with such capable young people to guide them. Rounding the foot of rock that marked the eastern boundary of the anchorage, the happy ship slipped from view, and I was alone once more amongst the kelp and sea cliffs, dipping and pulling, moving at the pace of one man under his own power.

I came to a broad cove in about an hour, where a good wave stood in a peak and poured across a reef shelf in front of a high sea cave. The surf here was not the intense plunge of the reef break back on Santa Rosa, but it held real ocean power nonetheless, the wall of each swell bending inward, back towards the tumbling foam rolling shoreward. There was no one around although the surf was good enough to attract 25 or 30 surfers had it been Orange County. It is a known spot, but the main part of the swell had come the previous day, and it being a Monday I guessed that the other boat surfers must have returned to the mainland.

I paddled the *Californio* over to the peak but soon realized that its sharp rails and flat rocker would not fit these compact wedges of water, so I headed back to *Cormorant* to trade it for the 6'7". Once in the lineup again I found the wave difficult to judge, the water pulling hard off the reef, and the swells bending so intensely that they were hard to catch. Finally I forced myself into one, paddling almost on top of the cresting lip, then getting to my feet too late and too high in the wave. Down I went, sucked into the foam like a fall into quicksand. Tumbling underwater a swift knock caught the top of my foot. The numbness that followed suggested an injury.

I surfaced and pulled my board in by its leash to paddle back out. There was no pain yet, but when I lifted my foot clear of the water, I saw a gaping mouth of a wound, with a strand of white fat, or perhaps a ligament, hanging from the corner. The blood pooled up, obscuring the gash, and then ran over the sides of my foot, inking up the water like some exotic tea. The marine layer had long since lifted and the water was sparkling clear in the sunshine, the green and brown shades of the reef readable from the surface, and shark attack did not seem in the realm of possibility. Another set of waves approached and I nabbed one from a better position this time, making an arcing turn across its bending curve, and kicked out at the end.

I paddled back to the boat, my foot starting to throb, and once on board I got iodine from my first aid kit and soaked a bandage with it, then scrubbed the cut deeply with a clenched jaw. Still stinging from the scrub out, I squeezed a good dollop of antibacterial ointment on another bandage and smeared that into the wound, then wrapped the works with a flexible band.

High, hot sun and an increasing texture on the water followed by a breeze, signaled the time for leaving. I sailed well seaward to stay clear of the kelp beds closer in, and my course led east by southeast on a divergent line from the run

of the coast. It was another long afternoon of no thought
in particular but the vague anticipation of making the next
anchorage. The eastern half of the south coast of Santa Cruz
seemed more sheltered the further inside I traveled, the mini-
range that runs down the spine of the island providing more
protection from the prevailing winds than the other coasts,
and by late afternoon I was two miles or more off Smugglers
Cove at the southeastern-most corner, in a dead calm.

There was nothing to be done but take up the oars and
pull and pull until I made the cove. I had not yet learned to
judge my distances from sea, and I laid into the strokes once
I could see the masts of the sailboats and the pilothouses of
the cruisers at anchor, but stopped to rest after a time when
none of the boats seemed to have gotten any closer. Breathing
deeply, I set to it again, still pulling strongly but more steadily
now, refusing to look over my shoulder and be disappointed
by my progress.

I finally made the cove late in the evening, well after
sundown and into the purple light of dusk. Passing one of
the RV-looking sailboats with two couples in late middle age,
sitting together in the cockpit, I heard one of the women say to
her companions, "He's coming over here," and I avoided them.
I slept as far from the other boats as I could, and pulled anchor
early the next morning, slipping out of the cove under oars.

I was hopeful of a breeze down the channel to ride across
to Oxnard on the mainland not 12 miles away, but there
was none. The sea was more still than I had ever seen it, as
if the gray sky pressed the surface smooth and held it down.
Anacapa Island lay six miles away on my chart, but it looked

much closer. I set off across that still ocean, the water so unmoving as to be more like air, the distance between the islands a deep canyon that I was floating across.

———————▶

In my sleeping bag under the boat tent the night before, I thought about the next step with *Cormorant*. I would journey down the coast of Baja, that much I knew. In all my time building the boat and putting in the days at the office, I had gnawed at the idea of a better time in history, before mass industry, a time of homesteads and wilderness. And since I was re-imagining the past, I could easily sidestep the unpleasant parts – slavery and social immobility to name but two. This "better time" went with my ideas of the life I wanted, but I could not solve the puzzle of where to go, or how to live within this particular vision, except with the thought of an expedition.

Cormorant would be the key, a means of escaping the technological maw of the present day. As I sat at my desk at work, my thoughts – tortured, anxious, overwhelmed – had me wondering if our involvement in this "future," in "modern technology," was anything we had a say in. How far would I be willing to go, and what were the consequences of stepping aside? Traveling in *Cormorant* would be a way to see differently, if I had the courage to pursue the vision.

Yet despite my critique of the current age and the antidote to it that *Cormorant* began to represent, I had to acknowledge my long utilization of and the benefits I derived from almost every aspect of contemporary life: the computer, the automobile, the cell phone, penicillin, international flights, a university education, supermarket groceries, and my ever-growing pile of surfboards composed of man-made chemicals – all of it financed at 12.25 percent on a credit card. I was not seeking an animal skin wardrobe, only the magic of the natural world, having lived too long enmeshed in and dulled by suburban convenience.

Sailing Baja would be a journey not only to test the feasibility of a non-motorized, sail and oar approach to surfing remote waves, but an attempt to tap a physical, ancestral memory of the natural world. We cannot know ourselves in a world that never gets dark completely, but perhaps the life of the past was the same for so long that it finally had to change irrevocably, and the real challenge is to fully experience our own time, and everything that characterizes it.

Still, a wholehearted embrace of the technocratic future leaves us bereft of the magic of the forest from whence we came. In his book, *Nature Revealed*, Edward O. Wilson writes, "Human nature today remains Paleolithic even in the midst of accelerating technological advance. Thus corporate CEOs impelled by stone-age emotions work international deals with cellular telephones at 30,000 feet." Open wilderness formed us. We are wild in nature, made of the same stuff as the dolphins and whales, the island foxes, sea birds, and every other creature – bones and sinew, muscle and blood.

I just wanted wind. I was tired of rowing. Anacapa Island lay unmoving before me even as I determinedly kept at the oars for long, uninterrupted stretches. After four or five hours, I made the north end of Anacapa and sat in the kelp about a mile off, but at least even with the island now. Still, I was becalmed on a great placid sea. My only option was to continue under oars, angling in to the rocky shore to at least have a better look. The prospect of spending another night out was upon me, and while that would not be so terrible, having made the decision to head home, I was now in the mindset of reaching a destination – or more precisely, of not being able to reach a destination.

The island was interesting closer in, with a vast bird rookery in its pitted and cave-riddled face. The kelp lay thick, but *Cormorant* just glided across, and now that there was something to see, the rowing was less tiresome. A gray inflatable boat with two outboard motors came roaring upon me. It was a park ranger checking to see that I was not fishing in this closed area. He mentioned that he had seen me setting out from Ventura, a week before.

"I thought you were a little crazy," he admitted. "But hey, you made it." We talked a bit about the waves and about poachers. I looked at the pistol on his belt and the carbine and shotgun racked by the console, the bulk of his bulletproof vest under the gray uniform shirt, the ball cap and sunglasses.

"I guess there are some rough customers out here," I offered.

"Nah," he said, "not really. Most of 'em are just having a good time."

I suppose I wanted some justification for the heavy arms he carried.

"If you're crossing," he offered, "I can give you a tow to get you out of the shipping lanes."

I put any qualms I had about traveling by internal combustion aside and thanked him. Running my bow line through one of the gaps in the starboard gunwale on *Cormorant*, then around a post at the console on his craft and back to my vessel's stern section, we secured the boat. As I climbed onboard, the ranger asked if I had any weapons on me, and if I would please leave my knife on my own vessel, which took me back to the other night on the tall ship when I was asked to "refrain from nudity."

The ranger throttled up, and we cut swiftly over the water, seawater jetting up through the opening of *Cormorant*'s daggerboard case. Because he was doing me a favor, I did not want to ask him to slow down, even with the seawater pouring in and starting to fill my boat. Despite the twin outboards churning up a great vee-ing wake, and our skipping over the swells, it seemed to take a long time to reach the oil derricks.

I had a hard time talking with him – not because he wasn't friendly enough, but because we missed on every point of potential connection. He mentioned the game on TV the week before – had I seen it? No, I replied, and had to ask what sport the teams were playing.

When the ranger pulled up a few hundred yards beyond the outermost derrick, untied *Cormorant*, and let me off,

I stood in water up to my knees, my boat dangerously swamped. He was a good fellow to help me, and so I said I was fine, that I could bail *Cormorant* quickly, although I was quietly alarmed by how low in the water my boat rode, wallowing dangerously in the swell.

The ranger backed away in his boat, perhaps as relieved to be free of my company as I was of his, then throttled up to serve and protect back on the islands. My gear was soaked, with bags and various articles of clothing I had shed throughout the morning afloat under the thwarts. The wind started in now that it was midafternoon, but the sky remained gray, and just that little breeze put enough movement on the sea to push wavelets lapping at the gunwale. I set to bailing, realizing that I had left myself in a bad situation, and it was hard work – something akin to rowing in terms of the ratio of progress to effort. I got the water down to the level of the floorboards, and rigged up to sail the final five miles into port.

I was back at work in early September, but I wouldn't be there long. I did not however, want to put the magazine in a bad spot. The dissatisfaction I felt was a product of my own unsettled spirit. I had been given a great opportunity, which I accepted, and despite facing some personal challenges during my time there, I did good work – put together articles, wrote some pieces, and met a lot of like-minded people. I carried a solid load of the line editing, and although the editor seemed to have the major content well in hand throughout each production cycle, I wanted to give my colleagues as much lead as I could before leaving them a man short.

The boss, Steve Pezman, asked me to go to lunch with him. He was a big man, with a great head of white hair and a powerful, rotund build. I always felt affection for him as he was simultaneously unsentimental about and benevolently detached from professional struggles. As associate editor, I regularly went to lunch with the boss and the editor, but this was unusual – just the two of us.

We got our Mexican take-out and headed to San Onofre to sit on a bench and watch the waves. A south swell was in, and guys were getting good, long rides off the main peak. We talked a little, about nothing really, and then he asked, "So, Christian, what are you going to do after the magazine?"

With *carne asada* spilling down my hand, I said, "I'm going to sail my boat down the length of Baja." I started to explain how I had planned to wait another 10 days until after his vacation to tell him that I was leaving, and how I would try and get as much material produced as I could before I left so as to not leave them in the lurch…

"Stop," he said. "We're terminating your position."

We sat there for a moment. It had been four years that I worked for him.

"Well," I said with a chuckle, "that makes it easy!"

He went to some effort to tell me that he had been pleased with my contributions, and that it wasn't about my performance but that the economy was starting to tank and that they just needed to do it and that he had been agonizing over having to tell me.

I understood that and accepted it because, like everyone at *The Journal*, he had treated me with respect and been more than generous in pay and in time to surf, to build, and to sail.

It had been a good run, but now there was a new run before me.

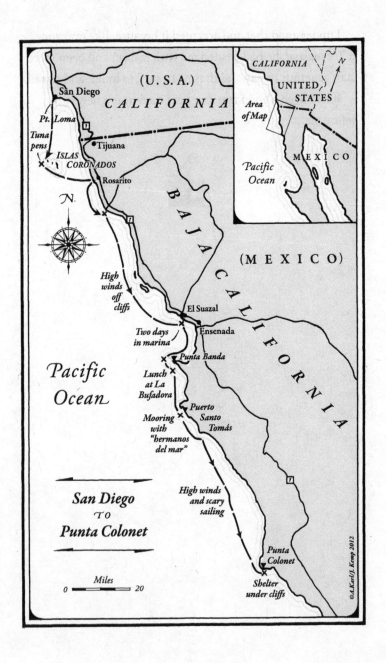

San Diego
TO
Punta Colonet

CHAPTER THREE

UNDERWAY

My plan was to sail from San Diego to Bahía Magdalena, about 800 miles down the coast, but not all the way to Cabo San Lucas. The final 150 miles from Mag Bay to the Cape was open desert beach with no shelter, which seemed like too much to tackle in an open boat, while to the north there were many little coves and bays to tuck into. I did, however, make a big mental leap over the 75 miles of open coast that lies between Punta Abreojos and Scorpion Bay, and again from Scorpion down to Mag Bay, which is also a mostly shelter-free stretch.

I had been making the shorter trips for more than a year, starting with the first Baja run, and the adventures near Point Conception and on the Channel Islands. I knew my vessel by now, and I felt confident. Still, a good friend called me, checking-in to see that I wasn't, on some level, trying to disappear at sea. I assured him that that was not my intention, on any level, but even having to respond to such a question seemed to place me in a certain category of people.

I always wore my life vest with a waterproof strobe light attached, used a lifeline, carried a VHF radio, and a SPOT GPS satellite beacon in case I really got into trouble. "Hey," I told my friend, "the trip has its risks – a small boat off a desert shore is no joke, but I'm going into it as prepared as I can be."

I had rigged a better boat tent since the island journey, with 10-foot flexible fiberglass sail battens that I set into blocks in the gunwales and bent into hoops as if *Cormorant* were a covered wagon, over which I stretched the marine canvas. With the edges tied down I had a cozy place out of the nighttime damp and cold wind. The daggerboard, laid across the benches, made a good sleeping platform. I cooked on an MSR camp stove with a set of stainless steel pots and whittled my food supplies down to the essentials, knowing that I would re-supply as I made my way along the coast. I secured a plastic cooler to the floorboards with a spare bicycle inner-tube, and in it I packed: rice, beans, lentils, dry soup powder, yams, onions, garlic, salt and pepper, olive oil, four pounds of chocolate, oatmeal, eggs, pancake mix, syrup, many bags of trail mix and dried fruit, and two large cans of coffee. I secured a fishing rod with a bait-casting reel and 12-pound test line along the starboard rail, forward of midships, to leave room for the oars.

With my job went my health benefits. I had been feeling pretty good about things in general and figured that, since I was getting back to essentials on this journey, I would simply ease off the Prozac as I made my way south. I had 30 days of pills remaining, and I read somewhere that people went off Prozac slowly, easing the dosage down. My plan, then, was to take a pill every other day until they were gone.

December 31, 2008: The big day had finally come. I moved out of my studio and placed my books, desk, and some boxes at Dad's apartment. I stowed the wagon and trailer with a friend in San Diego. Mother cried as we said good-bye on the phone, and I told her not to worry – that I was built for this kind of stuff. My best friend and his wife followed me in a skiff through San Diego Harbor out to Point Loma, with my buddies Patrick and Richard filming and snapping photos. From here on out, I would be taking my own snapshots.

We embraced, my friends and I, leaning over the gunwales, and then they turned back, leaving me to prepare as *Cormorant* swung to anchor. My first goal was the Coronado Islands, but I made no more than five knots (six at best), and that would not get me there before nightfall. At any rate, no matter my hull speed, I was too damn tired to make the trip that day. With all the frantic preparation of the last few weeks and the stress of leaving my whole life behind – regardless of how excited I was to be embarking upon a true, single-handed expedition – I sat in the boat wearied before I had even begun.

Something at the waterline of my boat caught my eye – a dead cormorant, its drowned head lolling back, tangled in a clump of seaweed. My mind raced with the omen of it, superstition battling rational thought. Cancel the trip? And do what instead?

"A dead bird, it's just a dead bird," I told myself. But of all possible dead birds, a cormorant? Then another thought occurred to me as I examined its body – the thick dinosaur skin on its feet, its hard little claws and saber-like beak, – and that was that my vessel was very well named indeed.

I have never been one for New Year's resolutions, and so sitting in my sleeping bag in my boat tent on the last night of 2008, I did not make any plan for the year ahead but to read the conditions each day and to make prudent, seaman-like decisions. I brought no watch, but I did not stay up to see fireworks at midnight, choosing instead to curl down into my bag and sleep deeply.

The following morning I pulled anchor and sailed out on a light offshore breeze, pleased again at the prospect of starting the New Year with a voyage. Later in the day, well past Tijuana, I examined my chart, determining the compass-bearing for the islands, and took a westerly turn and sailed outward. Golden rays shone down through the clouds and fog – inspirational as all get out, but no islands. "How is it," I asked myself, "that big rock islands just a few miles off the coast can hide?"

It felt as though an unseen hand was buoying us up, pulling us along. It is the quiet I love, like holding one's breath, but easier – just gliding all day. I heard the wing beats of pelicans as they passed, a little creaking of the masts, the lap and slip of the water. I caught a glimpse finally, the merest hint of a ridgeline, and I sailed for that spot into the evening, coming to the southern-most edge of the islands in the very last light of the day, and anchored alongside a series of tuna pens.

Fishing trawlers were anchored along a half-mile stretch of the island, their lights glaring off the afterdecks over the dark water, their generators running. It looked very industrial and made me want to button up the edges of my tent so that none of the light from my lantern escaped.

Men came around in the morning in launches to check the pens – circular nets 30 feet across and suspended from buoys with a raised fence, about 10 feet high, all the way around. These pens dot the northern coastline of Baja, filling up many of the coves.

"*¿Estás solo?*" The fishermen called to me. "*Si*," I replied, my first interaction of many to come.

"*Es muy pequeno, su barco.*"

"Yes, it's a very small boat," I agreed, and then added, "*pero muy suave con las olas.*" – very smooth with the waves – as some sort of rationale. As I got further down the coast, and the conditions grew wilder, this reasoning would come to seem less logical. But at this, my first anchorage in Mexico, it all sounded reasonable enough.

"*¿A dónde vas?*" the men asked.

"*Bahía Magdalena,*" I told them, "*poco a poco.*"

The day was gray. Not with a marine layer, but with dark clouds, darker underneath, storing up to rain. And there was no wind, so again I faced the prospect of a long row to get anywhere, as the Coronados lie eight miles off the coast at Rosarito. At that distance I would have done best to stay at anchor and wait for the wind to come up. Only one day into my journey, however, I was keen to make miles southward, and I set out under oars, counting on the wind to come up later and find me already well under way and ready to be whisked 15 miles to my next anchorage.

That was not how it happened. I rowed for a couple of hours and then set sail when a phantom breeze came up, but a phantom was all it was. I had brought a transistor radio and listened to a San Diego station interviewing the surfing world champion Kelly Slater. It surprised me to learn that he was a fan of ultimate fighting, and I thought that we were involved with two entirely different kinds of surfing.

The clouds got darker, the ocean remained still, and I waited for wind.

--------------------→

An anemic breeze, like the waft of someone's breath, brought us over the water not much faster than driftwood. The town of Rosarito, dilapidated and perpetually under construction, stood in a jumble along the edge of an eight-mile shoreline bluff. A refinery marked the north end of town, and three enormous tankers lay offshore at anchor like slumbering beasts. I closed the final mile to the point at the south end of town under oars, pulling into a thick kelp bed, throwing the hook, and tying off to the thick, tangled strands on the surface for extra safety.

The wind had finally come up, out of the south, suggesting a storm, and the swell seemed to have increased as well, coming through the kelp paddies in slow rolls and breaking on the rocks a few hundred yards inside. Setting up the boat tent as evening came on, I looked at a house on the cliff in front of my anchorage, its patio undercut with erosion, and cinder block walls with reinforcing steel spiking out for another story that did not look likely to come. Next to the house, on the opposite side of a trash-strewn ravine, stood a 20-floor apartment building that had not been there when I used to visit as a kid. Another tower rose next to that one, but it was skeletal and vacant as if its workers had forgotten they had a project. A light came on in the completed building – one light in all those floors of apartments.

I wondered what *Cormorant* must look like from shore, with the first raindrops starting to fall and night coming on, rocking heavily in the swell. I imagined I looked pretty vulnerable. I fired up the camp stove to make soup, still catching the San Diego radio stations on my transistor with straight-ahead jazz. The rain increased as I ate, the drops silver in my headlamp when I peeked outside the boat tent. The tent kept the weather out, with only a few drips from the saturated points over the batten-hoops. I crawled forward to check the set of the anchor and kelp tie, and the easy roll inside belied how much wind there was.

Morning was ugly with a confused sea and the rain clouds dissipating but not letting sunlight through – only an opaque sky behind. A panga with three fishermen in foul weather gear pounded through the chop further out, and I waved from beneath the boat tent, its hem across my neck and shoulders like a shroud. The three of them waved stolidly back, spray lashing at them over the bow. Hopeful of a brisk clearing wind out of the northwest after the rain, I rolled and stowed the tent, hauled the anchor free of the tangling stands, and then rowed clear of the kelp.

However with the sails up and rudder hung and the sea all a-jumble, I merely rocked heavily, without enough breeze to travel on. Rowing was even more tortuous than normal with the roll of the boat, and there was nothing to be done finally but to coax what movement I could from the light air, bracing myself with a free hand on the more extreme lists from side to side.

Gaining the first point south after two hours, still wallowing at a top speed of one-half-knot, was so frustrating that I had a moment of doubt concerning the entire undertaking. And I was hardly "immersed in nature": I was in fact a half-mile out from the actor Russell Crowe's film set on the point, with a hulking wooden ship from *Master and Commander*. I felt no less an actor myself – a Civil War re-enactor perhaps – in this ridiculous boat, trying to replicate a past that was so far gone as never to have existed.

Like every other situation, this one eventually changed. Throughout the afternoon I made my way a little farther south, to the low rock shelves and cobble stone coves at Las

Gaviotas – a gringo enclave of red-tile-roofed condos not unlike the houses in San Clemente. Here I slept again, redoing the boat tent and camp stove routine for my third night at a spot that would have taken 35 minutes to drive to from where I had departed in San Diego.

The monotony broke the following morning with glorious purple and gold light and green little waves peeling cleanly in both directions just in from my anchorage, mist blowing back off their tops. A lone egret appeared to stand on the water, as if defying natural law, balanced on the thick kelp just under the surface. I pulled my wetsuit on and went surfing, riding the smooth green slope of a wave into a tight arc that immediately put me back into the purpose of my journey.

I came ashore to hide under one of the shelves and have the bowel movement that had been a few days in coming, counting on the tide to come and take the waste away. This was the rough nature of small boat travel. I had pine tar soap on board *Cormorant* that was meant to lather up in salt water, and this I used regularly. I did not have enough fresh water to bathe, other than to perhaps wipe my face clean. In my planning for the journey, I had conveniently overlooked the impact that not bathing completely could have on my well being – along with the stretches of coast with no shelter and the prospect of weather that could overwhelm such a small craft as *Cormorant*.

In wild seas later in the day, with foam rushing out from my bows and myself wrapped in foul weather gear like an arctic sea rover, I surfed my 18-footer down large, rolling swells. The sails pulled stiff and full, and *Cormorant* raced too fast, reaching the edge of control. I dropped the mainsail and steered the boat around into the wind to tie-in a set of reefs as *Cormorant* bucked and rolled. The cliffs were high and sheer with no sheltering places, so I brought the boat before the wind again and *Cormorant* roared out – the whitecaps terrible all around and myself in a gleeful rage with the sea.

Night caught me 10 miles north of Ensenada, with the trawler fleet running in and out of the port at El Sauzal keeping me on my toes. Faint lights appeared 300 yards off my stern, and then another set of lights, much closer. I wondered how that boat had come up so close and unseen, just off the port bow. It was unnerving to think how easily a trawler could run one down in the early dark of winter. Still under sail in a light but steady breeze well into the night, I steered closer to shore, approaching a breakwater. I had trouble judging my location because of all the lights of the city ahead. Binoculars did not help. I sailed further in, peering into the darkness for any detail, until breaking surf appeared just off the port side, which forced me to jibe and run for deeper water.

I decided to drop sails and go to oars, angry at not knowing where I was, angry that all the lights looked the same, angry at being in my boat for 10 hours and coming on five days now. I ground my teeth and pulled hard on the oars, muttering oaths. A deeper shadow appeared ahead – the entrance to the marina at the Hotel Coral. I rowed in, in the still black water, passed the multi-million dollar power yachts, dipping the oars quietly, lights rippling across in reflection. I worked my way all the way to the back-most corner, to a small dock space where I tied off and put up the boat tent.

———————→

It cost $232 all told, for two nights in the marina, along with the fees I paid clearing customs at the port captain's office when I took the bus into town the next day. I told myself all would be well, because I had an additional $300 in cash, wrapped in plastic and duct-taped to the underside of one of the benches aboard *Cormorant*. From here on out, there would scarcely be any towns, much less anything else, to spend money on.

Nevertheless, 230 bucks seemed excessive in my mode of transport, and I approached the clerk at the marina office with the observation that, since I came in so late the previous night, shouldn't the current day count as the first requiring fees: Shouldn't I pay for one night only? His face twitched, and he trembled as if it took all his will to control himself. He then informed me that he would call the police if I did not care to pay for both nights.

"Do you accept *la tarjeta*?" – a credit card – I asked, feeling a little sick to my stomach at how unpleasant the guy was.

I had dinner at the hotel restaurant that night, sitting alone at a table with a starched tablecloth and the waiter in a bow tie and black jacket. I wore my cleanest T-shirt and army pants and did not feel entirely out of place, since I had managed a shower in the locker room earlier. I said good evening to the couple at the next table, but they seemed not to want to see anyone. I knew how that can be, but there is nothing lonelier than being alone among other people. I would be better once underway again, I told myself. Alone in nature, alone on the sea – that never felt awkward.

———————————

I set sail again on a workable northwest breeze, gliding across the wide bay out to Punta Banda, with the islands of Todos Santos off the starboard rail and the water be-sparkled by sunlight all around. This, finally, is what I have come for, I thought. The rocks off the tip of Punta Banda glowed blonde in the afternoon sun, standing in columns and squat platforms with the open Pacific rushing around their bases. The sea out there felt open and raw like it did off the west end of Santa Cruz Island up in the Channel Islands the summer before.

The land at the base of the point appeared to have been recently surveyed, with stakes driven into the ground and plastic ribbon stretched between them as if marking off parcels. Other than these signs, there was nothing but a slope facing the ocean above the broken coastline. A series of small coves ran farther down the coast with thick kelp again – thicker than any I had seen thus far on the trip – and I soon pulled the rudder onboard with the daggerboard as well and went to oars, scouting for the best anchorage.

The late afternoon light was beautiful on the kelp and the high boulders along the shore, and the water had a deep blue clarity with the fresh current that swept across the top of the point. I explored three coves, each one farther down the coast, and then came back against the wind to anchor in the middle cove, which was the widest and the deepest of them. This felt like real Baja, even though I knew that Ensenada, with its commercial port, sprawling neighborhoods, and downtown clubs and bars, was bustling just across the bay on the other side of the point.

La Bufadora, the blowhole, lay in the farthest corner of the run of coves, about two miles on from where I was anchored. A longstanding tourist attraction, it brought forth memories of a visit with my mother when I was a kid: I remembered *churros* and the great rush of the sea. Early the next day, after making coffee and eating granola, I rigged up my fishing rod and lowered one of the rubber jigs down into the kelp, almost immediately coming up with a nice kelp bass of perhaps three pounds. I looped a line through his gills and tied him off to the gunwale to fillet later. Some urchin divers motored up in pangas, and we said good morning and talked about the conditions, the men saying something about the coming tide stirring up a wind, which seemed almost like superstition to me. I asked them about the ribbons marking the land on the point, and they shook their heads disgustedly and said, *"Mas hoteles."*

Rowing down the coast that morning a wind did stir, strangely enough, first from the south and then switching around to the northwest before falling off again as I prepared to sail. Back to the oars, I pulled onward, skirting and rounding the rock fingers that plunged in at the ends of each cove, and surged forward with the moderate swell. Rounding

the point at La Bufadora, I saw the deep cove before me, the clear water shaded with reefs, and little holiday houses built along the opposite bluff – big, empty *discotecas*, built as open, multi-level *palapas* on the cliff above the blowhole itself, with loud music blaring, but no tourists present.

I anchored and swam to the beach in trunks in the cold January sea, forgetting to zip my dry bag properly and

soaking the trousers, T-shirt, and jacket I planned to wear ashore. Wringing out the shirt and pants, I put those on over my wet trunks, and spread my jacket out over my shoulders and backpack to dry. I made my way up a dirt trail to the shops and restaurants of La Bufadora. Every stall was open, and the place was crowded with vendors, but there was not a single visitor there besides me. There were pharmacies advertising Viagra, and men standing out front promising "*the* best price for you my *frien...*" The stalls offered the usual bullwhips and ponchos, the wallets and blankets, the plaster statues of La Virgin and Porky Pig that one sees in the line to cross the border at San Ysidro.

I walked to the end of the narrow walkway that led between the shops, the club owners trying to lure me inside for *cerveza* or tequila. The empty tables overlooked the stunning bay, and the men hustled for something resembling the parties they must have had in the days before drug killings and strewn bodies in Tijuana kept the college crowd away. At the point itself, a man stood in full Aztec dance regalia: a headdress and a shield, feathers circling his ankles above orange moccasins. At his feet sat a can with a note asking for 10 pesos per picture.

Walking back through the gauntlet of shops, the pharmacy guys offered some kind of pills I had never heard of, and the pancho vendors again asked me to feel how soft their panchos were, and the club guys, with their empty and depressing halls, again invited me in. I pictured my throat getting cut and body thrown from the cliff as they poured the shot of tequila they had set before me back into the bottle so as not to waste the liquor.

At the top of the long row of shops was a dirt parking lot, and here two restaurants stood with tables and chairs set under plywood roofs. Some local men sat eating, and I saw the ladies behind the counter grilling up great flanks of steak and smelled the delicious *caldos* and *frijoles* and the *tortillas de maiz* that an old *abuela* was pressing on her stone platform, then flipping onto the grill next to the meat, turning them and sending them out in basket after basket to the men who were eating.

The lady smiled. "*¿Sí?*" she asked.

I ordered *carne asada*, and she nodded as if I had made a wise choice. The *abuela* looked up from her tortillas and smiled at me as well, her deeply lined face like something out of the Corn Mother myths of the Indio ancestors. She said, "*Sí, mi hijo.*" Three busses pulled up to the lot as the lady put a plate before me with a basket of those perfect tortillas wrapped in a clean kitchen towel.

Down they came out of the steep steps at the front of the busses – hefty *Americanos*, or perhaps *Canadienses*. They squinted in the morning sun and flipped the tinted lenses of their glasses down, and then waddled forward with perplexed but determined expressions, until suddenly, the gauntlet of vendors that awaited them made sense.

The food was delicious, and I munched away happily, watching the parade as the bus drivers came over and took tables once their passengers were discharged to their fate amongst the vendors. Behind the counter, the lady asked where I had come from, and I told her, "San Diego in my little *barquito*," and explained that I was anchored in the bay below and that I was sailing south along the coast to go surfing. She made the sign of the cross and said something I took to be a prayer or a blessing, and then asked me if my mother knew where I was.

I had to tack a few times to work my way out of the cove at La Bufadora, but once in the open water, I ran free and swift before a good and helpful wind. I set the next headland off the bow and let *Cormorant* ride the swells and sailed on for two or three hours until at last the point at Santo Tomás was less than a quarter mile off the port rail. As I came on to a port tack to sail in to the cove, the wind swung before me and gusted, suddenly much stronger than it had been all day. I sailed on, as close to the wind as I could get, but the daggerboard and rudder got fouled in thick kelp outside the anchorage, holding me fast.

I first dropped the main, then furled the mizzen, and shipped the rudder. The last step before going to oars was to pull the daggerboard in, but when I did, the wind took *Cormorant* swiftly across the water, the daggerboard having been our last hold on the kelp. I was in open water in less than ten seconds and heading seaward fast. Even pulling with everything I had, I could make only the barest movement windward, but I managed to edge into another stretch of kelp and grabbed at a handful of strands and wrapped the bow line around to hold us steady. The little pangas and a lone house on the point looked far away in this blow, the water a series of tight rows of ripples driving at us from the shore. *Cormorant* strained at her kelp tie as if the wind were leaning against her, forcing her bow upward in an effort to pry her free.

I put all three reefs in the main, unfurled the mizzen and re-hung the rudder, then undid the kelp tie and sheeted-in the sails. The wind took us tearing off across the bay. I put the dagger board down and came about to try and tack against the wind and regain the cove. *Cormorant* made progress, fully reefed and sailing close hauled, bucking through the chop, through two or three tacks. But closer in to the cove, between the outer bay and where the pangas lay at their moorings, the kelp once again seized *Cormorant* by her daggerboard and rudder, putting me right back in the fix I was in before.

A bow wave appeared inside the cove, close to shore, then closer to me, more distinct – it was a panga, with three men motoring out. I had just cut my way free of the kelp and was again fighting to windward and making progress, when they reached me. The pilot put his boat about and came across to my bow, and the men in front motioned for me to throw a line. They caught it and tied *Cormorant* off, but the panga hit my bow with a splitting sound, and one of the men in front made a wincing face as he glanced at the stem of my boat. From where I sat amidships, I could see a thick, ugly splinter sticking sideways out of the stem like a badly broken finger. That was the price of the rescue.

The men hunkered in their boat, motoring back to the cove with *Cormorant* in tow as plumes of spray shot overhead off the bow. They were nearly expressionless as they pointed out an empty mooring can that I could tie to. I thanked them profusely and called them *hermanos del mar* – brothers of the sea – as I shook their hard, work-scarred hands. They nodded as if it had been nothing more than their duty to help me, and then they motored the last 50 yards to shore.

I sat and felt *Cormorant* pull to the solid hold of the mooring in the strong evening blow.

————————➤————————

After the men left me on the mooring I set up the boat tent and then put a pot of rice on the stove to boil. Retrieving the burlap sack with the bass I had caught that morning (which I swept overboard from time to time throughout the day to keep cool), I cleaned the fish, fried the fillets and head in a pan with oil, onion, and garlic, chopped a yam, put the works in the half-cooked pot of rice with a bullion cube, and covered it to cook a while longer.

The stew was hearty and tasty, the best meal of the trip so far, and I felt re-energized for the journey – warm food so essential to one's sense of wellbeing. An orangey glow came over the cove and the rock-strewn hillsides, but even so, it was a somewhat dust-filled and desolate-feeling place. The transistor radio did not pick up any signal, and the dial moved stiffly with salt crystals already accumulating under the face. Once the sun went down, I snuggled into my bag and started in on *Leaves of Grass* by the light of my headlamp, Walt Whitman an appropriate companion for my 19th century mode of travel.

I made coffee in the morning as I do everyday, and these cups aboard *Cormorant* – fine grounds boiled straight in a pot of water cowboy style – have been the best cups of my life. The men who had given me a tow the evening before motored past and idled for a minute to say good morning. They were divers also, like the men up at Punta Banda the previous morning. The oldest fellow had a coarse black beard and a boxer's scarred face creased by sun and salt air. He smoked a cigarette and nodded sagaciously when I admitted that I had gotten myself in a bit of a fix the night before. "*Que te vaya bien.*" – go well – he said to me, which is always heartening to hear, with its quality of a blessing, and they were off.

The morning unfolded slowly, the sun warming the cove as it rose higher. I hung my damp sleeping bag from the halyard on the main mast after folding and stowing the boat tent. Getting under way each day involved a precise system of shuffling, repacking, and then restowing my gear, as in such a small craft each space had multiple uses. The sleeping platform had to be taken down to place the packed dry bags, and the pots washed before I could stow them away with the stove.

I gave the divers a beach towel I had brought, because from the first day out it was soaked, and I saw that it would never dry out enough to serve its purpose. The radio no longer even registered static, the dial refusing to turn past 103.9 and the little screws holding the body in place already encrusted with rust. I wanted to pitch it overboard, but my conscience wouldn't allow it, and I packed it deep within one of the dry bags.

By midmorning I was hungry again, and with the boat pretty well squared away, I heated the rest of the fish stew and finished it off, enjoying it even more this time as the flavors had settled throughout. With a quick scrub out of the pots over the side, I finished stowing my sleeping bag and galley.

I untied from the mooring, stood up, and waved to the empty houses on the beach and then bowed in thanks and set off under oars through the thick kelp for the open water beyond.

A light wind had already started up, and my best guess was that the time was near eleven as I hung the rudder and hoisted sail, running about a mile off the coast and keeping an eye out for kelp beds that would impede our progress. Not two miles on, *Cormorant* got mired, which forced me through the awkward process of first cutting away the kelp and then bringing the rudder aboard, switching to oars, and then redoing the process in reverse once free.

The afternoon turned out to be another day of gentle sailing, the rolling hills leading down in ravines to wide, sloping beaches. The winds were steady and light enough to allow reading, and holding the tiller under the crook of my knee, I continued with Whitman, channeling him to the occasional pelican or gull: "Swift wind! Space! My Soul!" I was so consumed that I sailed right past the cove I had thought to shelter in.

With a sailing guide for Baja, I had some information on good anchorages (or anchorages that would serve), and I regularly spread out my charts and noted my location off the more prominent headlands and points. But as night began to fall, I realized that I had passed the secondary shelter I had identified, so involved was I in reading aloud. That meant I had to push on through 25 miles of darkness to the next possible anchorage. This loose reckoning was not at all in keeping with my generally focused approach to my journey. I had been lulled into complacency by Walt Whitman, the fine breeze, and soft winter sunshine.

I sailed to the edge of another vast kelp bed that looked to be three or four miles long and two miles across, and surveyed my situation. A little town was perched on a rocky bluff, and although I scanned the coastline carefully through my binoculars, I could not see any place that seemed like a landing – no place where pangas sat in rows on the beach, no obvious ramp down to shore. I was not overly concerned at first, and decided to sail on into the night, as I was running easily enough before a 12-knot northwesterly breeze and keeping well offshore.

A full moon rose over the arroyos, the desert held a pinkish glow, and stars shone down like a compliment in a million points of light all across the water. I sailed along, swaddled against the cold in a parka and outer shell, drifting in my thoughts deep into the night. Eventually, the wind fell away, and the ocean settled into a broad, glassy sheet. I smelled the clean desert scrub on the suddenly warmer air. The lines and sails and my outer jacket seemed to crackle in the dryness.

I knew that this was all the warning I would get.

Lashing the tiller in place with a bungee, I scrambled forward and dropped the main sail. Not one minute later, I saw and heard the wind line across the water behind, roaring down and tearing at the surface like a swarm of locust: the dreaded *Norte*. People call it the devil wind because of the fires it breathes to life and, I suppose, for the madness too. It is a terrible, mindless thing.

The wind did not slam into us so much as gather up and consume us, then sling us forward with spindrift and foam flying all around. Both hands on the tiller, I pulled hard to keep *Cormorant* running before the short and steep waves, surging ahead on the bigger swells with a strange vibration shuddering throughout the hull. A couple of steep lurches put us right on the beam-ends, the very scenario of capsizing in a raging sea that I had imagined, and cold water slurped in over the rail and filled the boat to her bilges with a frigid footbath. But the danger was too immediate to think of anything beyond keeping the boat upright, even if somewhere in my consciousness lurked the image, inevitable it seemed, of going over.

How long did I run like this? It seemed a lifetime, as the intensity of the flashing spray, the points of starlight dancing weirdly, and the moon gleaming off the waves kept my gaze locked just ahead of the bow – the steeper swells catching my peripheral vision as they swept alongside and hurled us faster on.

My hands ached with the strain of holding the tiller, and then my upper arms and shoulders began to burn. There was no option for relief. Steering through the steep troughs was the only way to remain upright, and although I was sailing on the small mizzen alone, it seemed even bare poles would have been enough for the wind to drive us dangerously fast.

I had come in closer to the shore and found myself a few hundred yards off a wide sandy beach. The wind here blew straight offshore over what appeared to be a series of dunes, and lumbering swells rose up with spray sheeting off their tops like fireboat hoses in full harbor display.

In the blue dark of the night, which for all its violence, had a magical quality, I thought I saw a light in the dunes. The surf was well shaped and eight to ten feet. I imagined a longtime surfer set up here in a camper, and the thought of an old bro and his dog made me smile. I was so sure he was there that I considered making for the beach through the big surf. But I read the conditions for a moment longer and realized that I would lose everything if I tried to make it in. I sailed on.

The wind still hurled us down the coast, the occasional tendril of kelp wrapping the rudder blade like a tentacle and then breaking free with the inexorable force of our momentum. Though my hands, arms, and shoulders were knotted with fatigue, I was prevailing in the fight to keep the boat steering in line with the waves. I even got the hang of riding out the bigger ones, and actually hooted once with the fun of linking one wave with a second and then a third steep swell for a shooshing toboggan slide of more than 100 yards.

I recognized that *Cormorant* was handling herself and that her pointed stern split the waves like cordwood, allowing them to roll off to either side. I had only to maintain my course, and if I managed to avoid running up on a reef, I would eventually make the sheltering cliffs of Punta Colonet. It was an absurd situation nonetheless – the roaring wind and desolate shore, this long winter night and the ghostly moonglow illuminating the whitecaps off into the distance – completely alone in my open boat, 250 miles down the coast.

Then I sang. For the ridiculous peril I faced, for my folly, for grace, and for a prayer. I sang the old Anglican hymn "Praise for Creation," and the wind became almost funny at that point – the absolute opposite, the utter rejection of morning and calm. The fact that no one in the world had a clue as to my predicament, or even, precisely where I was and, even more so, that I had put myself here struck me somehow as humorous. "Blackbird has spo-ken," I belted out in the rage, "like the first bhir-hi-hi-hirrrd!"

I had come in close now, spray blowing back off the crashing surf just a few hundred yards in, and the high cliffs of Colonet loomed ahead. As I had hoped, when I sailed to the base of the sheer walls, the wind passed overhead, 300 feet off the mesa, and left the water calm and strangely still, even as the ocean went ragged not 100 yards outside.

I could have scrambled up the boulders to kiss that old cliff face for the shelter it provided.

I set anchor and then put booties over my wet wool socks, slaked my thirst with deep draughts of fresh water, and mashed handfuls of trail mix into my mouth. My body shook with fear, exaltation, and relief. I wrapped myself in the mainsail, too exhausted to arrange the boat tent and sleeping bag.

The moon and stars had burned into my irises, and light patterns swirled hypnotically behind my lids. With these strange points of light in my vision, I wondered if this was what dying might be like.

CHAPTER FOUR

LETICIA AND THE WHALES

I awoke the next morning to a calm sea under a hot sun. I sat up, unsure for a moment of where I was, and startled a mama and baby dolphin that had been lounging just along *Cormorant*'s starboard side. My charts and binocular case were floating in the bottom of the boat; I reached for the bucket and began bailing. With everything so calm and sunny, it seemed the world could have no other face, and the night before was from some other lifetime.

Punta Colonet was an enormous, horseshoe-shaped mesa that protruded about a mile out and two miles across, the tall, sheer bluff rounding seaward like the ramparts of a great fortress. After bailing *Cormorant*, I rowed in the languid sun along the base of the cliff, working in along its long curve. I shed my layers until I wore only trunks and a T-shirt, the morning as still as if after a hurricane. Much farther in, but still a good quarter-mile from the innermost corner where the bluffs met the run of a cobblestone beach, I set anchor off a cut in the cliff line. An old man was fishing from the rocks with a gaggle of boys around him.

I packed a dry bag with a water bottle, binoculars, a sweatshirt, some granola bars, and one of the big bars of chocolate to give to the kids. Even though I valued my chocolate like a precious commodity, I thought those little guys would like it even more. I slipped over the side with flippers on and the dry bag over my shoulder, feeling like some hybrid of Santa Claus and a Navy SEAL.

The boys were milling around like puppies tumbling over each other, their grandfather a smiling old fellow. It was a Sunday, and he had brought them out for the day from their farm a few miles down the coast. There were five of them, the youngest perhaps six years old and their leader, the eldest, about 13. He was a beautiful child, his face finely made with dark, arching brows and delicate lashes over clear and intelligent eyes. I left my flippers and dry bag with the man, and his grandsons followed me up a narrow path in the cut to the mesa like a squad of awkward soldiers. Using driftwood sticks for swords, the boys lopped the heads off the dried thistles and ran up and back on the trail. When we reached the top, I told them they had better go back down to the beach.

With binoculars on a strap around my neck, a water bottle, and a sweatshirt tied around my waist, I set out for the end of the mesa. It was good walking ground, the desert clean and yuccas in bloom with bright yellow flowers off the tops of their shooting stalks. Isla San Martín showed in distant silhouette, and here and there the dark humps of migrating grey whales surfaced with soft spouts.

Standing on the cliff edge was heady, as it was a long, sheer drop to a fringe of boulders below. The coast drifted into haze to the southeast, but the extinct volcano cones near San Quintín stood out like tropical islands. Red and white checkerboard panels sat at the very headland of Colonet, with a small light on top of a tower of narrow-gage steel – none of which seemed significant markers for such a prominent point of land. I walked back slowly along the edge of the mesa and took the trail down the cut again to the old man and the boys.

He had caught a nice bass while I was away, and the boys were poking at it with sticks. I gave them the chocolate, and the old man and I talked about the previous night's wind; he said it had been really bad on land too. The boys had rimes of chocolate around their mouths by now, and I was so glad to have someone to talk to that I just stood there smiling at the phenomena of an old guy passing the morning with his grandkids.

I noticed a wave breaking in a nice peak in the corner of the bay, and I told the man and kids that I would be on my way, and we wished each other well: *that you should go well*, as it is said in Mexico.

The water was invigorating in just board shorts, but the swim back to *Cormorant* wasn't long, and I felt better for having made the plunge. It was so warm and still that rowing was a pleasure, and I soon glided to the inside and looked across to a cobblestone crumbler that broke a lot like the famous wave at Trestles in San Clemente. I maneuvered *Cormorant* inside to get a better look at the wave and then moved farther off again to anchor in deeper water.

The beach was formed of a high berm of cobblestones, backed by thickets of sickly-looking willows. Its north end cut off abruptly at the tall cliffs of the mesa, and the coast led away to the south beneath a series of bluffs and swales. *Cormorant*'s gunwales gleamed amber-colored and felt warm to the touch in the afternoon sun. A honeybee alighted there, next to the oarlock, and then another one landed on my forearm.

Another set down on the gunwale, and then a few more, and I looked up to see a swarm flying about in a thick cloud overhead. In a moment they were crawling over the entire boat – as if *Cormorant* had been sprayed with adhesive and dragged through a vat of bees – giving the oars, now the thwarts and benches, and finally my entire body the aspect of swollen, undulating, movement.

The bees didn't seem perturbed, and I gently brushed them aside to lay my oars down and then turned to sweep away a place for my foot and stepped forward to gingerly drop the anchor. The dry bag was still packed from my mesa walk, and

I grabbed it then jumped into the water, taking a bunch of the little guys with me, but only catching one sting on my upper butt.

From shore I could see the bees enveloping the boat like a blanket, and like a refugee forced from home with only the possessions I could grab, I took stock of my supplies: one power bar, a liter of water, and a sweatshirt. Although it was only midafternoon I knew darkness would come fast this time of year, so I walked inland towards the sound of tractors cultivating a field, mud squishing up between my toes.

I figured a farmer in the area might keep bees, and if the swarm hived up it would be an easy score, and I could get my boat back – everybody wins. But the man on the tractor wasn't interested in trying to figure out what I was saying (I didn't know the word for bees, *"abejas,"* in Spanish), so I slogged back to the beach.

The afternoon progressed towards evening, the temperature dropped, and the bees massed up in a ball at the top of the main mast. I was wondering what to do next when a man, woman, and a small boy came walking down the beach. I stood up as they approached and said, *"Buenas tardes."*

"How you doin'?" the man asked me. He had a stiff gray beard and a tight mass of gray hair that lay back on his head in wavelets – not from a salon but from sun and salt water it seemed. The woman was far younger, a pretty Mexican lady with high eyebrows and attractive eyes. When she spoke however, it was clear that she was drunk, and the man told me not to listen to her. The boy, about four-years-old, threw rocks and watched them clatter off the other rocks.

I pointed to the knot of bees at the top of the main mast, and the man grasped the bottom half of his face and stroked his mustache and beard with his whole hand, raising his eyebrows as if astonished by the phenomenon. "Well," he said, "you got a situation there."

"I guess I'm not going to do anything about it tonight," I observed.

"Nah," the man agreed, "guess you won't."

"You come with us," the woman offered, and the man nodded.

"Yeah. We got blankets," he told me, "you can stay in the schooner."

His name was Cameron and his wife's Leticia – the little boy was Roger. We made an odd party, walking back to the corner of the beach. I hobbled along in bare feet over the cobbles, and guessing that Cameron was a surfer, I observed that the break here reminded me of Trestles.

"The real wave is over there," he said, pointing to the cove where the high cliff met the coast, but he seemed preoccupied so I didn't ask more.

Their home was a single story adobe house on a raised earthen platform. There were two closed shutters that served for a window and a patio area with an awning made from cut-off, gnarled tree trunks that supported a trellis of interlocking strips of used drip irrigation. When he opened the door, the man disappeared inside for a moment then emerged with a plastic jug of tequila.

"Drink," he said to the woman. She made a waving gesture as if she didn't want any more. He said it again, more forcefully, and she took the jug.

When he passed it to me, I said I was all right, thanks, and was relieved and surprised that he accepted my answer.

He lit a joint and toked on it severely three or four times, brought it down to inspect the quality of its burn, and hit it again before holding it out towards me. The little boy, Roger, stood by his mother on the patio, and I half expected Cameron to pass it to him when I told him that I was all right without the smoke, either.

"I love-*ee* the *mota*," Leticia said with a high cackle as she took the joint, but before she could get much of a hit, Cameron gestured for it impatiently, and she quickly handed it back to him.

The schooner, 50 feet long, stood in an eight-foot-deep trench in front of the adobe, its starboard side staved in, with a washer and a rusted box for steps alongside.

"Couple of old guys," Cameron said, taking a pull of tequila and another hit of his joint, "ran this puppy straight into the beach here."

"For *moneeey*," Leticia added with a knowing leer, rubbing her thumb and first two fingers together.

"Why don't you make dinner?" Cameron said to Leticia, but it was not a question, and she went inside and turned on a single bulb that seemed to leak the barest gleam of light.

The boy was squatted on his haunches now, petting a mewing kitten so hard that its four legs spread out on the patio floor.

"Too hard," Cameron told Roger. The man laughed, looking at his son and the kitten through reddened eyes. "Little guy rubbed that cat's lower lip right off," he said to me. And when I expressed surprise, he said, "Bring the kitty," and the boy picked up the kitten by its forepaw and then held it by the neck with his other hand like he was strangling it. Cameron took the cat and held it up for me to see, and sure enough, its bottom lip was gone, rimmed by scabs, the lower teeth exposed as if it had a chew of tobacco in. "Just came outside," Cameron related, "and there he was, rubbing away with his hand on the back of the cat's head."

The boy made no expression, and the father said nothing more about it. Through the open door I could see Leticia at the kitchen counter, carrying on a conversation and laughing with invisible companions.

"Goddamnit!" Cameron roared. "How long does it take?"

"OK, OK," she said, stifling a giggle as if she had heard something she didn't want him to know. She pulled a pot down from a hook in the ceiling and set the water to boil, and began chopping onions, laughing, and chattering away in a mocking tone: "You *do-ee* the *cook-ee*! Hey you!" she said in a mock tone of a stern man. "You *cook-ee*!" and she laughed again.

Cameron shook his head when we sat at the patio table, "She's fuckin' nuts."

Leticia periodically came out to tell me about the bats flying around in the night air, pointing them out – the darting shadows that flitted just outside the awning – until Cameron screamed at her to finish the goddamn dinner and made her drink more tequila, which I guessed was some attempt to medicate her. Dinner, when it finally came, was a pasta salad of canned tuna fish with a lot of mayonnaise.

The night grew cold, and I was uncomfortable in shorts and bare feet with just a sweatshirt for warmth. I tried to remain the unruffled guest, making light conversation when I could and saying, "Ah, don't worry," or, "It's OK," when Cameron apologized for almost attacking his wife – not, of course, that there was anything remotely OK about this situation. But there was little, if anything, that I could do about it, except to prevent him from actually physically attacking her, which seemed more and more possible as the evening wore on.

"Thank you very much," I said to him, "for taking me in." And, trying for something like normal conversation, I said, "Man, bees on my boat – I never read about that in any sailing manuals!" Cameron smiled in a sort of wince and nodded as if he appreciated my effort.

"And Leticia," I continued, feeling that I might be straying into dangerous territory by addressing his wife, "dinner was delicious."

"Thanks-you," she said, nearly falling back in her chair with a hiccup. "I mean, *gracias*."

The wind was up again – another *Norte*
but less intense than the night before,
and Cameron told Leticia to get me the
blankets. Roger, the little boy, had gone
inside some time earlier, and I guessed
he was asleep in the small dark room
beyond the kitchen. After taking the plates
in, Leticia came back out with a stack of
blankets, which she handed to me with a
candle. Then the three of was walked over
to the schooner, the stars like cold, hard
bits of rock in the night sky and the hulk of
the ship an incongruous form on land even
in the dark.

"Careful climbing up there," Cameron
said, staying on firm ground as first
Leticia, and then I, stood on the thin metal
box that wobbled under our weight but got
us up to the slightly more solid footing of
the washer. Once on board, she slid open
the companionway hatch and lit a candle to lead me to a berth
amidships. She set the thick pile of blankets on a cushion in
the berth and left the candle burning on a shelf. The locking
cabin door made me feel secure, and I settled in to sleep and
to forget about the day.

Perhaps an hour later, despite how tired I felt, I was still
thinking about the events of the day. A banging noise on deck
jarred me from the cusp of slumber, and the companionway

hatch slid open. I heard footfalls on the passageway and a knock at my door. "*Es Leti,*" came a whispered announcement.

Leticia stood in the hatchway with a candle before her and a blanket over herself like a cloak, smelling thickly of tequila. She came and sat on the edge of my berth and put her hand on the blanket over my thigh. "You like to feel a woman's body?" she asked.

"Ah, no..." I said gently. "*No es correcto.*"

"*Es OK,*" she said, leaning towards me with that cutting breath.

"*No*," I said, "*su esposo....* – your husband – unsure of why I was speaking to her in Spanish.

"*Es OK*," Leticia repeated, "he don't care."

I said no again, and she seemed to take that answer, and leaned over to use her candle to light the one she had left me.

"This place," she said, waving a hand like a wand, "*es mágico*." The candlelight caught the raised brows of her face, and her cheekbones held darkened hollows underneath, her hair a wild, coursing thatch of black waves. "The little, how you say, the bobcat, she call, she go '*ayee, ayee, ayee,*' in the nighttime," she said laughing, as if at the antics of a friend.

"And the *ballena*," Leticia continued, "she sing to me when she pass out there," pointing towards the sea. "I hear she voice."

I went to check on *Cormorant* at first light, climbing down from the schooner and making my way across the cobblestone beach, ungainly in trunks and bare feet in the icy dawn. A little puppy, sleeping by the pangas parked on the berm, woke to follow me. When we reached the middle of the beach, I saw *Cormorant* at anchor, the bees still clustered in a ball at the top of the main mast. The boat rolled heavily in the offshore wind.

I wanted my vessel back, and I considered just swimming out right then to bring her ashore under oars, but Cameron had told me the night before that he would have the fishermen tow *Cormorant* over when they showed up for their workday in the morning. Feeling obligated somehow to wait for the help my host had offered to arrange, I hobbled back to the house.

They were awake by then and Leticia had hot water prepared for the coffee. Sipping my Nescafé, I glanced at Leticia and then at Cameron to see if anything moved between them. Dawn seemed to have given them a fresh start. Any tension from last night had diminished or been forgotten.

Roger picked up the puppy, and I kept an eye on him, listening for any yelps. But all was peace this day, and even Roger was playing nice, dragging a stick with a frayed piece of line that the puppy chased after and nipped at with bounding little lunges.

I asked Cameron how he came to live in such a good spot, and he said he'd just stayed down here after one of his surf trips. "Haven't been back to the States in 12 years." He explained that when Leticia got pregnant, her family arranged for them to stay in the adobe in the cove. "I used to pay rent," he said with a raised eyebrow, "a hundred bucks a month." He shrugged, "They just stopped asking for it after a while." Taking a sip of his coffee, he said, "I keep an eye on the pangas."

He added, "They're all Melings here."

Meling, it turned out, was a Scandinavian sea captain in the 19th century. He was shipwrecked here, Cameron told me, and built the adobe with salvaged timbers from his ship. "Come and look," Cameron said, rising from his chair on the patio and walking over to a shed. He pulled on a loop of rope to swing open a thick-planked door – presumably made from the wreck. Inside, a decrepit rowboat stood vertically on its transom, and various coils of ropes, floats, traps made haphazard piles, against which and a few fishing poles with missing eyelets and absent handles leaned here and there.

"They're all Melings," Cameron said. "You'll see. The fishermen have blue eyes." As Cameron told it, the sea captain made his way to the governor's office up in Ensenada after the wreck and made a deal to survey the coast and build wharves in exchange for land grants. To this day, the Rancho Meling still hosts visitors up in the mountains near the Parque San Pedro Martir.

The fishermen arrived soon after, and Cameron, as promised, talked with Jorge Meling, who did, incidentally, have blue eyes.

"*¿Es OK?*" the fisherman asked me, "We get you boat when we come back?"

"Sure," I replied – what else could I say? "*¿Cuándo regresan ustedes?*" – when will you be back? – I asked.

"Two, maybe three hour," the man told me.

"*Gracias,*" I said, wishing even more now that I had brought the boat over an hour-and-a-half before, so that these men could just help me heave her out now, rather than four or five hours from now, which is what Baja time would amount to.

Cameron stood to the side, watching as the men prepared their boats.

"Today you come fishing?" they teased, and he turned and walked to the house.

They slid the boats down the steep cobbles and splashed them, one man rowing with skimpy-looking oars over the short swells and the other pulling the outboard to life. Each boat then tore off across the smooth water, and I went up to the house as well.

Cameron had a clunky-looking laptop set up in the room at the back half of the adobe. "Solar panel," he said, by way of explanation. A cleanly shaped 8'2" surfboard hung from the rafters in the kitchen-half of the house. "Check it out," he said, and brought up grainy photos on the screen of good surf, groomed by offshore winds. "That's the cove," he said, indicating the wave out front. "Only works sometimes, though." He lit a cigarette and swiveled around in his chair.

"Looks good," I said of the surf in the photos.

"On a big swell the whole point lights up – I've surfed it fifteen, eighteen foot."

On a shelf above his desk – a card table with cigarette burns in the vinyl where the surface showed between old papers, dirty socks, and an overflowing ashtray – stood a plaster skull painted black with silver swastikas on each side. A bumper sticker, attached to the edge of the shelf with a pushpin, showed a series of playing cards with a drawing of an eye and a heart on the left side of the row that formed the message: "I love to ace spades."

He trembled noticeably. "I fucked my back up racing," Cameron said, and brought up photos of riders on Harleys sliding into the corners of dirt flat tracks. He spoke of La Jolla. He would have been a young man in the 1970s and seemed formed of the dark underbelly of that era, when surfing meant brawling – not a little tussle in the sand, but full on fistfights – and when surfing was for outlaws.

I never knew that time, but I remembered seeing guys like that when I first started surfing as a boy in 1978. They seemed like survivors or holdovers from another era. Huntington

Beach was a place for that class of petty criminal wave-rider, often low-level drug pushers who had spent time in prison.

Cameron brought up a game of solitaire on the laptop, and I went back outside, happy for the air.

———————

The bees were still at the mast top when the fishermen brought me over to *Cormorant* late in the morning. I leaned off the bow of the panga and pulled the anchor on *Cormorant* and then ran her bow line aft to an eye on the stern of the fisherman's boat. My hope was that the tow would be enough to dislodge the bees: It was not.

Cameron, the fishermen, and I all gathered to discuss the next plan of action.

I was with the fishermen, who thought the best thing would be to drop the mast and pour seawater on the clustered bees, but Cameron was already engaged in cutting away strips of an abandoned tire.

Through his tremors, his eyes got wide, and he said, "We'll burn 'em out!" with such zeal that it was clear that this was in fact the next thing that would happen.

The fishermen now watched Cameron as he hunted around behind the adobe, coming back down to the beach with a 12-foot two-by-four, holding some nails in his lips, and carrying a hammer. When he had nailed the tire strips to one end of the two-by-four, he told Roger to bring the can of gas, which the little guy did even though it nearly reached his waist, and he had to drag, as much as carry, it down from the patio.

His dad then doused the strips and lit them, and I couldn't help but picture a cross burning as he raised the contraption to the bees atop the main mast.

Bits of melted, flaming rubber dripped off the end of the two-by-four, and I was afraid he would foul the sails or the halyard with the noxious stuff. Copious billows of black smoke wafted into the midst of the bees and at least some of them peeled off the hive and swarmed around angrily, as I imagined they would do. But the main group remained, squeezing down into a tighter ball to protect themselves and their queen who was surely at the center of the sphere.

I persuaded Cameron to put the two-by-four down, even though he had worked himself into a fury, shouting "Ha!" and poking his stick at the hive. This was modern man in all his folly, the tire strips burning down, coating the rocks in bubbling tar and still trailing a thick cloud of smoke. The mast top was blackened and a good portion of the halyard as well, but somehow no rubber had fallen on the sails or aboard my vessel. The bees that had swarmed off the surface of the ball seemed to settle back to the main group, which remained unmoved by the performance.

I put my wetsuit and booties on, with gloves, a diving mask, and a scarf wrapped around my head so I could approach the hive more directly. Taking the cleat out of the block at the base of the mast, I then lowered it gently. I then waded into the water, and dunked the whole hive. I hated this. It was not working, and the bees clung on tenaciously. They were sluggish now from their plunge, and some were drowned, floating on the little waves in a needless waste. I finally just laid the mast aside.

Cormorant was a mess, with dead bees strewn across tangled lines and gear, and I began to unpack everything, hauling it farther up the berm to dry out in the heat of the day. Once I laid out all of my clothes and my equipment, recoiled the lines and sorted my food stores, I washed down the interior with bucketful after bucketful of seawater, scooping dead and dying bees down toward the two drain plugs I had opened in the bottom near the stern.

With that all done, I sat down and leaned against the low wall in front of the adobe patio, and looked out over the reef that was now exposed with the low tide. It was a beautiful, warm winter day, and the sun poured down with an almost liquid quality. Cameron had long since gone inside, I saw no sign of Leticia or the boy, and the fishermen had all left as well. The only people I saw were out on the reef, perhaps four or five of them, turning over rocks, hunting for something.

I thought of writing in my journal, but the sun felt so good that I just let the tiredness run through my body, and I remained there, looking out on the scene. In a little while, a fellow came walking up from the corner of the cove. He wore a ball cap and a red and white jersey with horizontal stripes, and he carried a sack full of octopus he had caught with a mean-looking piece of rusted iron bent into a hook and lashed to a long dowel for a handle. His bicycle was parked along the wall where I sat, and he heaved his catch into a milk crate that he had on a rack over the rear tire.

We introduced ourselves. His name was Marco. He had been to a lot of places in the U.S., he told me, crossing the border and hiking over the desert many times. Ultimately, he decided it was better for him in Mexico; he didn't like the life up there, he said. Seeing my boat, he seemed to sense that I had my doubts about it too. He offered to share his lunch of delicious little rolled tacos, insisting that he had too much to eat all on his own. I went to my supplies and brought back water and a bag of pistachios. There was something of a seer about him, a gentle quality that suggested he didn't pronounce judgments, but only offered observations. He lived about eight miles away he said, as he stood to ride home.

Later in the afternoon, packing my gear as the shadow from the mesa crept across the cobblestone beach, Cameron stood nearby smoking a joint. "That guy," he said, jutting his chin towards a man in a new pickup who was parked on the berm about a hundred feet away, "is buying up the whole mesa." I clipped the dry bags shut and set them in the bottom of the boat, and looked over at the man. He was watching the cove with a woman in the passenger seat. He looked towards Cameron and me, and honked the horn of his truck, motioning for us to come over.

"*Buenas tardes*," he said with a smile beneath a substantial black mustache. Cameron glanced away nervously it seemed, with his hands in the pockets of his grubby sweatshirt.

I shook hands with the man, and Cameron mumbled something about the house and walked away.

"You *eh-stay* with him?" the man asked, and I explained the situation with the bees, and again he smiled, the mustache almost like a living thing over his mouth.

"*El Presidente*, Calderon, he come here last year in a *helicópeoro*," he said, looking over the cove as if over the future itself. "Gonna make this whole thing," he continued, with a wave of his hand that was not unlike Leticia's magic wave the night before, but took in the whole sweep of the headland, "a big port, like Ensenada."

I nodded and glanced at the woman in the passenger seat – her makeup and big earrings, her manicured nails – and I thought of babies reaching for shiny things.

"We let your *frien* stay for now," the man said.

I excused myself to finish stowing my gear and walked back to my boat.

To fix the split bow I got from the panga-hit back at Puerto Santo Tomás, I had asked Cameron for a wood screw and a dowel. He drove Leticia cruelly to find those things, forcing her to crawl over stacked boxes in a shed, and barking orders so that I regretted asking for anything at all.

She did, however, come up with a screw and a dowel, and using the hand-cranked drill I had in my tool kit, I drilled a hole into the stem at the middle part of the break and then drove the dowel home with a cobblestone. With a smaller bit I drilled a hole through the center of the dowel and screwed the wood screw in. Cameron had found wood glue and a can of black spray paint in the house and I used these as well to make a pretty good fix – or at least one that would keep the split from growing larger. It was too late in the day to travel, and Cameron said I should have dinner with them again.

The man in the pick up honked once as he drove past on the road out, the woman looking straight ahead in a silhouette of curls and earrings.

———————

Leticia seemed better that night, not as drunk or maybe a little mellowed by the weed she smoked. Cameron, on the other hand, was agitated and continued shouting orders at her, while the boy played with a toy car in the dirt, apparently oblivious to all around him.

"Why can't you just cook a meal?" Cameron wailed from the patio.

"I *cook-ee*!" Leticia called back from the kitchen, understandably annoyed as she dropped three fish into a frying pan of oil.

"You getting smart?" he threatened.

"I not smart," she replied meekly, as if the conversation had gone this way before.

The puppy was curled up, sleeping by the corner of the adobe near where Roger was playing. The kitten was not around.

"*Su perrito, es muy amable*," – your puppy is very friendly – I said to the boy. "*¿Cómo se llama, él?*" – what's his name?

"Chuy," Roger told me, and then left his car to climb the steps and sit by the dog.

I moved over to sit by the dog as well, and we petted him, the little boy leaning against my knee. *"Muy amable,"* I said.

I was leaving in the morning and I tried, as I had the night before, to be relaxed and undemanding – to be an understanding buddy to Cameron and sympathetic to Leticia without alienating either one of them. This, of course was an impossible task, and as we sat to eat, I thanked her again for her wonderful cooking – a generous assessment. Cameron said that it was a wonder we were eating at all since it took her so damn long to do anything. Leticia told him that I would make a better husband than him, and we sat eating in silence for a time.

"If it wasn't for the kid… " Cameron said to me.

I settled in the schooner again to sleep, listening to the wind though the fittings that remained on the deck. No one visited, and it was a deep and quite night in the arroyo. At the first hint of light I was up, stowing my gear in *Cormorant* and lining up the skids to slide her back into the water. Leticia brought me a coffee and smiled shyly – looking sane and sober, pretty and a little sad.

Cameron came out to the patio, and I walked up to him to shake hands and thank him for the shelter and the help.

The tide was high, and the water came well up the berm of cobblestones with the surges of swell that seemed to have increased throughout the night. A wave feathered in the corner of the cove, brushed by the offshore wind, and cupped across for a moment before disappearing in the deeper water inside the reef.

Cameron saw it too, and said, "That's where it breaks when it's on."

He walked down to help me shove *Cormorant* off, and she slipped down the skids so fast with our strong heave that I had to scramble after her, only just leaping aboard before she splashed and glided out on the still morning water. I set the oars in the locks and sat down to row, facing shoreward with the bow heading out.

Cameron stood with his arm around Leticia, and his other hand on Roger's shoulder as the boy stood in front of his parents, and I waved goodbye.

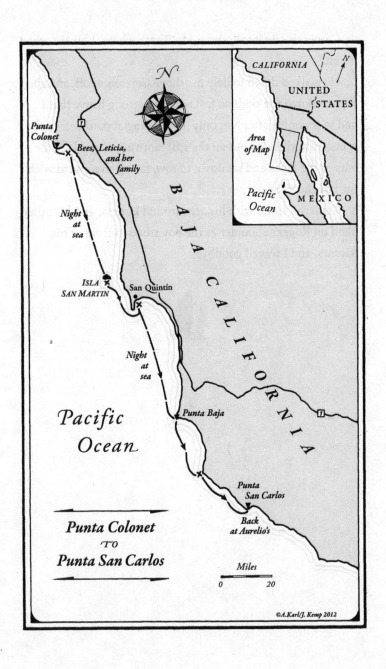

CALIFORNIA

UNITED
STATES

Area
of Map

Pacific
Ocean

MEXICO

Punta
Colonet

Bees, Leticia,
and her
family

Night
at
sea

ISLA
SAN MARTIN

San Quintín

Night
at
sea

Punta Baja

Pacific
Ocean

Punta
San Carlos

Back
at Aurelio's

B A J A   C A L I F O R N I A

Punta Colonet
TO
Punta San Carlos

Miles

0   20

©A.Karl/J.Kemp 2012

CHAPTER FIVE

SLOW CROSSINGS, BIG WAVES

Nightfall out from Punta Colonet found me in deep, open water, somewhere along the 15 miles to my destination of Isla San Martín. The wind had been light to non-existent all day but had nevertheless carried me miles enough for the tall cliffs of Colonet to have slipped from view. Now only the dome of the island rose out of the horizon, visible to the south. I sailed south by southwest to Isla San Martín, which is only a few miles off the coast, but my course took me well offshore to avoid the thick kelp beds that lay between Colonet and San Quintín.

The wind went completely calm at sunset, but the sky was so clear, the water so still and wide, that I was not at all alarmed by night coming down. I enjoyed the feeling of being aboard my good little ship.

I dropped the main, shipped the rudder, and furled the mizzen before setting the drogue to minimize whatever drift there might be. I made tea on the stove and ate trail mix. The oars I set near the locks and pulled the sail over my sleeping bag, rather than putting up the tent in case I needed to maneuver at some point in the night. Adrift as if among the stars themselves, I lay back and stared skyward – enveloped, cradled by the universe.

In the stillness I heard the exhalations of whales passing in the dark.

A cold offshore wind started well before dawn, and I came to regret not getting up to take advantage of it, so warm and comfortable was my sleeping bag. By eight in the morning the wind was gone. Another gorgeous, calm, sunny day lay before me, with nothing but open sea in every direction and just the outline of the island away to the south.

Baitfish broke the surface a hundred yards off the starboard side, followed by the thrashing of bigger fish, their tailfins cutting the water and making great boiling patterns. Soon gulls, terns, and pelicans were wheeling out of the sky and plunging in, and although I rigged up a silver spoon on my rod and reel and rowed in the direction of the action, but I got no hits.

I waited for the wind until late morning, realizing finally that it was to be one of those "perfect" winter days and that no wind would come at all. So I set to rowing. Concentrating on my technique, trying to be as efficient as possible with my movements, I used the length and weight of my body to lean through the strokes, not pulling too hard with my arms. I would row for 45 minutes and then break long enough to drink some water and check my progress from both the land passing far off the port side and the details of the island ahead. But any changes were a long time in distinguishing themselves.

The hours went by neither slowly nor quickly, and I felt a tremendous fortitude in taking the situation for what it was. I decided that rowing was no more difficult than riding a bike, and with that thought fixed, I worked through the whole, calm day in 45-minute intervals.

The ocean and sky went golden and a high formation of pelicans passed, gliding straight on for the island. By now, far too regularly, I was turning to see if I was any closer. But I kept on. What else? A line of cormorants coursed by just over the water as the sky reddened in the last light of day. I was fatigued, but I rowed on in my drive to reach the island. I heard the waves gurgling finally among the rocks on the north coast, and knew from the sailing guide that I had only to follow the curve of the circular isle eastward to come into a nicely sheltered cove.

It was dark now, and I could only decipher shapes as there was no moon, but a marker light for navigation stood on a pole at the end of a natural jetty, marking the cove. Once inside, I rowed towards the dark shore to lie in close. The island rose in a wall of blackness from where the waterline should have been, and I inched in until the bow nudged a rock wall. I then backed away and threw the hook. Some seals got spooked and splashed from their rocky perches, and I saw the smooth curves of four heads in the water in the quick flash of the marker light across the little anchorage. I set up the boat tent and gratefully fell into a deep sleep.

Morning – another morning – but I had the unique experience of waking up in a place I had only seen in the deepest of shadows of the previous night. Harbor seals watched me from where they lounged on the rocks and from the water. An abandoned fish camp stood on the small beach. One shack had fallen in, and another was on its way down, with sun-bleached boards hanging akimbo through the roof.

The chart showed a second cove just past this one that was even more sheltered – practically sealed off from the sea except for one gap in the jetty that a small boat like *Cormorant* could easily slide through. Moving across the water was like rowing over an aquarium, and once around the end of the jetty that formed my first anchorage, I glided above a kelp forest of a luxuriance I had never seen. Purple urchin dotted the bottom, and big red and black sheepshead floated serenely amongst the fronds; the sleek forms of seals, swift and effortless, slid past.

A flat rock came very near the surface at the keyhole entrance of the next cove, and as I edged in I saw 30 harbor seals sunning themselves on the opposite shore. Not wanting to disturb them, I kept to the furthest side and dropped the anchor as gently as I could. They watched my every move, each seal with both its head and tail pulled up taut, ready to wriggle off the beach at the first note of danger.

The sailing guide noted that a nice trail led to the summit of the extinct volcano and offered a view of the island, which is no more than a mile or so around, and I decided to bring my fishing gear and walk down the opposite side from the peak and come back to my cove via the southern coast, casting from shore as I went. The tide had gone down quite a bit, and I stepped over *Cormorant*'s rail into knee-deep water and waded ashore, scaring the seals into a furious dash for the sea. I felt badly because they had looked so warm on the sand – storing up, no doubt, for their time in the water hunting.

Wherever the trail was that led to the top of the volcano, I could not find it, and I had to walk through thick, spiny bush, working my way around the cholla cactus that grew in dense patches on the slope. I held the fishing rod above my head much of the time and felt lucky on the few occasions that I could leap from one rock to another.

The view from the top was a perfect panorama of the island and the mainland at San Quintín, not four miles across the channel. Shinning blue sea stretched outward and a fresh wind, which I could have used the day before, blew from the

northwest. Starting down the backside of the cone, I was soon
into thicker and deeper brush than I had dealt with on the
way up, and I had to backtrack in a number of places to pick
a route past the more formidable stands of cholla – the thick
spines of which have barbs on the tips.

Eventually, I made the back edge of the island, but an edge
was all that it was. A sheer cliff plunged 40 feet down to a
swath of boulders, over which a slow-moving swell washed
and receded. Walking the cliff edge, I found a rope tied off to
a spike and let myself down hand-over-hand, with the fishing
rod in my teeth, to a platform from where it was an easy
scramble down to the boulders.

I had not followed anything that resembled a trail, not
even an overgrown trail, and yet there was the rope I needed.
It seemed obvious that it should be there.

Climbing out on the boulder that sat farthest seaward, I
cast a rubber lure and promptly snagged it in the kelp. I had
only brought the one, and unwilling to let my expedition be in
vain, I stripped and waded into the cold, clear water, and then
swam the length of the fishing line underwater, found the
lure, and worked it free.

My next cast brought a streaking form out of the kelp, a
blur of green and white spots, and the rod doubled over, the
line whizzing off the reel. My heart pounded, as this was
clearly a real fish, and a little ridiculously I felt a moment of
fear at what the thing might be. It was a beautiful, glistening
calico bass, probably five or six pounds and golden at the base
of its fins. With the fish came a surge of contentment with the
rightness of what I was doing.

The flat rock at the entrance to the cove stood clear of the surface with the low tide in the late afternoon, and *Cormorant* sat on the exposed sand. Checking my tide chart, I realized that I would have to move with the high tide at one the coming morning to clear the shallow entrance to ensure I could sail out the next day whenever I was ready. In the meantime, I nestled in among the sand dunes back from the cove, trying for a windbreak where I had set up the stove. I chopped an onion and set that to brown in oil and then laid a thick fillet across the whole pan, the ends of which curled back as they cooked.

With the rice boiling and my last yam cut into chunks, I had another good fish stew in the works. I ate the fillet on its own while the rice cooked and then fried the second slab of fish with lots of Spike spice peppered over the top, and I got so full that I lay back like an engorged python. I threw the rest of the fish – half of the second fillet with the head and spine – into the pot with a bouillon cube and covered it for later.

The temperature dropped as the sun went down, and I packed up my camp stove and pots, and waded back out to the boat. Tiredness always brought a suggestion of a deeper world-weariness, or an awareness of my solitude, which left me a little sad. I was cold now, and so I put on a down jacket and set up the boat tent, and disappearing into my shelter in the late dusk, I read by the candle lantern, and I wrote in my journal. These were the evening activities, my private occupations.

Late in the night I woke up when I needed to, pulled the anchor by starlight, and with the edges of the tent rolled up for visibility, I rowed out of the little cove to re-set in the kelp bed. The sea felt swollen with the tide and lay perfectly still and dark. I let the tent edges back down and slept again, the whole operation taking no more than 10 minutes and done as if having never woken.

Morning broke sunny and clear, the land and sea in their richest colors with the early light. I set up the camp stove and made a pot of coffee followed by a heaping stack of pancakes. Using precious butter, and one egg for the mix, I ate to fullness and was happy. A panga motored into the cove and soon pulled abreast of *Cormorant*. The three men on board said good morning and asked where I had come from. When I told them that I had sailed from San Diego, the surprise that registered on their faces reminded me of the scope of the endeavor I had undertaken.

I offered them a pancake, but they wanted cigarettes. I had brought a pack of roll-your-own tobacco for the occasional evening smoke, and I held out the papers and a pinch of tobacco, but the men didn't know how to roll, so I rolled each one a cigarette. They asked if it was marijuana. They were an urchin crew, with one diver, who had the most confident attitude and seemed naturally in charge, and his tender, a young man who worked the air compressor and kept the hoses from tangling. The pilot of the panga was older than the other two and more grave in his bearing, sitting aloof in the aft part of the boat, his hand on the tiller of the motor.

Later, well after breakfast and the last of the coffee, and after I had stowed the boat tent and gear and read more *Leaves of Grass* aloud while waiting for the breeze to come up, the men in the panga motored over again.

"*¿Qué pasó?*" – what were you doing? – the diver asked. The tender leaned out to hold *Cormorant*'s rail so that the boats wouldn't bang together.

"*Leyendo,*" I told him and held up my book with the picture of the hoary-headed old bard on the cover. I said that Walt Whitman was a 19th-century American poet and that he wrote about how we are integral to the natural world, as some explanation of my situation I suppose.

The men nodded as if it all made perfect sense, and the diver held up an urchin like a big, purple softball with spines for me to have. I did not know how to go about eating such a creature and asked the men how I should do it. The pilot deftly cleaved the urchin with a machete and separated out the roe, then handed the shell halves over to me.

The taste was like the kelp forest – clean and a little salty, invigorating in its light but powerful sustenance. Soon after, I pulled anchor and waved to my new friends as I made my way over the kelp under oars before preparing to sail. A light wind ruffling the water was all I had to go on, but it moved us along anyway, back to the coast south by southeast. About halfway across the channel, the conditions so steady and *Cormorant* making perhaps three knots, I dropped the green rubber lure in and jigged it along behind, about 30 yards off the stern, not really expecting to catch anything in that open water, moving so slowly.

But then a sudden, urgent pulling on the rod in my hands – the line reeling off, and then another greater, more violent pull downward – startled me into action. I put the tip of the rod up, but the fish pulled even harder, and the line being so thin I had to relent and let the rod fall again. The battle continued for some minutes, my mind reeling with what this thing could be. Midwinter, a couple of hundred miles into Mexico, the water still cold – these were the elements. A shark, I wondered? No, too much sustained fight. A bonito? This was bigger than a bonito. I settled on white sea bass, and just as I got this mental picture, the line went slack and I lost the fish.

Coming into the coast, I surveyed the shore through my binoculars, noting the volcanic-looking shelves and a nice clean wave that seemed to stand up on a reef and peel across a little cove with a house perched above, and it looked like a fine place to live. A yacht approached from up the coast and overtook me, running wing-and-wing but with the motor on as well. I waved to the man at the helm and he waved back to me. A beautiful planked craft, painted white, she resembled vaguely Joshua Slocum's famous *Spray* but ran narrower in her outline.

Throughout the afternoon I lolled southward, running about three-quarters of a mile off a long stretch of beach and then closer in to another reach of rocky coast as I neared the point at the big bay of San Quintín. Red and white panels, like the ones on the mesa at Colonet, affixed to a tall pole marked the point and just underneath lay the wreckage of a yacht, high and dry on the reef. The wind picked up as I rounded the headland and ran into the bay. *Malia*, the white yacht I had seen earlier in the day, lay at anchor, and I sailed well inside before tacking and reaching upwind to her. The man was on deck, and I called out to ask him if he minded my anchoring there. I know little about yachting customs, but I figured it was polite to ask – even if 25 yards lay between us.

No problem, he told me, and for the first time in my journeys I felt a twinge of envy at the large deck space he had and the cozy, dark cabin he would descend into after his glass of wine. An old dog was sailing with the man, and she barked at me before losing interest and curling next to him in the cockpit. It turned out that we had covered some of the same territory, not only in our obvious run down from San Diego, but in times up around Santa Cruz and out at the Channel Islands.

In the last light of day he wished me goodnight and went below as I set up the boat tent. The wind came on harder, and as I reheated the fish stew from San Martín, I peeked under the edge of my boat tent at the glow in the portholes on *Malia* and felt the desire for a real ship. It was unsettling to find myself wanting more than what I had. I am a long way from being a bodhisattva, but I rarely yearn for material things. Still, it was the shelter, the solidity of timbers and a cabin to sit in, that made me covet a more substantial craft. *Cormorant*, after all, was the kind of boat that Shackleton and his men made a desperate self-rescue in. These are workboats, not yachts. But if I thought too much about it I would get depressed.

I had another round of transcendental reading, another round of Walt Whitman expounding on this great American soul who takes in all modern experience and the very pulse of

the land and the sea. After that I felt better and slept deeply in
my warm bag under my perfectly suitable boat tent.

Malia was gone when I awoke. It was still very early in the
day, and it seemed some accident must have happened, but I
counted it as an impressive piece of seamanship to have pulled
the anchor and slid off without so much as a knock to wake
me. The skipper had said he was heading south to rendezvous
with his parents in a week's time down in Mazatlán. That was
another point that worked on me: to travel by sea with some
timeframe of when one might actually arrive. I had no doubt
of *Cormorant*'s ability to get me wherever the water might lead,
but that depended upon a right balance of wind and sea that
neither overwhelmed the boat nor left her wallowing in vast
calms.

The captain of *Malia* had told me that a swell was forecast,
and farther inside the bay, I saw broad, heavy waves rolling
into foam over a shoal and shuddered at the thought of getting
caught by the surf after dark, trying to find one's way in. I
worked my way out to the point under oars and felt the fuller
heft of the swell in the open water. Anchoring in a rocky cove,
and tying off to a long strand of kelp with the stern line for
extra safety, I paddled my shortboard in and then walked the
mile or so north, back up to the long beach I had sailed along
the afternoon before.

Atop the red and white markers for the point sat the huge
jumble of sticks of an osprey nest. Perched on top, a bird

looked down on me nervously before taking to the sky and flying a large circle over the dunes and reef around the nest. The wreck, an old catamaran with a cabin, lay at an angle, stripped bare on a rock platform like some warning of how wrong things can go. The surf, when I finally reached the beach, was not so good. There was plenty of swell, but having came from far across the ocean, it was organized into long lines that came ashore and folded over all at once and did not offer much of a ride. This was a quality swell for which an average stretch of beach was not well suited – a proper reef or point set-up was what it needed.

At the south end of the beach, where the rocky part of the coast began, a wave formed and offered a short ride before shutting down. I paddled out, almost duty bound to surf. I made a few waves, raced fast and then straightened out for shore as they closed out, and it reminded me of summers in Newport as a kid when my friends and I would pull into impossible, pounding closeouts, just to have a sense of being in the barrel for a second or two before getting totally destroyed. We learned a lot about taking off on hard-breaking, steep waves and about how to drive through the tube, and so when we finally got to places that had those same steep, fast-breaking waves that a surfer could actually make – places like Hawaii or Indonesia – we were well attuned.

The winter sun was warm, the day clear. I peeled my wetsuit down to my waist when I came in from surfing and walked back towards my anchorage along a dirt track just in from the rocky coast. A bluff ran parallel to the track, and looking up, I saw another gringo watching me – clearly a surfer, with sunglasses on and board shorts. I raised my hand in greeting, but he just stood there impassively looking at me like a person with no humanity, and I thought of running up there to sock him in the nose just to force some interaction.

The wind had come up offshore by the time I reached the cove where I had left *Cormorant*, and she rode her anchor line taut with her bow facing shore. A wave broke off the rock finger on the north side of the anchorage, groomed by the wind as it advanced, spray peeling off the top and flying seaward until finally spilling over in a concentrated cylinder. I pulled my wetsuit back on and walked carefully in bare feet across the tide pools and then waded in and paddled to the top of the point.

I waited for a few minutes, sitting on my board, before another set of waves approached the reef. Spotting a bigger one behind the first two, I paddled out to meet it. The takeoff was clean, and I got a good turn that gave me a lot of speed and shot me well ahead, and I put the board over and let it run fast through a swooping cutback into the pocket. That was all, just one wave, and I paddled back to *Cormorant*; I needed this wind to travel on.

———————➤———————

Changing out of my suit amid my scattered gear back on board, I watched the wind on the water out ahead across the wide opening of Bahía San Quintín and tried to guess if I was in for trouble. But I was anxious to get under way, and I put on my layers – my wool sweater and jacket, my board short pants, and my ball cap – and then stowed the surfboards. I untied and coiled the stern line from the kelp and pulled anchor. The wind drew us out like a leaf on the water, out past the long fingers of rocks, and I zipped my lifejacket, rolled up my sleeves, and laid down to hang the rudder, checking to see that *Cormorant* was clearing the boils where the reef came near the surface.

With the rudder hung and pinned in place, I lashed the tiller along the starboard rail with a bungee cord. Moving forward, the daggerboard went down easily and nested in its slot. I turned and stepped aft again to unfurl the mizzen sail and run the sheet through the block on the rudder head and secure it to the cleat at the base of the mast, with the American flag whipping smartly in the breeze and *Cormorant* now rounding up into the wind. I went forward again to raise the mainsail in a motion that was as much pushing the yard aloft with one hand as it was a downward pull on the halyard with the other – all while leaning forward on the mast and hooking a leg around for safety.

Now she sailed. *Cormorant* heeled over in the stiff wind, the Mexican eagle and snake flying from the main, higher than the stars and stripes, and headed for the open water at a determined clip. The next headland lay some 20 miles distant, and I could see it out there, a dark rectilinear shape jutting into the sea from the long run of coast south of San Quintín. The wind carried us for about 25 minutes before starting to fall away, as if someone were slowly turning off the tap. After an hour the sea lay flat and calm as it had days before, and the sun shone down and *Cormorant* floated, adrift. It was perhaps a mile or so back to shore, and I considered rowing in to at least have an anchorage until the wind should come up again, but I decided against it and instead organized my dirtiest clothes for a seawater and pine-tar soap washing in the warmth of the midday sun.

Cormorant crept along, slower even than a slow walk; a wake rippled off the hull as if on a pond. Time goes indeterminate in these conditions. The markers lie so far off that no noticeable change occurs in one's surroundings hour after hour. With no watch, I concerned myself only with the number of hand widths I had above the horizon to determine the hours of daylight I had remaining.

A whale appeared, a big gray accompanied by a calf. They surfaced 10 feet off the starboard rail, the big one's body far longer than *Cormorant* and bending gracefully in the clear blue sea. The baby floated alongside and they both came right to the rail of the boat. I grabbed my camera and stood to take my *National Geographic* cover shot, but the mama exhaled a huge flurry of bubbles, covering an area 20 feet in diameter, making it seem as if *Cormorant* were suddenly in sea of 7UP soda. Both whales descended downwards horizontally, like submarines – a large blue-gray form and a lighter gray shape adjacent, fading, fading, until they merged into the color of the deep.

Nightfall saw me again on a vast and open sea, far from any land, with the headland I was aiming for only a slightly larger silhouette after a full day on the water. Again I deployed the drogue and spent the night in the open with my lifejacket on and my sleeping bag over me like a blanket, the sail pulled across to keep the dew off. The quiet was so profound that when I heard again the soft exhalations of the whales passing in the night on their long swim southward, I could not be sure it was actual breaths I was hearing, or just the turnings of my imagination or even the hiss of the nylon sail material against the sleeping bag. But the sound came regularly enough, finally, to be unmistakable – the sudden vapor release of the spout and the easy sipping in again of cool night air.

I awoke periodically throughout the night to check that all was well. *Cormorant* lay on the calm water as if sleeping, every surface wet with heavy dew, the air cold and damp. I only dozed periodically in the later part of the night, until finally, in the couple of hours before dawn when I sensed more than saw any light in the eastern sky, I began to prepare to sail on the next breeze that came. A cold offshore started at the first hint of a purple glow, and I quickly raised the main to catch it. By sunup however, the breeze was gone, and it did not seem that I had made any appreciable progress.

Sails again hanging limp, I attempted to row, but the main wiped the side of my face with wet licks, and the tiller slid back and forth under the elastic cord so that *Cormorant* swung wildly off course with each stroke, making the effort futile. Finally, I dropped sail, made a pot of coffee and ate some granola, and considered the dismal prospect of another day of either drifting or doing my best galley slave act.

Big, smooth swells passed slowly beneath the boat, and it seemed I had been carried some distance closer into shore.

Through binoculars, I saw big surf rolling in and crashing into great cataracts of spray. These were the conditions for seriously good surfing somewhere, but I was out of the equation as the headland still loomed a good number of miles ahead. Although now, at least through binoculars, I could make out details like tall sea caves and off-lying sea stacks. How many hours did I sit? How many hours going nowhere?

Towards midafternoon I had approached within two miles of the headland, mostly by drifting, but partly by rowing. A *pangero* motored passed and offered me a tow the rest of the way, and I was sorely tempted, but I said only, *"Es mejor"* – it's better – and then gestured that I would continue under my own power by patting myself on my chest. *"Pero muchas gracias, amigo,"* I called as he pulled away. A breeze came up later, and I rode it onward.

It was late in the afternoon by the time I approached the headland, and with the rising wind I sailed well outside as there were heavy patches of kelp and large swells lumbering onto the point ahead. I sailed standing upright to have the best view of the kelp and whatever else might lie in my path, running in now with the swells. Heavy surf broke hard on the reef but lurched too suddenly and pinched shut too fast to be any good for surfing.

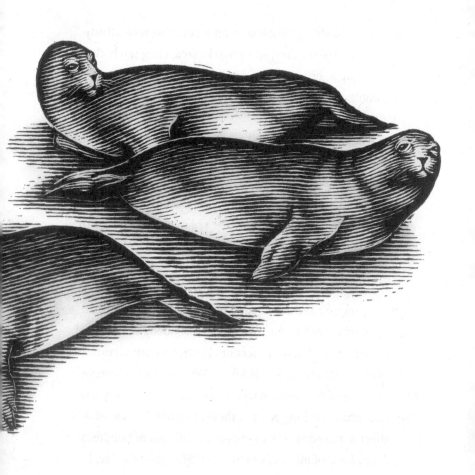

Farther along the point I saw a 4 x 4 van that I thought I recognized. The lights of the van flashed on and off, and the horn sounded. Two figures ran down the steep track to a little landing cove waving their arms, and I knew then who it was: the Long brothers, Rusty and Greg, professional surfers from San Clemente.

I dropped the sail, calling out in shouts to my friends, pulling up the daggerboard and the rudder, and then going to oars and skidding ashore on a little dumping wave. Rusty grabbed hold of the bow, and when I asked, Greg ran back up the ramp to bring the van down and pull *Cormorant* across the cobblestone beach to a level spot alongside a broken concrete slab.

To see friends after even such a short time of solitude was such a wonderful feeling, to remember that I was known in the world, particularly after the trials of night winds and bees, long crossings and strange people, leavened by meeting the kind ones too. And always only the sea under me, always this tenuous relationship that was only as good as the changing conditions allowed.

The boys were set up in a bungalow on the bluff top with a campfire and a well-supplied camp table. They had a photographer with them, Todd Glaser; a videographer, Noel Robinson; and a fellow professional surfer named Grant "Twiggy" Baker from South Africa. With visages reflecting an epic day of surfing in glazed-eye smiles, I knew they had gotten into something good in these environs. But we were all a-jabber at the odds of hooking up like this out of hundreds and hundreds of miles of desert coast. Sitting by the fire, I related the journey so far.

———————

The fishermen maneuvered their boats down the ramp in the darkness of early morning, shouting to each other over the roar of the truck motors and the squeals of the brakes on the steep drive. I emerged from the boat tent and the men glanced over at me – at the canvas tent, the scarred and re-oiled planks, and the gear in piles of dry bags – with nods of acknowledgement.

I arranged a daypack with water and a couple of granola bars, but I was getting low on food and had only oatmeal and dried apricots to cook for breakfast, but I knew there would be no time for that as the boys would want to get to the reef as early as they could. We had to wait for the fishermen to clear the landing before we could depart, and the last fishermen down the ramp told me to anchor my boat out in the bay. *"Más seguro, no ladrones"* – more secure, no thieves – they explained.

The men helped me pull *Cormorant* across the beach. Rusty brought me a cup of coffee, a kindred soul, knowing somehow that a little bit would go a long way to getting me in tune for the surfing to come. I drank it down in three scalding gulps, happy for the heat, happy for the vivifying effect. Barefoot on the cobbles, I shoved off with help from the fishermen and my surfer friends, wetting my trousers to the knee in the cold green water. I hopped over the rail dripping water on the floorboards, set the oars in the locks, and pulled a good 200 yards offshore, then dropped anchor near an oversized panga that the fishing co-op on the point kept tied to a mooring can.

My friends waited with their hired *pangero* idling a few feet away, and I moved as quickly as I could because with these particular surfers – buddies of mine though they are – there was no time to waste. Wave riding is their business, and they move like a commando unit, tolerating no delays. I tossed my bag to Glaser, who I had just met and who was quietly making a name for himself as a *Surfer Magazine* staffer, shooting the best surfers in the world. Passing my board in its padded bag across to Rusty, I then stepped to the panga and left *Cormorant* with her boat tent furled, rocking on the water at anchor like a good dog left to wait on a chain all day for a master with other things to do.

At full rev, the panga rode high over the water, and sitting in the bow with the golden light over the glassy green sea, I marveled at the speed. The wind pulled at the hood of my jacket, and the boat lifted gently over the swells, and I looked back at my friends, excitement welling up in me as to where all this speed and daylight and thin, foiled surfboards and surfers in the prime of their careers might be leading. After a while we approached the north end of a high set of dunes and rock shelves, which stepped down to a broken, rocky shoreline where a fringe of white foam danced.

Here the *pangero* swerved out to sea to avoid a wide area of dense kelp. The coast was jagged, with deep slot coves and off-lying rocks, and the farther along we went, the heavier the swell poured in, breaking with broad blue backs and great plumes of spray and foam. A lighthouse stood forlorn on the highest bluff, and the dark rocks of the shore, jutting out like catwalks into the frothing surf, gave an aspect of shipwreck and danger, even in the beautiful light of a clear morning.

The reef the boys sought slumbered under the tide, and the *pangero* circled in the channel so we could have a look. The ocean was a clear, deep blue, with kelp fronds swaying in the current like a forest bending to a breeze and the water swirling up in boils over an obviously shallower spot. We were at least three-quarters of a mile off the broken shore and about a quarter-mile seaward of a rock platform where some big seals lounged. It would have been quite a feat to paddle out here from the shore, as all across the inside a confused mass of broken water and colliding swells smashed and tore against each other.

Outside, where we sat in the panga, the waves loomed up over the reef and rushed into whitewater that stood so white against the blue in the morning light that it seemed like an avalanche in some remote, snowy range. After each wave rolled through, the trail of foam on the surface fizzed like it was electrified. But the waves weren't yet doing what they would when the tide pulled off the shelf, and with a few hours before this would happen, the boys asked the pilot to swing inside to get a look at another reef closer to shore. Here, amid the heave and wash of the water rushing by, the *pangero* dropped anchor, and we watched a thick wave, 12 feet in the face, break towards us with powerful, churning foam right to the rail of the boat.

The other lad with us was Noel Robinson, whom the Long brothers knew from Puerto Escondido in mainland Mexico and who would ride his last wave there a year-and-a-half later – a hard-breaking ten-footer that caught him wrong and took his life. Here, on this trip, he was filming while Glaser took still photos, and he was a solid, capable presence. Since the outer reef was not yet working, the boys decided to suit up and ride the wave in front of us. Glaser set up on a body board with his camera, and Rusty mentioned to Noel that he should just have a surf and not worry about filming until the afternoon. After all, he had been at it the whole day previously and was actually a surfer first, and then a videographer. Their relationship was built while surfing the enormous tubes of Puerto, and the three shared a camaraderie based on many past engagements.

I joined them, although my 6'7" single fin was not at all suited to the bumpy, lurching quality of the wave we were attempting. Twiggy from South Africa was the first to get a wave when he swung his board around under an already breaking section and got to his feet more from the board falling down the vertical face and he landing on it, than from springing up to a standing position. That is the difference between merely competent surfers and professionals – guys and women who have brought all of their focus to the art of surfing and so employ subtle moves like that one to extricate themselves from otherwise horrendous beatings.

The 6'2" three-fin Twiggy rode also fit the steep curve of the wave and allowed split-second adjustments down the face and carving turns back up, and he sent huge fans of spray flying as he snapped back down again.

My arms felt leaden as I paddled: the long hours of inactivity in my crossings, and even all the oar work I had put in, seemed to have drained more than increased my strength. A swift-moving blue peak advanced upon me, and I turned and paddled but did not have the jump on it, and the wave lifted me as I sprang to my feet, launching me as if from a springboard. I landed on my ass, hard, the wave crunching down on me with a rushing savagery. I am a better surfer than this, I thought, as I tumbled underwater, finally surfacing far inside amid a wide field of sparkling foam. I reeled my board in hand-over-hand by the leash and paddled wide towards the panga to get clear of the subsequent waves.

The warble went out of the conditions by late morning, dissipating with the dropping tide as if the receding flow dispersed the superfluous energy out to sea. What remained was a heavy, long-interval ground swell, moving through a perfectly calm ocean and meeting the outer reef shelf unimpeded. Wide, gaping tubes blasted out immense volumes of spray. The sheer velocity of the wave, perfectly shaped though it was, had me doubting my equipment.

Not having taken off our suits, the Long brothers and Twiggy and I jumped overboard and paddled out to the peak right as the pilot pulled up to the reef. Glasser and Noel dropped over the side with their cameras in water housings and swam directly over to the impact zone, which was itself a feat of ocean athleticism. Paddling over the first wave as it poured across the reef shelf, I felt the pull of the water up the face, and looking into the torqueing hollows, I knew my board could not track inside such cavernous hulks.

Still, the spectacle was amazing: legitimate, 12-foot barrels with perfect conditions. With only three or four waves per set,

I hung back and let them set up for the right ones when they came through.

Having only had that small cup of coffee and some trail mix that morning, and worn down from my light sleeps at sea in the past few nights, I felt shaky and out of it. I sat inside of the other three surfers, putting myself in danger of getting thwacked by one of the bomber waves that would inevitably come through.

I paddled hard for one that slid in under the others and made the drop. But this being a smaller eight footer, it only capped over and ran through in a great wash of foam. I looked back to the line up and saw Twiggy swooping into a proper one, his line high on the face as the wave threw out far ahead of him, and I knew that I would not get the rides that this place offered with the board I had. And I might well get injured too or foul up the scene by blowing it on a perfect one, and so I let the session go.

There was nothing for it. I was too tired, and I was unprepared for surfing at this level of intensity. I suppose it might have been a moment of aging – it certainly was a moment of acknowledging my limitations. But rather than feeling defeated, I just felt tired, dehydrated, and hungry, and was glad, actually, to have the panga to paddle over to. I put dry clothes on and ate my remaining granola bars and drank all the water I had. I still felt thirsty and hungry and the day was not even half-over. But the warmth of the sun was delicious, and the kelp forest was teeming like the one up at Isla San Martín. The *pangero*, named Angel, fished with a drop line as the boys went barrel for barrel out at the peak.

I sat slump-shouldered with fatigue on the center thwart of the panga, much like I would have sat on board *Cormorant*, only here I was not going anywhere, and it felt like I had a long time to wait to move anywhere, ever again. I had not even brought a book. The surfing was world-class of course, and seeing Rusty expertly stand tall through the deepest of tubes was worth the time, but I felt I had strayed from my mission.

Angel was having good luck with his hand line, and he brought up hefty sheepshead one after another, with happy little exclamations of surprise at each hook up. He tossed the fish in the hold of the boat, and they lay there working their gills back and forth in the deadly air, suffocating, and I wished he had killed them outright. I was feeling drowsy in the sunlight and he asked me if I was OK.

I mentioned that I was hungry, and he handed me a *carne asada* sandwich on a big Mexican *bolillo* roll. I told him I didn't want to take his lunch, but he lied and said not to worry, he wasn't hungry.

Could we share it? I asked, but Angel wouldn't hear of it. "*Come*" – eat – he urged, and guiltily, but needfully and gratefully, I ate.

Noel swam back to the boat after a few hours, and as he approached, Angel shouted out "*¡Tiburon!*" – shark – but he was only crying wolf, and Noel sparred with him in a friendly, fluent barrage of Mexican slang. Noel was raised on the coast in Northern California, in Sonoma County, and he gave a rugged, quiet first impression. Listening to him joke with the *pangero*, it was clear that he loved this life: this surfing and

this Mexico, which after all carried so much of the spirit of
old California.

By the fire that night, back at the fish camp, the mood was
quiet after our long day in the sun. Angel brought a plate
heaping with fillets of the sheepshead he had caught, and
Rusty made tinfoil boats for the fillets and stuck them in the
coals of the fire. He sautéed vegetables in a skillet over the
camp stove, and although hunger definitely enhanced the
flavor, the black beans and salsa and plain yogurt for sour
cream made these the best burritos I had even eaten. I was
desperate with hunger and the food was my lifeline.

After dinner, I felt fatigue like a sickness, and I went
into a room of the little house the boys had rented and piled
blankets over the top of my sleeping bag and sank deep below
the covers. I wanted only to sleep and could not pretend to
socialize. I hadn't felt exhaustion so keenly yet on this trip,
but the long nights only half-sleeping at sea and the days
under the open sky were catching up with me.

It was Inauguration Day in the United States the next
morning, 20 days out from San Diego. We listened to the
commentary on Greg's satellite radio on the drive back
to Mexico Highway 1, which the boys would take to San
Clemente for one of their girlfriend's birthday parties that
same night. I caught a ride with them so I could resupply,
and planned to hitch back out to camp that afternoon. As
we drove, the event of Obama's presidency, the significance

of the American political tradition, and perhaps the first stirrings of homesickness in all this Baja desert country – coupled with the fact that my buddies would be home in mere hours – began to work on me. The description of the crowd in Washington, D.C., and the thought of my mother traveling there brought tears welling in the bottoms of my eyes.

I wore shades. I was sitting in front as Greg drove and hoped he would not notice.

CHAPTER SIX

LOS NARCOS Y LOS PESCADORES

Greg let me off on a dusty street corner in town, where Highway 1 makes a sharp turn and a palm tree reaches over a cracked and listing block wall. I waved goodbye to my friends as the van pulled away north, picked up my two five-gallon water bottles, and walked to the market that carries groceries, hardware, and sundries. They kept the lights off inside, and the concrete floor was cool, but a strong smell of vegetables about to go off pervaded.

A purified water dispenser stood next to a cupboard with fresh *pandulces*. I bought yams, onions, garlic, instant coffee, rice, beans, lentils, and a sack of sugar, with a few sugar breads, and put them in my duffle bag. I asked the lady at the cash register if I could leave my water bottles while I went across the street to Mama Espinoza's to have a meal and use the computer.

Since I had told everyone I knew that I would be off in the desert wilds for months on end, I had no messages. Obama's inauguration speech came on the television, and I stood watching his address, and again the teary feeling came upon me. I felt pride – in that Whitmanesque sense of the boundlessness of the promise of America – in our tradition of peaceful transfer of power, even though we fall short of our democratic ideals.

The lady at the counter was the granddaughter of the old lady who first opened the place in the 1930s and who was herself an institution on the Baja highway circuit. Things here were not quite like a ghost town, although a quiet pervaded – the drug war was more of a newspaper phenomenon than anything I actually witnessed, but the stories were horrific enough. A woman in town was shot dead at a taco stand a couple of months before, along with two of her customers, the hit's intended targets.

I imagined the Mexican drug dealers, desperate to get out of poverty, were driven to inhuman extremes. And the American customers, desperate to escape the emptiness of their strip mall society, were driven to drugs with insatiable appetites. It was a perfect economy of supply and demand, with terrible consequences.

I told the lady that I had left my boat out at the fish camp and then asked if she knew anyone from town who was heading that way. She did not, but she said, "*Vaya con Dios*" – a blessing to be sure, but also a dismissal, my life so removed, so remote from any of her concerns. I used the bathroom and shaved my bristled cheeks, but left the thick mustache and a soul patch, thinking these appropriate for the *ranchero* country I was traveling in. When I returned to the market for my water bottles, I asked around for a ride to camp – *nada*. Grasping a heavy jug in each hand and with my duffle stuffed full and slung over my shoulder, I waddled down the dirt street for about 400 yards until I reached the spot where the fish camp track branched off.

"Where are you from?" a big guy with tattoos covering his forearms asked, in the parlance of California cities. Snap judgment though it was, I looked at the small car he drove, its dented body, faded paint, and Baja license plate – his obviously local connections – and I had the feeling that he was laying low out here in this small town. It was the smooth way he talked – an exaggerated easiness that made me uneasy. I told him that I was from San Clemente and he nodded, and we talked a little more, but there was nothing going on. He told me that someone would come by, and drove off.

Not long after, two men in a small pickup stopped and waited while I loaded my water bottles and duffle, and then climbed into the bed. They had windows stacked on a triangular shaped rack, and I grabbed hold. We started out, first across the sandy river bottom, through stands of willows on both banks, and then down the road past little houses, some of which had attractive yards with trees that cast desirable shade.

Around the next bend, near an elementary school, an old *vaquero* rode towards the truck on a roan-colored horse. His eyes were rheumy, his gaze penetrating like a shaman's, and when I turned to watch him as we passed, he also turned in his saddle. I raised my hand, and he turned back around and rode on.

The man driving stopped at a fork in the road and leaned out of his window, holding up his palm as if to ask which way. I couldn't be sure. The men in the truck were from San Quintín, and didn't know this area very well either. The track to the left looked like the steep path we had driven down coming out from the camp road, and so I pointed in that direction, sure that once I saw the view from the top I would be oriented and find we were going in the right direction.

The track dropped down again after the short steep rise, and we followed its twisting course between ever-steepening arroyo walls. The walls gave way to open, rolling desert scrubland after awhile, and I kept thinking that at the next junction another path would present itself and bring us up to the plateau and then out to the west where the camp was perched on the short, narrow peninsula.

That junction did not come, and after 40 minutes the man driving pulled up on a section where the track ran along the top of some dunes and said the gas was getting low. Standing up now on the wall of the pickup bed, I saw the flat profile of the point away in the distance to the northwest. I apologized and pointed out that the camp was back the way we had come. Without changing expression, neither angry nor worried, the man got back in the truck. It was later in the afternoon now, the light just starting to glow as he turned around on the narrow track.

A coyote came over a dune and watched us as we drove away.

———————————→

Afternoon had slid into evening by the time we made the camp, and I asked the man who lived across the street from Angel, the *pangero,* if we could buy a tank of gas from him. He agreed to pour a jerry can's-worth into the window repairmen's truck, and they said for me not to worry, and paid for the gas themselves. Angel and his wife came out (I had kept my surfboard and gear in their yard, and *Cormorant* out in the bay at anchor), and Angel's wife took them over to the bungalow and pointed out some windows that needed replacing.

The light was going fast, and I changed into my wetsuit to paddle out to the boat and bring her back in to load my supplies. Anxious to reach *Cormorant* and see that all was well, I called out to her as I got close, like one might reassure a dog left behind. Once onboard, with everything dry and as I had left it, I quickly stowed my board, pulled anchor, and rowed for the beach cove. Still in my wetsuit, I made a series of quick dashes up the beach for the water bottles, my duffle bag, and the dry bag I had left at Angel's place. Then I shoved

off and rowed back out to anchor again and set up for the
coming night.

It was dark by the time I had the boat tent up and all of my
gear organized. I cooked lentils and rice by the light of my
headlamp. The steam from the pot made the inside of the boat
tent nice and warm, and I felt good about this little place that
I had made for myself in the world – this little boat and scrap
of marine canvas for a roof. And now that I was on my own
again, with the whole coast ahead of me, my enthusiasm for
the trip returned.

Sleep, as always, was my balm, and by morning I felt
that I was completely back to the rhythm of the trip and was
immersed in the quiet flow of my thoughts. There was still
plenty of swell in the water, and I paddled the 8'2" into the
corner of the point where it met the beach. Easy, peeling
waves made for smooth, gliding rides on the bigger board, and
I just stood there on the ones I rode, watching the water get
steep all down the line before me.

My plan was to sail to the stretch I had been to with the boys,
but I wondered about tackling those waves again, not only
with my boards that were not suited to them, but alone this
time. The trip there amounted to a crossing, as there would
be no shelter until I reached the anchorage, which lay beyond
the farthest point. I watched the wind all morning as I surfed,
unsure whether it looked to blow steady or if the dry air hinted
at a brewing *Norte*. I decided finally that the conditions were

manageable, and paddled back to *Cormorant* at about midday, after a long session surfing the small, easy peelers.

I reheated the rice and lentils for lunch and then prepared to sail.

The breeze carried us steadily until the camp and the point became a low smudge behind, and the sun neared the horizon out over the sea. It was a golden-green evening and the wind fell off, leaving us on another calm expanse of water. The lighthouse point was only slightly more visible now than it had been from where I started. Long tendrils of kelp began to show in the water with thicker beds visible ahead in the last light of day.

I shipped the rudder and daggerboard, furled the mizzen, and dropped the main. Going to oars once again, I placed the bow in line with the flash from the lighthouse and settled in to a long distance row. None of this was a trial when I had my head right. And as the stars appeared in the sky and sparkled off the calm water, *Cormorant* slid across the kelp like a serpent through the grass – my head was definitely right.

It was a long row nevertheless. I turned regularly to see the flash and the outline of the ridge where the lighthouse stood, until I knew just from the angle of the kelp in the water and certain stars reflected on the rippling surface exactly the course I should be on. At some point in the night, I began to hear the roar of breaking surf, and as I approached, I held the oar blades out of the water and turned my head to listen. There were the little crashers slapping in amongst a rocky shore, and these sounded fairly close. Then there was a deeper sound, an occasional *boom-braarr* that I might not have known to listen for had I not already visited this strange place of reefs two days before.

My heart beat more heavily as I approached, as there was no place for shelter but that one beyond the heavy surf. The night held no moon, and the lighthouse light was more blinding than helpful now that I was within the direct path of its beam. Besides stopping where I was in the open water and trying for a kelp tie, the only option was to continue on, working far outside the possible extent of the reefs, and then circling back to the sheltered water inside. I saw the smaller surf crashing white against the low rock shelves now that I was approaching, but the coast lay black and barely distinguishable from the dark sea.

I put directly out from shore here, knowing that the off-lying reefs were still a good distance south but that once I got far enough outside – far enough for the lighthouse again to define the ridgeline – I could row south again until I put the light behind me, and work back in, reasonably sure that I had cleared the reef.

The plan came off as if I had known those waters like a local *pangero*, and I even caught a glimpse of the dark waves washing the reef off the port side. Once inside, the calm water lay still, as if there could be no other state for water to lay in, and I scanned the cove with a flashlight to see if I could spot any rock heads standing clear.

The lighthouse on the ridge above was to the north of me now, and I was surprised by the sound of a dog barking at me from shore. I was sweating, I realized, now that I had finally arrived, and I pulled my sweater off and took my wet T-shirt off and dug out another.

Anchor. Boat tent.

I performed these tasks automatically, and slid into my sleeping bag and was asleep before I had taken three more breaths.

Morning broke calm with gray skies, and I rowed ashore to the cobblestone landing beach, nosing *Cormorant* onto dry ground and heaving her a few inches further up by the breasthook, before tying the bow line to a rusted truck axle and wheel. The dog appeared on the low bluff above the beach and barked at me again. A German shepherd with a hint of blue in his dark coat, he might have been a little intimidating if he wasn't such a puppy under all his barking, and bringing my fishing rod was enough to scare him off when I went to walk the coast.

The feeling of desolation was great. There were abandoned shacks that wouldn't have been much to look at even if their roofs weren't caving in, and on the bluff were odd pieces of machinery that had long since melted into amorphous shapes with rust, but that may once have been mining or fish processing equipment. The ground gave way underfoot, the entire bluff area a warren of burrows and bird feathers, but no birds. I saw the dog standing there, watching me, and took a knee and called for him to come over, but he would have none of it. He barked half-heartedly and trotted off, disappearing around the next wall of cliffs.

I watched a wave break hard onto one of the rock platforms, whitewater rushing across like a flash flood, and decided that that would not be a good place to fish. The lighthouse stood a few hundred feet above, and I climbed up there to get an overview. From the top, I took in the whole stretch of coast 10 miles north and south – the point I had sailed and rowed from way away up the coast and the high mesas of the Viscáino Desert plains farther down. The big wave out on the reef was not stirring, but a series of reefs directly below the lighthouse held good-looking surf.

Walking back down, I tried to pick a path over steady ground that would not cave in beneath my feet, but by the time I reached the water my shoes were caked with the fine, tan dirt of this place. I sloshed along a keyhole beach of white seashells, trailing plumes of mud in the clear seawater. The farthest rock shelf to the north stood higher than the others, and the swells seemed to pass it by, and here I set up to fish. My second cast brought a solid strike with a sharp pull on the line, which disappeared into a thick patch of kelp. I was unsure whether I had a fish or not, but either way, I didn't want to lose the rubber lure. I patiently pulled and reeled, pulled and reeled, until the kelp lolled in a big lump like a subdued whale against the wall of the shelf where I stood.

Carefully, I climbed down the face of the rock, the water surging into the keyhole and back out again, welling up to my knees. This would be a great way to get sucked in by the swirling water, but the footholds were wide enough that I could lean down and lift away the strands of seaweed. I discovered that I had hooked another bass, though not as big as the one I caught back on Isla San Martín. Still, it was a good fish and I lifted him out of the water onto the rock shelf, smacked his head to end it, and then walked back to the boat the way I had come.

The lighthouse on the ridge had a metal roof and lens suggestive of the classic lighthouses of maritime age America, although the structure it sat on was an uninspired block of concrete. I walked a path below the lighthouse, holding the fish by its gills, and clomped over the bluff again to drop into the little cove where I had left *Cormorant*. After filleting the bass, whose coloration was a darker, more olive green than the previous one, I went through what had become my routine of making fish stew.

I set the pot aside to cook, enjoying the sound of the hissing stove and the look of the steam billowing out from under the lid in the cool gray of the day, and then pulled the dry bags out of the boat and spread my things on the cobbles to at least air them out before repacking to be better organized.

The winds remained slack and the sky gray. I climbed to the bluff top to look out at the rock shelves where solid, clean waves were still coming in. Stowing everything back in the boat, I put a big, flat rock over the top of the pot with the remaining fish stew so the dog couldn't get it, and then put my wetsuit on. I walked slowly across to the rock shelf that held the wave I thought looked the best, and made my way out to the end, breathing deeply, watching carefully.

It was a long, keyhole cove between two jutting rock shelves, but rather than leap from the very end and risk getting caught by the surf, I chose to paddle from the inside, keeping to the deeper water as I found my lineup for the spot. The wave rose up in a peak about 30 feet off the end of the shelf, and broke fast across, hollow, and then dissipated in the keyhole channel. I was a little spooked being alone and did not like how hard my heart was beating, worried that I was transmitting signals of solitary, mammalian vulnerability. After all, with the seals that lived around here and the remote, skeleton coast feel of the place, why wouldn't there be great whites?

The water was aquarium clear, and I watched the dark shadows sway in the current, pushing and pulling. Gray sky and a slate gray sea, darker gray rocks, and the waves pouring open with silver roofs –this was true wilderness surfing. I let another set come through and just paddled up the waves, watching how they stood and advanced on the reef before throwing over. I looked down from the tops of each one to gauge the line and how much room I would have before running up on the dry shelf.

After watching a few, I saw that it was OK – that I would be fine if I could hang through the eight or 10-foot drop and make the bottom turn. Although still wary of the environment, I hunted down the next wave that came. It all went perfectly, and for some seconds the world was framed by a sheeting crystal water roof and curved and shimmering surfaces. And then release, and a burst of speed, and a skimming across the water with no evidence of any wave remaining but the froth of the spent foam and crash of white water on the rocks behind me.

Paddling back out, I put my head underwater and watched the blurry shapes of the reef and sea grass and darker forms of fish. Once outside again, waiting for the next set, a few harbor seals swam near by and then a few more, until about seven of them floated in a loose circle around me, keeping about 20 feet off. These are the seals of the selchie legends in Ireland and Scotland, and the way that they watch, silent and intent, lends a sense of fellow feeling. The seals darted away from me nervously when I paddled for a wave, but they seemed to figure out what I was doing after a few times, and as the session wore on, I saw them swimming under me in the swells as I lined up to take off. Since they were hanging about so contentedly, it didn't seem likely that any big sharks were lurking, and I was able to relax and enjoy the surfing.

The sky hung low and gray throughout the afternoon, and when I pushed *Cormorant* off the beach to anchor again in the cove, a light wind started up from the south, ruffling the surface slightly. The thick kelp outside kept the swell action down in the cove, and I put the boat tent up and slept for an hour or so before dark. A light rain was falling when I awoke. I saw the dog walking the cove beach, his coat soaking wet, and he looked at me across the water, and then turned and walked back up the bluff, disappearing like a ghostly apparition. I heated another helping of stew, and then made coffee with the smaller pot I had, and sat drinking it and looking out at the dreary evening.

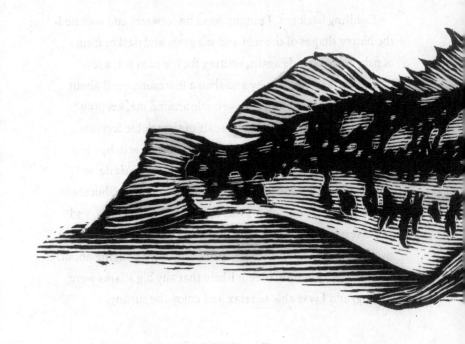

Morning came and I rowed out to the edge of the kelp
and set sail to continue the journey, but the wind fell off not
20 minutes after I started, and with no shelter for another
15 miles, I decided to turn back for the cove anchorage. I
felt anxious to move on, but not so anxious that I wanted
to drift again in open water, and so I waited. The wind did
not come up that afternoon, nor did it come up the next day
either, except for very early in the morning, before first light.
I scrambled to sail out, only to get tangled in the kelp, and
I worked myself into a fury cutting the boat free from the

heavy, slimy clumps, dunking my arms and getting soaked in cold sea water.

My cove anchorage was beautiful in its rugged isolation, but the coast here had an oppressive quality that began to work on me. There was a reason no one came around except for a few *pangeros* who pulled traps and then went home. The swell had subsided when the front came in, but the gray sky persisted and it seemed the weather was in a holding pattern – completely undecided about what to do next and content to hang in its gray mood.

On the third day, I resolved to leave no matter
what. Perhaps it was that I could not shake the habit of
accomplishing things, moving from place to place. Perhaps
my culture had made me unable to accept and to wait, but
I could not wait – not any longer anyway. And then I was
granted a reprieve once I cleared the kelp, and a breeze, a
true steady breeze, started up from the northwest. Soon I
was coursing along again, with that lovely sense of tension
and pull the sails give and the solid-yet-giving feel of the hull
through the waves.

The headland of Punta San Carlos lay below the prominent
mesa, and there I hoped my friends Aurelio and Rudy would
still be doing their daily fishing runs. With luck I would arrive
in the evening and see them. I had sent a Christmas card to
Aurelio at his home in Ensenada before I left, telling him that
I would be coming through again, but I was a couple of weeks
later than I had predicted.

Aurelio shouted to me in my boat tent, "*¡Buenos días,
Christián!*" I was awake but had not yet roused from my bag.
The sunrise, or the part of it I could see through the V-shape
at the back of the tent, was golden and the day seemed
especially glowing and clear after the long stretch of gray skies
up the coast. I sat upright and fumbled with the edge of the
boat tent, calling out "*¡Buenos días, amigo!*"

The camp lay before me a short distance across the water
– the bunkhouse and veranda, the steep track down to the

sand where the men launched and retrieved their boats, and the high mesa looming over the coast just as I remembered it. And here was Aurelio, standing in his panga with the throttle in his hand as if we had just pushed through the surfline like we had almost a year ago to the day, preparing again for our respective days at sea.

He gestured that he was heading out and that he would see me when he returned, and I nodded and waved him on, and then slipped back inside the tent as the sound of his outboard droned off into the distance. The run down from the lighthouse cove the previous day had been steady for most of the way in an even, 12-knot breeze with the shore about three miles off. I sailed for the headland at San Carlos, lifting and falling in the easy roll of the water. About two hours into the day's sail, a panga motored alongside from farther out to sea.

The two fishermen aboard were young men, and the pilot in particular seemed very interested in *Cormorant*, asking questions about where I sleep, how much the boat was worth, how far I was going, where I had come from. None of this felt at all threatening, I could see that he was merely intrigued, but in motoring down to my speed and coming up alongside, he got too close and bumped the rudder arm on *Cormorant*. The impact reverberated all the way through the boat and felt like it could have done damage – the rudder and tiller assembly strong enough for its intended purpose, but not to sustain a blow that could stress the joints or bend the pins on which the rudder sat.

I sailed on, quiet after our preliminary greeting, but the pilot motored right alongside, smiling a kind of shy smile

that I responded to with a nod and grin, before returning my
gaze forward, hoping he would power up and continue on to
wherever it was that he was going. His partner amidships was
staring intently at a cell phone, trying to make a call on this
open sea off an undeveloped desert shoreline. I was annoyed,
and I felt badly about that, since I also felt that I should take
some interest in these fellows as I was traveling in their
country. But I just wanted to be alone, even if alone was what
I most certainly was and would be for the foreseeable future.

The pilot offered me an orange, and I thanked him as he
tossed it over. Then, after another few minutes of silence, he
offered me a whitefish. I had nothing to offer in return, and
however mean-spirited it might have been, I just wanted them
to go. I suppose, like so many before me, I was just another
gringo seeking to disappear in Mexico, without the trouble
of having to interact with the people there. The fumes from
the outboard wafted across in the breeze, and when the pilot
finally waved and sped away, the quiet and fresh air he left
behind and the return to my own slow progress came to me
with a physical sense of relief.

I had come in closer by now, and though I could not pick
out details at this distance, the set of the land was plain
enough to see – steep slot canyons cut inland, perpendicular
to the sheer bluffs along the coast here. One canyon in
particular almost formed a cylinder, its steep walls polished
like an enormous gun barrel. San Carlos is a windsurfing
destination, and the winds in this part of Baja are notorious
for coming up quickly and blowing ferociously. And they
came on stronger as the day progressed.

Although *Cormorant* sailed swiftly now and whitecaps scoured the water all around, the headland seemed to hover in the distance, never seeming any closer, but by late afternoon I had finally covered the miles. The ocean had a cold green look, and the wind was heavy as I came abreast of the point. An off-lying reef boomed with surf just ahead, and the light was fast fading.

Making a few points seaward to clear the reef, I glanced at the mainsail that was straining full, and turned to look north at the run of sea behind us, which came on in an endless procession of spilling runnels. The challenge now was to swing crossways to the wind to reach for the shelter of the cove without getting knocked over in this hard blow.

Letting out the mainsheet while grasping the line closer to the sail's tack, I eased *Cormorant* to port and yanked down on the main to keep the yard from getting blown vertical and fouled with the mast. With the sail wrapped awkwardly around the mast, most of the sail's body flapped ineffectually downwind, and I was able to reach into the bay on the mizzen and only the forward part of the main.

Aurelio hailed me in the morning, and then I lay back down before getting up to heat water for granola and coffee. That rolling sea and hard wind the night before had been no small event, and again I felt tired and listless in the aftermath of what felt like a real action. This journey was a mental test, I was realizing, as much as a physical one.

The wind started up by nine or so and came on stronger throughout the morning. By the time Aurelio came in, his panga bucking heavily in the chop as he rounded the reef, the wind was so strong that I could not row against it even far enough to pull up the anchor. He motioned for me to hop aboard, but I asked if he could give a tow-in as I did not want to leave *Cormorant* in these conditions.

"*Como quieres,*" – whatever you want – my friend said, and I passed him the bow line as he pulled up alongside, and then he towed me forward to bring up the anchor before taking us in through the surf. Once on the beach, he brought his battered old pickup down and dragged *Cormorant* up to where the other boats lay on the dry sand, and then we went back down to heave his panga onto the truck-axle trailer and bring it up as well.

Solid land felt heavy underfoot, but welcome after days of rocking confinement aboard *Cormorant*. Sitting down in the cookhouse out of the cursed wind felt even better.

Aurelio brought a kettle of hot water to the table, and we made cups of Nescafé, and like our first greeting earlier that morning, the similarity to last year felt so immediate as to make this seem a regular occurrence between us. There wasn't much to say, however. Although a year had passed since last we spoke, he had been doing the same routine of ten days to two weeks in camp and a week up in Ensenada. Regardless of the decisions I'd made regarding this journey, for all Aurelio could see, I was the same solitary traveler that had shown up on his beach 12 months before.

He stood up after drinking his coffee and said, "*Me voy*," and walked outside, crossing the camp in the dust-swirling wind. Again I stood at the screen door, as if the past year had evaporated, and looked out on the torn ocean. I was grateful not to be out there, and amazed at the timing of my arrival, as the wind was gusting now to 40 or 45 knots. I was relieved that I had thought to ask for the favor of Aurelio towing me in, as my usual inclination would be to not say anything for fear of making a burden of myself.

I went down to my boat, the wind whipping the hood of my jacket about, and grabbed the bags with my clothes and sleeping bag, as well as my books, and went back up to the kitchen. With early afternoon sun streaming in through the screen door, I set my books and journal on the end of the table at "my spot," and put the kettle on the burner for another cup of coffee. I was not as cavalier in moving in as it might sound, and was, in fact, very conscious of being a guest, but I also knew from my experience with him that Aurelio would be first to ask if I wanted anything. I would also leave money for his trouble as I had the year before.

The thing was, while not wanting to be a mooch, I had a real need for the shelter. I could have, I suppose, rowed ashore at first light before the wind came on too strong, emptied my gear and water from *Cormorant*, and worked her up the beach beyond the tide line and set up my tent (I brought one in case land camping was required) somewhere out in the desert. Aurelio was a friend and I was excited to see him, but I didn't have anything to share or to bring to the reunion. I felt hollowed out somehow, and wanted only to read and to write in my journal about what I planned to do next in life, with an interminable list of the months ahead, and what I would do first, and then next, and then after that.

My present circumstances were rarely sufficient for me, except when startled by splendor – and then for those moments only. I wanted something more wonderful than the sensation of marking time that my regular jobs had been, that serving in the Navy had been, that much of my schooling had been. But there was a bleakness now. My hair had gone sticky with salt and every bit of my clothing smelled of dried sweat and balls. The shacks were broken down and there was dirt over every goddamned thing in camp. The trash that blew around in this driving wind – even the trash – was coated in dirt. This was all becoming too much.

———————————————▶

I felt better after a shower. I shaved, and soaped and rinsed my hair twice. The T-shirt I had been wearing was greasy, and I hung that on a line and wore a sweatshirt and board shorts under wool-lined army trousers. Back in the cookhouse I started in Thoreau's *Walden*, which, after *Leaves of Grass*, kept things right in the same era. Those two, Thoreau and Whitman, sought what I was seeking – to reach beyond the impositions, social and technological, of their time to a freer plane, a more expansive way of living.

But what did Thoreau find when he visited Whitman, still living at his parents' place in Brooklyn and sharing a bed with his developmentally disabled brother? An unkempt room and a chamber pot in need of emptying – a lot like what my mission was starting to feel like. While Whitman proclaimed his vision of a transcendent self that took in all worldly experience, Thoreau championed an escape from the dull routine of earning a living by living so simply that his time was his own.

Although my time was certainly my own now, I did not really have a place of my own to live – no benefactor like Thoreau's Emerson on whose land he was allowed to build his cabin at Walden Pond.

Like Whitman, I had been seized by a vision. In my case, the vision of this perfect little boat, and of going, slowly, to extraordinary places: To "loaf and invite my soul" as brother Walt put it.

It was not so long ago in history that one could pull off a simple life in Southern California – diving for abalone and lobster off the beach and hunting rabbits, quail, and deer in the open chaparral just inland. But I have to stop the fantasy and remind myself that, in those supposed days of milk and honey, the Great Depression was on and that most of the land was private ranches. Still, before my grandfathers' times, the *Californios* made it work, but theirs was an intricate system of families and customs, and the U.S. taxman eventually drove them under too.

Thoreau only lived in his cabin for two years anyway. None of this makes a complete life.

Looking out Aurelio's screen door again a little later, I saw a catamaran round the reef outside, come a little way into the bay, and set anchor. The wind was still howling terribly, but the men on board got the anchor down, and with two hulls the vessel seemed fairly stable. They went below, and I returned to the table, took out my journal, and made a sketch.

It was the next boat I wanted to build. With a cabin, I decided, I could actually live this life. The hard benches and canvas tent on *Cormorant* made only a bivouac, not a home. I decided on a length of 27 feet, because that was a size I would be comfortable building. The building technique would be the same as *Cormorant*, but with the addition of frames throughout and watertight compartments.

Yes, this would be home.

Aurelio returned later in the afternoon from tending to something out at the windsurfing camp on the point, a mile up the coast. He put the kettle on and began chopping onions.

I sat at the table and watched him.

"Tomorrow," he told me, "you make the dinner."

I said that I would be happy to. He brought over the kettle and the Nescafé. There was something different this year, but I look too carefully sometimes and see things that are not necessarily there. On the one hand, I thought it was good that Aurelio spoke so directly to me. Alternately, I feared he was annoyed at my being there, as if perhaps I expected him to cook for me.

When we sat down to eat though, everything felt like it had before – Aurelio seemingly content with the well-ordered life he lived, and pleased with a simple, well-made meal. He was the one living Thoreau's ideal.

Somehow the conversation came around to drinking and smoking, and he said that I was lucky I was staying in this camp, because at all of the other fish camps the men were "*marihuaneros.*" Aurelio repeated his statement that he did not drink, and then told me the guys who had murdered the woman and two men at the taco stand in town a couple of months previous had come up from Guerrero Negro, as if to confirm what he'd said about the "marijuana men" in the other camps.

I washed the dishes, and Aurelio had a cup of coffee, and a little while later a few men from camp came in. The Rudys, father and son, were not here just now, and I had not met these guys before. They were younger, two of them thick set and jovial in sweatshirts and work boots. The third one was quiet with a serious expression under a ball cap pulled low over his forehead and sharp-toed cowboy boots and a *ranchero* shirt that was the *narcotraficante* style. An ugly, dimpled scar marred his cheek with a jagged line running up to his ear. Their talk was so full of local slang and half-spoken phrases that I could not follow the conversation, except in the general outlines of how rough young men can talk – about how one guy was stupid or weak, about how a particular woman in town was a *puta*. They talked about the killings.

I didn't much like these guys. They were probably friendly enough by themselves, but together – particularly the scarred guy who sat apart from everyone else and looked on with a menacing silence – they talked too loud and brought a vibe like they wanted to see what I was made of.

Aurelio glanced at the sullen *hombre* in the ball cap, and then at the other two, and then to me with a nervous smile.

"You like-*ee* the *marijuana*?" one of the big, jokey guys asked me.

"*Ahorita, no,*" – not just now – I replied.

"*¿Cerveza, o tequila?*" his buddy asked.

"*No,*" I told them with exaggerated gravity, "*estoy como un angelito.*"

"*¿Pero las muchachas?*" the first one continued, rising up in his seat with a lewd thrusting of his hips.

Raising my eyebrows and tilting my head slightly, I said, "*Pues…*" as if admitting that we all have our weaknesses, and at this they threw their heads back in great blustering laughs, Aurelio almost looking relieved, and even Scarface on the opposite side of the table gave in to a very brief flicker of a smile.

When they left, we all shook hands in the street-style of slaps and fist-bumps and I felt like an idiot for playing the game to this extent, but at least they were leaving.

A few minutes later, after we'd been sitting there in silence, I asked Aurelio if they had been fishing here long. He told me that they only sometimes came around. And then I asked if he knew how the one guy had gotten the scar. Apparently, he'd been shot in the face in a fight at a *discoteca*.

Aurelio was off fishing before first light, and although the wind had subsided somewhat overnight, it was far from calm. The day, with its sharply defined edges and crisp wavelets on the surface out off the point, seemed ripe for another hard blow.

I spent the morning with Thoreau, looking up from the pages with the gusts, which were coming on stronger now. The catamaran must have left in the night, and the other fishermen had not gone out. I saw them gathered by the boats down on the beach, but rather than go and state the obvious – that it was a hell of a blow coming on – I preferred to stay in, read, and have another cup of coffee.

"Most men," Thoreau writes early on in *Walden*, "even in this comparatively free country, through mere ignorance and mistake, are so occupied with the factitious cares and superfluously coarse labors of life that its finer fruits cannot be plucked by them."

Not wanting to be one of those men, I decided to head out a little later and walk to the point to see what "fruits" I might pluck from the surrounding desert or shore. A narrow path led out of the camp and followed the bluff out to the first point, then dipped into a swale and continued up the other side onto a plateau with another long, curving bluff over the water.

The windsurf camp at the point consisted of a few trailers set at a 90-degree angle to the prevailing northwesterly, with an area of artificial grass staked down over the dirt in front. A wide cove sat before the camp, with the main point of San

Carlos a couple of hundred yards off to the right as one stood facing the sea.

One of the caretakers, a gringo, was there, and I introduced myself and we talked briefly before I continued my walk. I asked if he knew Rudy from down at the fish camp, and he gave a little snort of a laugh and said that he knew him all right. I asked if the money I had sent to the camp the previous year had reached him.

"Yeah," the guy said vaguely, "I heard something about that. Are you the guy with the boat?"

Taking this as some manner of confirmation, I said that I was. We talked a bit longer about some of the waves in the area; there was a little cliff wall down the coast a few miles that could get good, he told me.

A few hundred yards farther down the bluff, heading back towards the fish camp, I came upon a trailer with a satellite dish and a well-constructed set of windbreaks made from PVC frames and tarps tied off. Two big, shaggy dogs, huskies or malamutes, lay curled in the sun in front of a man and woman who sat side-by-side on plastic chairs, reading.

"Good morning," I said, in a tone that I hoped would startle neither the dogs nor the people. The dogs each opened an eye but didn't bother to lift their heads, and the people looked up from their books serenely, and said hello.

"You must be the guy we saw in the boat off the point last night," the man said.

I told him that it had been me out there, and we agreed that the conditions were pretty wooly for such a small, open vessel.

They had been coming down here in the winter for years, he told me. "Mostly to windsurf, but I ride the bike a bit too," he said, pointing to a dirt bike propped up on its kickstand.

Their windsurfers were laid neatly side-by-side on the edge of the low bluff, just a few feet in front of their camp – clean, plastic-looking things with nylon sails.

One of the dogs stood and came over to give me a sniff, his fury, slowly wagging tail like a dust broom.

The couple had come down from Salt Lake City. The lady had recently retired as a librarian, and the man was an equipment operator who was off work in the winters. They had a tidy little arrangement with their truck, trailer, dogs, and toys, and the man asked me if I wanted to check my email, as just this year he had worked out the satellite system.

He seemed eager for me to see what he had pulled off, and he showed me a voltage regulator, solar panels, and a propeller for additional power. They had to keep a light on, he explained, because they generated so much electricity.

I thought about avoiding the email, as my check of it in town the week or so before had been so disappointing. But the novelty of it – knowing that we were a good four-hour drive off the main highway in the remote Baja desert – was too tempting. There was only one message from my buddy Dave, who wrote, "Don't know if you might check this somehow, but here it is," with a link for me to follow.

The editor at *Surfer Magazine* had written a profile about me and my proposed journey, and the link went to the forum where magazine readers weighed in with their opinions.

Commentators ranged from those who thought that I
had to be insane to attempt such an undertaking and that
I would likely die at sea to those who thought it heroic.
The general consensus seemed to be that I was foolhardy,
which made me wonder, just as my buddy asking me if I
was trying to disappear at sea had made me question my
motives. The interior of the trailer, with its seamless plastic
surfaces and synthetic seat cushions, along with a sudden
knowledge of a public debate of which I had been blissfully
unaware, made me want to get outside and breathe in the
wind off the ocean.

On my way out I saw two volumes of John Muir writings
on a shelf – his *Mountaineering* and *Wilderness* essays – and I
really wanted those. I asked the librarian, guessing that they
were hers, and she said that she had read one of them a long
time before, hadn't gotten to the other one, and why didn't I
just take them.

What a gift! My 19th-century conversation had just
expanded, and I had the makings, along with *Moby Dick*,
of a respectable survey of American writing from the era.
I explained this to her, and she seemed pleased. I could not
have been more grateful to her, and I promised to take good
care of the books and to send them to her in Salt Lake City
after my journey, and she said finally, "Really, its OK. I'm not
reading them!"

Providence!

A great blue heron stood on the mossy-looking reef, stalking the shallows as I climbed through an opening in the rocks to begin my walk back to Aurelio's. The bluff ran for a few hundred yards, and stood about 30-feet high, with an occasional sea cave and long chute cut out of the reef platform that extended seaward. Anemones clustered together in the pools, the ones still underwater opened like light-green, exotic flowers.

Later in the afternoon, back at camp with the sun getting lower over the ocean and the wind having stayed strong at 40 knots all day, I became concerned that Aurelio's boat had not yet returned. There was no one stirring, and I went into the cookhouse and put the kettle on, then stood by the screen door watching the water. As I drank my coffee, I finally saw the bow of a panga working past the outer reef, and went down to the beach to help Aurelio with the boat. He smiled broadly when I told him I had started getting worried with how strong the wind was, and he said it hadn't been too bad far outside where he was working.

After we got the boat up the beach, Aurelio changed clothes and said he was heading into town and asked if I would like to go. So we set off across the desert on the long, winding track, past the boojum trees in the arroyo, up the winding road along the wide plains under a purple sky. We slowed at a rancho to greet an ancient man and his wife. The wind blew cold and the land felt immense, the two old people like wraiths at the dilapidated gate of their property. A tiny ranch house sat a mile or so off in the distance. I nodded and said hello to them, but they didn't seem to see me, and only exchanged a word or two with Aurelio.

It was dark – the deep black of a desert night in winter – when we reached the highway. The headlights from Aurelio's truck cut across the embankment on the opposite side of the road, the rocks and dirt and a bit of cactus showing in a fragmentary snapshot. The asphalt felt smooth and fast. Small points of light shone from the town in the valley below, and the hum of the tires changed pitch as they went from asphalt to the concrete of the bridge over the wide wash. The first houses appeared a few hundred yards past the bridge.

"Allá," Aurelio said, pointing to a taco stand that was shuttered closed, and made a motion with his hand as if he were shooting a pistol.

There were one- and two-story buildings now – a general store, a Tecate distributor, a beauty salon. I saw a store a little farther down from where we stopped with a *"telefónico" and "larga distancia"* sign, and told Aurelio that I would be over there, making a call. A lady behind a counter took down the number I wanted to call and told me to go to a booth on the other side of the room.

"Hello?" came the querying voice of my dad, and when I told him it was me, his relief was palpable, and I sensed how worried he must have been, alone in his little apartment with no way of knowing how I was doing, or what I was experiencing.

He had always had a general distaste for Mexico, always warned me of sleeping on the beach down there, and could never understand my draw to the place, even as I came back with stories of how good the people had been to me. We had the conversation we always do, which is a back-and-forth of him expressing his worries and me assuaging them (even to the point of lying).

He was concerned about what I was going to do for work when I got back, and I told him that I would have plenty of work, that everything would be fine. Then he asked where I was staying and was happy to hear that I was with Aurelio again. I told Dad that I loved him and that we would spend some time together when I was back. We said goodbye, and I walked over to the counter and paid 43 pesos for the call.

I walked outside into the night again and felt like a ghost. Disconnected from the life I had been living in the U.S., I was now adrift. Or, if I was going anywhere, it was only because I had chosen a spot on the map on a whim. The map for the territory I sought to explore did not exist.

Aurelio whistled for me from across the street. He was sitting at a taco stand with a plate of tacos and a soda in front of him. The two ladies working away on the grill behind a dull sheet of plastic for a window glanced at me and then back down to their work.

A man and a woman sat at another table on a concrete walkway above the parking-lot patio where Aurelio sat.

I approached the stand and saw the *carne asada* the one lady was chopping on a well-worn block and asked to have what Aurelio was having. She smiled at me, attractive in the genuine graciousness that shined from her face.

"Hey, where are you from?" the guy sitting at the table with the young woman asked. He had a shaved head and looked as if he stood barely five feet. With a gold stud in his ear, a gold front tooth, and a pair of snakeskin cowboy boots, which he propped arrogantly on the table, it was clear that he wasn't a fisherman.

"I'm from San Clemente," I said.

The woman with him smiled a kind of pained, nervous smile like Aurelio had the night before. She seemed to be trying to make herself smaller, though her nice broad shoulders and thin frame and the tresses of copper curls that fell around her head made her seem like she belonged to another species next to the almost freakishly small and feral-looking man.

"Yeah," he said in a long drawl, nodding his head and grinning as if he had just taken a toke off a fat and satisfying joint, "San Clemente."

Aurelio was standing by the ladies at the taco stand now, very involved in a conversation about somebody's niece – none of them paying any attention to this man or our interaction, until the lady called to me and said, "*Sus tacos*."

"Hey *amigo*," the little man said, taking his feet off the table and pulling a chair out for me, "sit here, with us."

I thanked the lady and took the plate with the two perfect-looking tacos in their hand-pressed corn tortillas, the steam rising and mingling with the smell of the meat.

Since Aurelio had already eaten and stood talking with the ladies, it would be difficult to refuse the man's invitation to join his table, and so I walked over and thanked him and sat down. I didn't feel particularly threatened by the guy. There was a theatrical quality to these supposed *narcotraficante* get-ups that I couldn't quite take seriously.

When he asked what I was doing I told him that I was sailing the coast and that I was a friend of Aurelio's, and turned my head to indicate him at the taco stand a few feet away.

The young woman smiled at me again, and then lowered her eyes almost coquettishly, and I glanced at the man, expecting him to start getting jumpy.

"I think she like you," he said, smiling big – the gold tooth doing little to improve his looks.

"*Gracias*," I said stupidly, looking down, embarrassed. I had gotten a Coke, and the tacos went down in three bites with a good, big slug from the bottle after each one.

The man's name was Chato, and the young woman's Elizabeth, and I shook her hand lightly and offered a fist bump to the little big man, which he accepted, saying, "All riiight," with the same exaggerated pleasure he had before.

"*Oxaceno*," Aurelio said of the guy with the boots, like he'd eaten something spoiled, as we pulled away from the taco stand.

It could not have been much past ten- or eleven-o'clock when we got back, but it felt very late as we drove into the camp, the shanties like a dilapidated movie set in the bouncing headlight beams of the truck. Aurelio pulled up between the cookhouse and the bunkhouse, and when he shut the motor off and cut the lights, the darkness fell like a blanket. But the still-darker shapes of the buildings stood like cutouts against the starry sky.

Out here by the sea, the night had an ambient glow, and the water reflecting the lines of whitewash in the surf added just that little extra illumination.

———————

Again, Aurelio was gone before sunup, and I had slept right through his leaving. At one point in the night I awoke in the blackness of the bunkhouse and felt the block wall next to the pallet bed I was on, and thought for a moment that I was aboard *Cormorant* and tied to a stone quay like one might find in an English fishing village. I reached my hand over the side of the bed, which I imagined to be the rail of my boat, to feel for the water, but finding only air, I had to think about where in the world I might be – a very disorienting 20 seconds went by before I realized that I was at Aurelio's place.

It was eight o'clock when I arose, the sun high, the day already on its course, and all the boats on the beach gone to sea. I read and wrote in my journal, and Aurelio came in later in the morning, saying only that he just had a little fishing to do that day, and that he was going back to town in the afternoon. I asked him if I could go along once again, as I should have picked up more supplies while we were in the day before.

"*Por supuesto, amigo,*" – of course – he assured me.

Not long after, the man and woman from the point came riding up on the dirt bike; she was carrying a pan wrapped in tin foil. The four of us stood in front of the cookhouse, and they presented Aurelio with the pan, which was a freshly baked corn bread.

"For the *langostas* last week," the man said in his best Mexican accent.

"No problem, *es* OK," Aurelio told them, everyone seeming a little embarrassed by the exchange.

The lady said to me, "You found a good place to stay."

"Yes," I replied. And then turning to Aurelio I said, "*Somos un equipo,*" – we are a team.

He smiled uncomfortably, and said "*Si, un equipo,*" and I felt like I had put words in his mouth.

They set off for a motorcycle ride, my mind swimming with thoughts of how Aurelio and I were in no way a "team." I had simply arrived at his place and he had taken me in because I was there.

What more I should have done wasn't clear to me. I had offered, the year before, to send gear down if he wanted it; I had a discount card for a marine store in California and thought things might be cheaper for him that way. But he said he didn't need anything.

Out at the bunkhouse, I got my shaving kit and took one of the remaining pills. I had about ten of them left and was letting two days pass between doses now, having been told by the doctor that Prozac has a long half-life in the body, and deciding for myself that meant I still had the active ingredient working. I went back to make another cup. The jar of Nescafé was getting low, and I felt badly about that too.

After the coffee, I walked down to the beach with my bags, and refolded my clothes, recoiled the lines, and restowed my gear in preparation for a morning departure the following day. On returning Aurelio was nowhere to be found, and his truck was gone, and after an hour or so, it was clear that he had driven to town without me. Having missed the trip, and without making arrangements for Aurelio to pick up food for me, I was low on supplies. Still, I did not want to linger here any longer. The weather seemed to have improved to a milder pattern of light offshore wind in the morning, followed by a moderate sea breeze in the afternoon, and these were the conditions I required.

Repacking *Cormorant* and washing the caked sand and dirt from the thwarts and benches with seawater made me feel better, clearer in mind, and back to the mission at hand. I had set a pot of beans to simmer before going down to the boat, and when I returned to the cookhouse I rinsed them and filled the pot with fresh water and turned the flame up. At sunset, I began chopping onions and garlic and set a second pot of water to boil for yams. Aurelio had a head of cabbage, and this I sliced into discs and added to the yams when the boil ran high. I let everything cook down and the smell in the small room was very nice. Well past dark, Aurelio had not returned, and I set everything aside, and covered it.

The beans were respectable, if plain, and I salted them now that they were soft. Still no Aurelio, and finally I made myself a small bowl of beans and yams boiled soft with the onion and garlic cooked down and caramelized with a touch of balsamic vinegar, and salt and pepper over the whole thing; the cabbage, which I had only lightly cooked, I placed on the side of the plate and drizzled with lime juice. I ate, then washed up and covered the food I'd cooked.

Combing through my equipment as I repacked earlier in the afternoon, I pulled out two of the extra headlamps I had brought, and a pack of AAA batteries. I wrote a note on a piece of paper thanking Aurelio for another year's safe haven on the coast, folded it with a $20 bill inside, and with the headlamps, left it on the table in the cookhouse. I turned out the light, returned to the bunkhouse, and went to sleep.

I was up at first light, and went down to the beach where the others were preparing their boats for the day. The two big fishermen I had met before helped me drag *Cormorant* across the sand, and as I was preparing to push into the surf, Aurelio drove up in the battered pick up he used to haul the pangas.

"Hey *amigo!*" he said, hopping out. "*La troca se quebró anoche, me deja en el pueblo.*" His other truck had broken down, something about a belt and the water pump, and he stayed in town. "*¿Te vás?*" – you are going?

"*Si amigo,*" I told him. I hugged him and then shook his hand. "*Gracias por todo,*" I said. "*Hay algo para comer en la cocina*" – there is something to eat in the kitchen.

Aurelio smiled. He was in his foul weather gear, all set for the day's work. He motioned for me to hop onboard *Cormorant*, and pushed us into the whitewater dribbling in.

With a final shove, he shouted, "*¡El equipo!*"

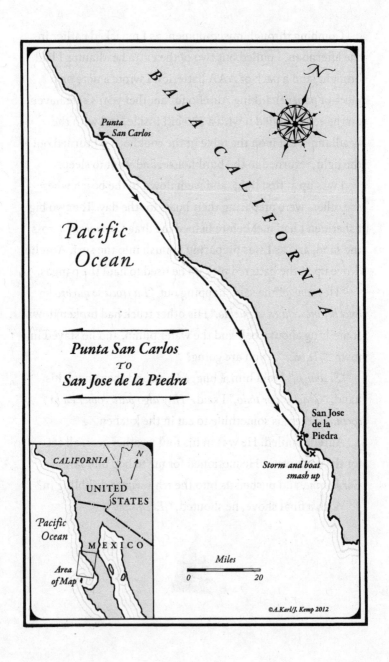

BAJA CALIFORNIA

Punta
San Carlos

Pacific
Ocean

Punta San Carlos
TO
San Jose de la Piedra

San Jose
de la
Piedra

*Storm and boat
smash up*

CALIFORNIA

N

UNITED
STATES

Pacific
Ocean

MEXICO

*Area
of Map*

Miles

0   20

©A.Karl/J. Kemp 2012

CHAPTER SEVEN

A SMASH UP
AND A FIX

In the open desert country around the San Carlos camp squalid shanties obfuscated the natural beauty of the setting, and even just 500 yards past the last structure, the coast took on a more vibrant sheen, as if it had gotten its color back. I ghosted along in a light offshore breeze, keeping close to shore, taking in the scrolling picture show of the cliffs and the beach as they went slowly by.

In a little while, the sand gave way to a rocky stretch with sparse strands of kelp reaching to the surface, and I rigged up a rubber lure to cast as I glided along. Right away I caught a little kelp bass, but he wasn't worth keeping and I let him go, watching him hover still for a moment, just a foot under, before twitching away. Then I noticed clean little waves breaking left and right in peaks along 400 yards of shore before the first headland down from camp.

The offshore breeze had dissipated and the water sparkled translucent in the warm morning sun. I dropped the main and anchored in deeper water outside, and put my wetsuit on. The ocean was cold, but on my 8'2", the *Californio*, I paddled with most of my body out of the water and was soon gliding into slick little peelers – trimming high in the pocket, dropping down, and then banking off the closing sections. After a few rides I took a wave in and walked the beach, just to feel the wonderful isolation of a pristine place again. I sat on the rail of my board, which I set on its edge in the sand like a low wall, and watched the pretty surf rolling in and listened to the little birds chirping just beyond the low bluff.

I paddled back out and rode a few more waves but was soon hungry and cold as I was only wearing a long-sleeve spring suit; the full suit would have been the better call. Back onboard *Cormorant*, I enjoyed a substantial stack of pancakes with the last of my butter and eggs and a transcendent pot of coffee. By the time I had scrubbed my pots clean in the clear ocean water, stowed the 8'2", and put the rest of my supplies to rights, the wind began to stir. In dry clothes, feeling refreshed and cleansed from surfing, well fed and warm inside from breakfast, I pulled anchor and set all the sailing gear in place and resumed my easy glide just offshore.

Wearing the headland close off the port rail, the wind picked up once clear and *Cormorant* heeled into a fine clip. Now, as in the year before, I ran a few points seaward from the general trend of the coast to the southeast. The next headland lay well ahead in the distance, but there was the whole day before me with sufficient time and a superb breeze, and that feeling of everything-being-right came over me once again. I made the cove with the high cliffs, where the panga hung over the edge the year before, by mid-afternoon. This year the panga was nowhere to be seen, and the surf was not happening either. A fisherman and a young boy pulled nets from a boat on the sand. I waved to them, and although it seemed they were looking at me, they did not wave back.

———————————➤

The anchorage made for a miserable night's sleep. It seemed the strong winds of the previous days had put a short-interval roll on the water, and no matter how much line I put out, or where in the cove I set the boat, *Cormorant* rolled side to side and up and down like some coin-operated horse ride. I did not want to go ashore only to read, make dinner, and sleep, but I would have been far more comfortable in my sleeping bag on the beach than in my boat tent turned funhouse. Morning was a great relief, not because the rocking was less severe, but because I could pull anchor and have those interminable little swells helping me now as I rowed on. It felt as though I hadn't slept at all, and I ate some dried fruit and drank water and then took up the oars again in a stupor.

The day was fine however, and by midmorning, like the day before, a light but steady sea breeze came up and filled the sails and carried us slowly but steadily onward. I got hungry by lunchtime, and with such gentle conditions I was able to set up the camp stove and cook a cup of rice while underway. As the pot simmered I fished, and soon came up with a fine bass, perhaps a foot long and two pounds in weight, and I filleted him up, tossing the guts overboard – gulls appearing out of thin air – and fried the fillets and made another stew.

These accumulating days stretched on at once very long and in some way outside of normal time. A deep familiarity had come to me concerning the working of the boat and the character of the conditions. No sound escaped my notice, and the significance of each was clear: I could distinguish a bird splashing down outside my peripheral vision from the slicing of dolphins' fins through the surface. I imagined that I could tell if the breeze would come on stronger or fall away. It was only perception, but full immersion was the essence of it – a prolonged "being with" – and in this way I was getting exactly what I sought from the voyage.

The wind fell off at sunset, and best I could tell, I was two miles from the cove at San Jose de La Piedra. I would not make the next headland south, another two miles beyond the light at San Jose on this night, and I dropped sail and went to oars. The short sea was still up, and it washed back off the cliffs about 200 feet away, making rowing a penance. *Cormorant* rocked so heavily that the blades popped free on every other stroke and the slight progress was miserable.

After such a poor night's rest and a long day at sea, this seemed unfair somehow, but there is no referee to appeal to and so I worked on, angry now that the going was so hard and that the daylight was all but gone. Heading straight out finally to get away from the washing motion closer in, I found somewhat more reasonable water. Although I could feel the cold dew in the night air, I was sweating heavily with the work. The light gleamed ahead like an old friend in a crowd, and I pulled on, less annoyed now and just intent on getting to the bay.

Passing the headland, I kept on for about a quarter-mile looking for the off-lying rock. The moon was not yet up and even if it had been, it was still just a sliver, and the night was dark. But through the gradually dimming evening and the cold blossoming of night, my eyes had steadily adjusted to the low light, and I picked out the dark forms of the humps of the rock in the middle of the bay after a short while, and rounded to them.

I put down my oars, and stepped forward to drop anchor. God, what exhaustion, and I sat for some minutes on the midships thwart with my elbows on my knees and my face in my hands as if I was sobbing, but I was just letting the fatigue drain. I had to change my T-shirt and dug a dirty one out that at least was dry. I put on my sweater, knit hat, and jacket before setting up the boat tent.

Everything was effort, all of it toil. The boat tent I put up with grunts like a power lifter. To get the stove set up and lit felt like the night's work, but I heated and finished off the fish stew and, desperate to rest, I crawled into the bag. The goddamn rocking was just as bad as the night before, and I was pissed off about it. Nothing for it of course, and I slept as well (or as poorly) as I could. I tried to wedge myself in with the surfboards on one side and dry bags piled against the rail on the other, but nothing seemed to work. At some point I must have slept, because I was awoken in the morning by fishermen calling out to me, checking to see that I was OK.

They said that they would be back in the middle of the day and that they would pick me up and we could have lunch together. There were three of them aboard – a middle-aged man and two younger men in their 20s. The land here rolled away in dunes beyond a white sand beach that ran in a crescent from a stubby rock headland. Mesas rose up from the desert in the distance, and to the south, hills with green shrubs and cactus slanted down to a wall of sea cliffs and caves. Where the cliffs ended, the land beyond emerged again low to the water in the distance on the other side of a bay.

I ate chocolate, drank coffee, and had a Clif Bar. I read Thoreau. "The wildest scenes had become unaccountably familiar," nodding my head in agreement. How great it was to be anchored way down in Baja with the side of the boat tent rolled up to let the morning sun warm my body but keep my face and my book in shadow, and to read good, sustaining words.

The fishermen returned very soon it seemed and motored alongside. I hastily packed a knapsack and stepped from

Cormorant to their boat, not worried about leaving her because the day was calm. The panga felt substantial after the lightness of my boat, and we rode high on the water as the pilot throttled up, lifting over the breaking waves and skimming right up on the wet sand as he simultaneously tilted the outboard up on its hinge.

We each shook hands on the beach: Mario, the younger pilot, his friend Juan, and Mario's dad, Jose. It was a friendly and easy conversation, telling one another about ourselves while walking across the sand to an RV parked behind the bluff at the headland.

Mario seemed to have the authority within the group; he spoke with confidence while his father hung back and smiled deferentially. His friend, Juan, was tall and skinny and listened intently to everything Mario said, as if it all pertained to his education in fishing. I asked how the surf was off the point. *"Algunas veces,"* Mario replied, and then in English, "Sometimes... *buenas olas,"* pumping his fist for emphasis. "I have the boogie board," he continued, his voice smoky, *"buenas, buenas,"* indicating long point waves running down the beach.

A small, round woman emerged from the side door of the RV as we approached. She smiled, and we shook hands. "Juana," she introduced herself, her decaying front teeth as matter of fact as the rolls of fat stretching the material of her shirt at her waist. The men removed their foul weather pants and boots, hanging these on various rusted traps outside. *"Ven,"* Juana said, motioning us inside.

She stirred a large pot of beans on a burner with
a hose running down to a propane tank on the
floor. In the cuddy above the front seats, a rumpled
pile of blankets marked one bed, and the other
two were in the back, down a narrow passageway,
behind the tiny kitchen. Juana ladled out plates of
beans and passed them to the fishermen and me
sitting at small booth tables on either side of the
RV. Mario and his father sat at one booth, and Juan
and I in the other.

Handing a plate to me she said, "*Estos frijoles son
los mejores del mundo*," with a satisfied and knowing
air, and one bite confirmed that they were, in fact,
the best beans in the world.

Each plate had a nice hunk of *carnitas* in it,
and the pork flavor went all the way through,
smoky and rich. Juana came and sat next to Juan,
putting an arm around him, and they made a funny
couple– she so round and he so long and thin. The
meat came apart when I pressed the side
of my fork into it, and as I took another bite I saw Juana
looking on with appreciation. "*Increíble*," I said, and she
nodded with satisfaction.

The *carnitas* had come from her family's rancho, about 20
miles back in the desert from here. I asked if they had water
there, and she said, "*Por supuesto*," – of course – with the
same prideful air she had regarding her beans. This wasn't
a haughty attitude but instead a self-appreciation that came
from knowing the value of the place and of her family.

After lunch, we stepped outside and I sat on an upside-down bucket while Mario and his dad, Jose, searched a box of discarded diving and fishing parts, looking for a pin they could use for the winch assembly on their boat. Juana and Juan leaned side by side on a plywood table over a discarded washer and an oil drum.

A pickup drove over the rise behind the RV and descended into the camp. An old fellow was driving and his wife sat in the passenger seat – her *Indio* face wizened an earthy, reddish brown with a ball cap turned sideways on her head, hip-hop style, that read "U.S. Border Patrol."

It was the slow talk of country folks, but the information seemed to be about who they had seen out on the four-wheel-drive tracks in recent days, in this way keeping tabs on the people traveling in their area. The old woman gave me no more than a glance, and I realized that it wasn't really rude on her part, but only that I was merely passing through. I did not actually exist for these people – my presence had no bearing on their lives.

With the fishermen it was different because we shared the perils of the sea, and one never knows when the only helping hand might come from a guy in a small, hand-built sailboat. It probably would have been different with the *campesinos,* too, if we had met out in the desert and one of us had a mechanical problem… then, we would be a factor in each other's lives. It was refreshing, I decided, to see people who did not indulge in extraneous communication.

The old man fired the truck up, and Juana said goodbye and went back into the RV. I raised my hand and nodded to the woman with the sideways ball cap, and she seemed to see me for a second after all and gave a barely perceptible tilt of her head in recognition. The men were getting their things together to head back out, and I stood up and put my knapsack on. Juana came back out with a mayonnaise jar full of the beans and *carnitas* and handed it to me saying, "*Que te vaya bien, Christián,*" – go well – and I leaned down to kiss her once on each cheek and thank her.

After the four of us shoved the boat into the water, Mario pulled the engine to life and accelerated through the line of little breakers, and again the panga took on a hovering feeling as we sped across the small bay towards *Cormorant* lying steadily at anchor in the full tide. I thanked my new friends for their company, and marveled that these men should have chosen to host me – to simply pass the middle part of the day, sharing their food and telling what little about themselves could be told in those brief hours.

I stepped across to my own boat, which felt small and thin comparatively. Still, all of my things were here, and dry, and I was happy to be back on board. As I began readying to sail, the wind coursed hot off the desert. I untied the tent canvas, folded it over and rolled it up, and then stowed it in its place on the starboard side. The fiberglass battens I unbent from the slots in the handrails and stowed them under the surfboards. I had only to stuff my sleeping bag into its dry bag and stow it with the other dry bags, before dropping the rudder in place and pulling anchor.

The wind blew offshore, although it came full and strong it did not have the intensity of a *Norte*. Nevertheless, I reefed the main down completely before setting the mizzen sail and lashing the rudder in its forward position so that *Cormorant* would draw up into the wind as I pulled anchor.

The shortened mainsail went up with one downward draw on the halyard, but once underway I wished I had only put in one reef, since *Cormorant* was running tame in what could have been a roaring sail. Of course the alternative of having too much sail up was worse by far, and it was these cautious moves that would help to keep me safe. The water shimmered light green and darker blue farther offshore in the bright sun, and the sandstone cliffs looked freshly scrubbed as I approached the headland. In this wind I really could have been heeling over smartly, but I had to be content with an even keel as I rounded the point and came into the bay, where the year before the dolphins had surrounded the boat in the night with the moon reflected off the shiny domes of their heads.

Here I dropped anchor about 40 feet from the cliff wall, trying to tuck in behind an outcropping of rocks for a windbreak. But I placed myself too close to the breaking waves and had to move a little farther off. It was midafternoon, but I set up the boat tent, laid out my sleeping platform, and made the stove ready for cooking. A nice little wave was breaking off the shelf with the offshore breeze holding up the wall as it peeled across, and I wanted to be able to come back and make a hot meal after surfing.

Sitting on the midships thwart, I pulled on my wetsuit. I saw a panga racing in from far outside and watched as the pilot steered towards me. I waved at the two men aboard as they passed. They waved back and looked over their shoulders at me as they sped in towards the beach. I pulled the 8'2" *Californio* from its board bag, and eased myself into the cold water, straddling the board so I did not have to dunk in completely, and then paddled shoreward. There were no campers this time, no one around but the fishermen's camp farther down the beach, and what appeared to be another trailer beyond that. The waves were small but shapely – all hollow pockets, spray, and the steep wall ahead.

I surfed until sunset, slouching down into a knock-kneed tuck, making myself small in the hook of the wave on some rides and standing to my full height across the steepest, fastest part on others. I enjoyed each wave immensely – the sensation of sliding over the surface of the ocean always novel, always seductive. This, of course, was why I had come. There was nothing particularly special about the surf, other than its fantastic shape and the even texture of the water groomed by the wind. The waves stood no higher than my waist, but riding them made a playground out of this corner of the desert.

Back on board *Cormorant*, dry and warm in my clothes under the boat tent with the beans Juana had given me heating on the stove and the candle lantern burning with its soft glow, I thought, *all's well, all's well*. I had started in on the Muir essays and farther, deeper now into my journey (about 350 miles from home), I felt buoyed by the great wanderer's stories:

"The days were growing short, and winter, with its heavy storms, was drawing nigh, when avalanches would be booming down the long white slopes of the peaks, and all the land would be buried. But, on the other hand, though this white wilderness was new to me, I was familiar with storms, and enjoyed them, knowing well that in right relations with them they are ever kindly."

This, from the first page of John Muir's *The Discovery of Glacier Bay*, published in 1895, contained everything

I loved most about his philosophy – his embrace of wild weather and the sense that Nature had a sentient ("kindly" as he put it) quality.

I ate contentedly and then picked up my book and read on by the light of the lantern held close to the page, illuminating just one paragraph at a time, the brass base getting warm in my grasp. Although I should have been tired out from the poor sleeps I had been having, I read on for a long while, so far away in my little boat, in that distant cove, on the edge of that vast desert.

"The weather was about half bright," Muir wrote of the Glacier Bay canoe expedition, "and we glided along the green and yellow shores in comfort, the lovely islands passing in harmonious succession, like ideas in a fine poem."

Coyote calls woke me in the morning. The sun was well up, it was probably near eight, and I lifted the bottom edge of the tent to see what was going on. Five young men sat on the rocks near the point yammering at the boat, and I stuck my head out and waved and called out, *"Buenos días."* One of them yelled back, but I couldn't understand what he said, and another one shouted something equally incomprehensible. They all giggled and it struck me then that they were a gaggle of Mexican children, the size of grown men, playing dress-up as fishermen.

"OK *amigos!*" I shouted across with another wave, as if we were all in on the same joke, and rolled the edge of the tent back down, happy in my privacy to set up the stove for coffee and hot granola. They let out a few more yips and yowls and there may have been the plunking-in of small rocks thrown near the boat, but soon enough everything was quiet again. I peeked through a little gap in the boat tent and saw that they had left, and then rolled up the sides to enjoy breakfast in the fine morning sun. This was another benefit of staying on board – the nice bit of distance the water provided.

I went surfing later in the morning. Two pangas had buzzed by heading out to fish. The water was clear and lightly green, tropical-looking as if over reef flats, although the bottom was sand. In an easy routine, I paddled into wave after wave, riding some of them on my belly. After about an hour, I saw two trucks come over the ridge behind the fishermen's camp. There were boards in padded bags secured to the roof racks, and I watched them come slowly down the track and pull up to a little flat area on a rise at the base of the point. These are the people I will be surfing with, I thought. But I was not alarmed as I might have been at other remote surf breaks where one goes to great effort to have a wave alone. Aloneness was a commodity I had a good supply of.

There were two men in each truck, and from where I sat in the lineup, they looked older – wide-brimmed hats and at least one silver beard. They leaned against their trucks and watched as I rode the little waves that came through. It would have been a disappointment to have driven the 50 miles across the desert and come upon such small surf, but the coast itself would have been some consolation with all of its desert mystery, clear water, and clean sand. One of them put a wetsuit on and pulled a longboard off the roof of the truck and made his way down to the water.

We said hello, and he asked me where my camp was and I pointed to *Cormorant* riding at anchor out in the bay, farther up the point.

He was a good guy, I could tell right off. An elementary school teacher from Los Angeles, he looked to be near my age (late thirties). We traded waves back and forth and made easy conversation, he telling me about living in Santa Monica and me talking about building the boat. The guys he was with were older, he said, friends of the guy he had driven with, who was an Australian surfer he knew from Malibu. When we went in an hour or so later, I met the other guys, two of them brothers from Santa Barbara, and the Australian.

The men were interesting fellows, each of them accomplished in their fields, which included teaching, archeology and architecture. As I told them about my journey, and how I had packed up everything I owned, left work, and my apartment, I felt like I was living the life one is "supposed" to live when young, avoiding the trappings of middle-class conformity. But it felt that I was only saying words about "freedom," and as we talked, sitting there by the trucks, I gave voice to the doubts I felt – the fear that there would be some permanent consequence coming from just cutting out like this, that I would go too far in a certain mode and lose the opportunity to have a regular life.

I felt it sometimes, even just six weeks into the trip, that I was removing myself from the normal experiences. While that is to be celebrated in youth, does it mean something else when a man stays alone too long and does not have anyone as he gets older? You see them, the old bachelors, and they always seem a little dried out and hollow – haunted.

I might have made the men a little uneasy, speaking so candidly. One loses one's sense of propriety; the line between normal communication and what goes too far into the personal becomes blurred when one spends too much time alone. But each of them told me not to worry, that this was a fine thing I was doing, and that I should continue in it.

One of the pangas motored down to the point out of the northwest, and as he came into the bay, the pilot circled over to *Cormorant* at anchor. I gave a shout and waved from where we stood at the top of the bluff at the headland, and the men in the boat waved and beckoned for me to come down to the water's edge. When I got there they had motored in close to the cliff wall, and the fellow in front held up a nice halibut, probably 12 pounds and about three-feet long. I patted my thighs over my front pockets, gesturing that I had no money, but the young fisherman shook his head no and said, "*es* for you," and stepped to the rail of the boat to hand the fish up to me.

"Hey!" I told him, "Wow. *Gracias*," and accepted the fish, and said, "*muchas gracias*," again.

I climbed back up to the brothers at the top of the bluff, and we made our way back to the base of the point where they had made camp. They had brought a small bundle of firewood and I suggested that we cook together. Everyone seemed happy with that plan and we agreed to meet just after sunset.

In the meantime I paddled back to *Cormorant*.

The flames licked up from the broken husk of a yucca stalk, and the Aussie split chunks of firewood with an axe and laid those over the kindling as I walked up to the men's camp site. Evening was deepening over the bay, and the fire stood out bright and made a dome of light in the falling dark. I took the halibut down to the edge of the rocks and cut open its small belly pouch and emptied the guts. Soon the fire was burning hot, and the brothers wrapped the halibut in foil and laid it on old fish trap we were using for a grill. It came out beautifully, the light flaky meat pulling right off the bone. We ate the fish by itself, and although each of the five of us had a nice slab of fish on his paper plate, there were still leftovers.

Later, after dinner but not too far into the night, I changed back into my wet wetsuit on the rock platform down by the water. Packing my clothes in the dry bag and swinging it over my shoulder, I stepped down to the dark water with my surfboard under arm – the whitewater shined luminous in the night from the little waves. *Cormorant* was a dark silhouette at anchor.

Later still, deep in the solemn night, I rose from my sleeping bag and crawled out of the boat tent as the moon crept out from behind a wispy puff of cloud, showing all the bay and the running hills of the desert. The sparkling water was so clear that I could see *Cormorant*'s shadow from the moon's spectral glow on the sand bottom fifteen feet below. "How wholly infused with God is this one big word of love that we call the world!" says John Muir.

And I say it too.

The next day we all surfed together, the waves still small, but still reeling across mechanically, cylindrical, speedy, and fun. A pod of dolphins came racing into the bay, hurtling themselves clear of the water, leaping right out of the waves, putting our surfing to shame. We hooted at them in appreciation. I surfed for so many hours that the brothers went in, had lunch and came out to surf again in the afternoon and I was still there – a ball cap on as a sun shield for my forehead. The waves were so neat that there was nothing else I wanted to do, and I glided and banked and trimmed all through the middle of the day and into the afternoon.

Finally, parched and exhausted, I paddled back to *Cormorant* where I ate the remaining halibut and poured a bottle full of water from my five-gallon jug and drank it down.

The day was uncommonly still – no harbinger of weather on the horizon or in the sky – just a languid sea as the surf diminished and the sun burned its way slowly westward. I decided to pull anchor and take *Cormorant* north around the headland and explore the cliffs and caves under oars. Every movement I had made with the boat thus far had been in the interest of heading south, and even though the going was easy in the still water, something in me needed convincing that it was OK to push north, even for just a mile.

Boulders rounded right down into the clear water, little flakes of quartz sparking in the light tan elephant hides of the rock. A sea cave rose up like a chapel and a thick snarl of branches with an attendant osprey guarded the entrance. Wanting neither to disturb the bird, nor risk getting shoved against the wall of the cave in a surge, I chose not to row inside. In such calm water, working the oars was nearly effortless. I fished for awhile, floating off a rock shelf out from the sea cave, and although I could see nice ones down there drifting in and out of undercut crevices, none of them took any interest in my lure.

By early evening the sky had changed, and though the sea remained calm, clouds billowed up on the horizon away to the southwest. A light breeze started in from that direction, and *Cormorant* swung around on her anchor back towards the rock wall of the bay. I reset the hook farther off, out in the middle of the bay where there was no protection from the cliffs. But with the wind from the southwest there was no protection there anyway. By the last light of the day, I noticed the clouds had stacked up more significantly and were darker out to sea. The breeze was blowing more strongly from the southwest.

No one stirred at the surfers' camp at the base of the point, nor at the fishermen's trailers down the beach.

I slept better than I had thought I would that night. The boat rocked heavily, but something in the movement of the water was more even and consistent than the short chop of other recent nights. I put my head outside at one point and felt the wind tousling my hair, a little spray whisking off the surface and alighting on my face. I could see nothing in the darkness, but I could tell it was a good blow coming on. A flag would have been snapping briskly. All I could do at that point was try and rest, and trust in the anchor and the 100 feet of line I had run out.

Whitecaps were running all across the bay at dawn, and
Cormorant rocked even more heavily with an added diagonal
roll. The sky was dark all the way across, with charcoal-bellied
clouds piling up from the horizon and stretching northward.
The air smelled of rain. I took the boat tent down and stowed
the battens, moving quickly now, having decided that I needed
to get ashore. Pulling the anchor line in hand-over-hand, I
piled the line, chain, and anchor haphazardly in the bow.
Once the hook let go of the bottom, the wind drew us quickly
across the bay, blowing us towards the corner where the surf
converged on the rocks.

The waves were a disorganized smear along the whole
stretch of beach, and I held myself off, back-pedaling with
the oars outside the farthest breakers, and surveyed a landing
spot amid the chaos of the rising storm.

I glanced over to the surfers' camp and saw the men
scurrying about, taking down their tents, stowing armfuls of
gear in the backs of their trucks. Three fishermen stood on
the berm of the beach straight in from where I sat aboard my
boat. One of them waved his arms overhead, then brought
them down in a sweeping motion before him, indicating that I
should run ashore right there.

With no perceptible break in the frequency of the waves,
I brought *Cormorant* around and started in. A slightly bigger
wave stood outside of me and I back-paddled to crash through
the top of it and let it pass. I then pulled hard on the oars to
move forward again, chopping with short, hard strokes to ride

the whitewater wake just behind, where the other waves could not reach me. But *Cormorant* cut too swiftly through the water and the wave drew us tumbling over it, the boat plunging down on her bows then swinging hard over, broadside to the crashing whitewash. I had no control over any of this, but *Cormorant* seemed to take over, and rode sideways into shore, rolling back on her rounded sides until the keel met the wet sand of the beach.

The fishermen ran down to me, and with two of us on opposite sides grasping the gunwale forward, and two aft, we dragged the boat up the beach and placed her between two of their pangas at the base of the berm. There was no time to stand around, as the wind was coming on harder now – the sky almost sweating with moisture but not yet raining.

I thanked the men and grabbed dry bags from the boat and walked quickly up the berm to the higher ground that rose up behind. I dropped the bags and returned to the boat for the rest of my gear, and in three trips I had it all staged in a pile next to a large shrub.

Looking over the area, I saw a broken down pickup, with its hood up and windows smashed away, that was oriented parallel to the shore and might provide some break from the onshore wind. I jogged the 100 yards there and saw a level spot just on the inland side of the passenger door. I shuttled my gear in three trips, unpacked my tent, and set it up with the fly staked out as taut as I could get it. I put my sleeping bag inside and then ran down to the boat once more to pull the 6'7" out of its boardbag and bring the bag along with the collapsible water jug up to the tent.

Just as I had gotten my sleeping bag arranged over the board bag, and put water on to boil for tea in the vestibule, the first spattering drops of rain began to tap down on the fly. The surfers drove by and honked a little later. I was well into reading Muir and happy, delighted actually, to pass the day so cozy in my tent while the rain came down, but I peeked out to see them waiting by *Cormorant*. After putting my rain gear on, I ran down to shake hands with them and wish them well and thank them for the company.

The schoolteacher gave me a *Playboy* magazine, and the Aussie offered a plastic bag full of packaged food and handed me a can of white gas for my stove. They were heading inland to a Native American site they knew of with petroglyphs, and then home a few days early with this weather. I waved goodbye as the two-truck caravan pulled away and stood there by *Cormorant* for a moment, looking at the churning ocean and the desert that looked brooding now under dark clouds and sweeping bands of rain.

Hurrying back to the tent, I laid out my bounty in the vestibule, peeled off the rain shell tops and bottoms I wore, and got back inside as quickly as I could. The boiling water had heated the tent. The fabric was orange, which made a cheery little cocoon in the dark day. My beloved coffee was running low, but I had a cup and then laid out the remaining food I had in order to take stock and make a plan.

There were three bags of instant beans and rice from the Aussie, and I had about a cup-and-a-half of rice, two cups of lentils, a tin of sardines, a half-cup of soup powder, a serving of granola, and perhaps a cup of sugar. The realization that

I had passed up on the opportunity to shop back in town the week before with Aurelio came down on me like the shock of an overdrawn account.

This was real economics – calories versus hours and the body's requirements. I had a pouch of tobacco, and though I hadn't felt much like smoking on the journey thus far, I rolled myself a cigarette. South of here along the coast there would be surfers camped sporadically, and I pictured myself rowing ashore and going tent-to-tent with my tin pot, begging for alms like some outcast sailorman.

The closest town was hardly a town at all, merely a place where an old fellow sold gasoline on the side of the road from a steel drum at twice the going price, just so motorists could have peace of mind until the next real stopping point, and this place was at least 55 miles across the empty desert. Perhaps the fishermen here could sell me some supplies. John Muir may have traveled the Sierra on foot with a couple of biscuits in his pockets, but I felt hungry and tired.

There is a town on Isla Cedros, noted on both my chart and in the sailing guide, and I had been considering making the crossing out there to resupply. If I continued to follow the coast I would end up far inside to the southeast, and have to work my way 35 miles out against the wind and current to clear Punta Eugenia – the big fish hook on the map, half-way down the pacific coast of Baja. The point I planned to cross from was a day's sail to the south – the same place I had ridden crystalline sand peelers the year before, the place where I had seen lion tracks in the smooth sand of the arroyo. It was 55 miles across to the island from there, and calculating a speed of three knots, I realized that I was looking at a full 24-hour's sail, and only if the breeze held steady, neither too strong nor falling away deep in the night.

I put my rain gear on later in the afternoon, grabbed the *Playboy* and tobacco, and headed over to the fishermen's trailer. It was a broken-down refrigerated delivery truck with no wheels; the big box had a plywood floor, which served as their kitchen and lounge. The men slept in tents clustered in front of the truck like a mini refugee camp, with multiple frayed tarps over the top for added shelter. The camp itself was strewn with discarded netting and a broken chair lying on its side.

I knocked on the roll-up door at the back of the truck, which was opened about a foot to let air in. One of them pulled it up, and I saw inside three of the men – who would have still been boys not three years before. An older man was with them, his face drawn and grey-whiskered, his hair gray, and his back stooped.

They welcomed me inside, and my eyes went right to the big pot of beans the old man tended on the table, boiling on a burner like Juana had up at San Jose de La Piedra, a couple of days before. I could not hope for such magical beans as she cooked with the blessed pork from her family's rancho, but still, this was food, this was shelter, this was human companionship, and I was surprised by how much I craved these things.

I offered the *Playboy*, and the boys looked it over greedily, laughing and pinching each other and exclaiming "*¡Oooh, chi chi mamá!*" I offered them tobacco; all I needed was whiskey now to complete the corrupting picture of the old fur trapper coming into native society to wreck moral havoc. The other two fellows showed up from the tents outside, having heard the excitement in the back of the truck, and soon all six of us young fellows, along with the old man, were smoking away happily, and looking at the voluptuous curves on the pages of the magazine. One of them asked if I had *mota*, and feeling like Lucifer himself, I said that sadly, I didn't.

The old man was named Jose; I called him Don Jose, as a slightly teasing title of respect, but he seemed to appreciate the notice of his senior status. When the food was ready, they offered me a plate of watery beans and rice as if I were one of their crew, and the fellow who had been sitting in the chair motioned for me to sit there. The beans, seasoned as they were with honest hospitality, tasted wonderful. The boys passed the one bottle of hot sauce they shared, and I spiced up my plate and looked at my companions and thanked them.

"*En serio,*" I said, "*muchas gracias.*"

Rain lashed through the night but it just drummed off the surface of the tent I had staked down so well, and the rhythm of the storm lolled me into a deep sleep. Solid, unmoving ground was a welcome change as well. The rain continued through dawn, and in the morning I boiled water for coffee and the last of the granola, not bothering to look outside as the buffeting wind and the steady funnel of water draining from the edge of the fly told me all I needed to know of the conditions.

A little later, however, some slight increase in the velocity of the wind or the intensity of the rain, made me pull my rain gear on and go out to check on the boat.

As I stood from the tent I saw two of the fishermen running toward the boats. Ugly, black-faced waves broke hard on the sand and surged across the beach, receding now with *Cormorant* and two pangas in the wash. I ran then too, and as I reached the beach, I saw two of the fishermen's boats smash *Cormorant* between them. The men had each gotten a hold of their bigger, fiberglass boats, and I ran in to grab *Cormorant*'s bow line.

There was no way that we could pull our respective vessels up the beach single-handedly, and when the next surge washed in, the boats smashed together again, this time with the horrible sound of cracking wood.

A battered old pickup roared towards us down the muddy track with the rest of the men from the fishermen's camp running behind. They ran a long line from the front bumper to my boat, and I quickly tied a doubled bowline to the eye in the bow stem, stood clear, and waved my hand for the driver to haul away.

The truck belched smoke and threw up mud and shrubbery, pulling *Cormorant* across the beach, right up the berm and into the desert behind. Whatever damage she had sustained from the other boats, this treatment looked enough to finish her off. But there was no time to assess, and

I undid the tie and ran the thick hawser down to the men still struggling to hold onto their pangas against the tide.

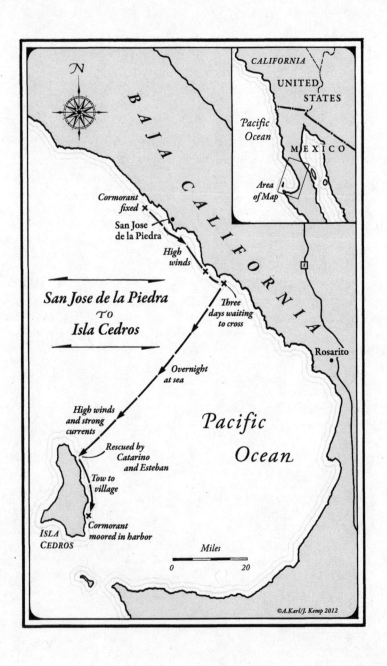

CHAPTER EIGHT

THE VALLEY OF DECISION

First thing the next morning, I made a strong cup of coffee with the last of the grounds, then walked down to have a look at the boat. It was cold and clear, the tide was high, and the water was still and no waves were breaking, which seemed odd just one day after the storm. A heavy dew covered *Cormorant*, and mud had been slung all across the interior in the previous day's action. The broken parts of the handrail stood out jagged and sharp in the early sunlight, the wood underneath exposed now and looking too clean, like bone or some tissue not meant to been seen.

I squeezed the broken pieces of the handrail and they snapped back in place, so I saw that I would be able to drive stainless steel screws in, put resin down, and hold the works steady with a clamp. The plank lands, on the other hand, were split apart lengthwise for a good three feet along two separate strakes in the port bow and needed to be relaminated. To get a good bond I would have to carve away the paint and primer down to bare wood, fill the gap between the planks with thickened resin, and then run dry wall screws through to pull the strakes tight together while the resin set. Once the resin hardened, I would back the screws out and fill the holes with another batch of resin.

My camp was about 200 yards from the fishermen's camp, but nearer my tent stood another trailer where two other men were living. I waved to them as I passed, and one of them nodded slightly, and then closed the door.

They had no boat that I could see, nor any fishing gear.

With the rain and the hard sea-use my vessel had been through, I wanted the wood to dry completely before I put resin on it, so I wiped the dew away with a cloth, and scavenged pieces of rusted fish traps to use as spacers to force open the broken areas of the handrail and let the air circulate. I took my scraper to the plank lands, and broke free the lengths of resined fiberglass rope I had laid down during construction – this after taking off the side benches, which were held in place by stainless steel bolts and locknuts.

I then pried the split planks apart with the scraper blade and inserted the quills of seagull feathers, doubled over, to keep the gap open. A hard, cold, clearing wind came up with bright sun, and the conditions could not have been better for drying out the boat. In the evening I would drape the boat tent canvas across the exposed places to keep the moisture off through the night.

My food supplies were virtually gone after lunching on another package of rice and beans. For breakfast I had used the last of the rice with sugar, and now all that remained was a last pack of rice and beans and the lentils. I visited the fishermen boys again that evening and shared my tobacco sheepishly, hoping for something to eat. They seemed to be getting a lot out of the *Playboy*, and their teasing was giving way to punches on the shoulder, protests, posturing and then play-fighting with a hint of potential escalation.

All the while, Don Jose stirred the big pot and checked on another pot of simmering rice on a second burner, ignoring the five overgrown boys yelling, pushing and jostling all around him in the close space of the back of the truck. Naturally, when the food was ready, Don Jose handed me a plate and I lined up with the others for a scoop of rice and a ladleful of beans. I sat to eat on the floor of the truck, leaning against the sidewall.

Two of the boys were brothers, their last name McLeish. They had blue eyes and sandy-brown hair, high cheekbones and thin moustaches. A great-great-grandfather had ended up in this part of Baja in the 19th century. When I asked them how he got here, they did not know and said only that he had come from "*Scotia*."

"*¿Te gusta el surf, no?*" – you like to surf – the younger one, Pedro, asked me.

I told him that I did like surfing, and when one of the others asked me what I did for work, I told them that I had been writing for a surfing magazine. Then Pedro asked me if I knew a young woman named Christina, who had been surfing here at this bay with some friends earlier in the winter.

"*Es una surfista profesional, en las revistas*" – a pro surfer in the magazines – he said. "*Muy linda, y amable*" – very pretty and kind. He described her with great admiration and affection. Although I couldn't figure out which surfing starlet he was talking about, I could imagine the shining, smiling face and the sense of fun a young girl can bring.

He was married and had an infant in the village, as did each of the other boys – not any of them older than twenty-three – one of them even divorced already and remarried with two kids from each wife. But there seemed to be a yearning in Pedro's questions about this Christina.

After dinner they passed around a boiling kettle of water and a quickly emptying jar of Nescafé, out of which each of us spooned a tiny bit of coffee into chipped mugs. I offered the tobacco package and each of the five young men, except Don Jose who held up his hand, took a pinch and rolled a cigarette.

I asked them when they would be going back to town, which prompted a heated exchange that I couldn't follow, but seemed to be about whose turn it was to make the run in. Pedro, the younger McLeish, said that he and his brother were going in, and two of the others looked down and shook their heads in disappointment. I explained that my supplies were getting low, and asked if I could go in with them, and if there was a bus that came through.

Yes, there was a bus twice a day, they told me, going all the way to Tijuana. I said that I might need more resin and supplies to fix the boat, and that I had even thought of going back to California for a week or so, and if I did, could I leave my gear and my boat here with them? Of course, they assured me, no problem.

When I offered to pick up supplies for them if I went over the border, the older McLeish said loudly and repeatedly that he wanted new foul weather gear. I explained that I wasn't sure that I was even going, but that if I did, I would see what I could do. Still he pressed for the foul weather gear, until his brother turned to him and told him to stop.

In the morning, as I prepared to start the repair project and the men got ready to fish, I saw why the older McLeish, named Jaime, was so desperate for new foul weather gear; his was a miserable scrap of a jacket torn up one side and sewn crudely with fishing line, and his bibs had holes above the knees that would have him soaked by the first crashing wave. The fishermen brought the pangas down to the water with the beast of an old truck, and heaved and strained to get their hulking fiberglass boats into the surfline, the water splashing up on them with the little waves rolling in.

Soon both boats were away – the McLeish brothers in one vessel and the other three in the other. Don Jose drove the growling pickup back to the delivery-truck kitchen. I pulled the canvas off my boat and decided to let the sun get at the wood for another few hours, although everything seemed nicely dried out from yesterday's conditions. In the meantime, I went in search of driftwood to fashion dowels to help secure the handrail back to the riser blocks. There were some small scraps of plywood on the beach, but no dried branches or roots. It seemed that that kind of driftwood didn't make it this far down the coast, as there weren't any trees in this landscape.

Some of the shrubs that grew on the flat ground behind the berm had woody, if slightly pliable, branches, and I snapped a short length off and laid a drill bit next to it, pleased to see that they were the same diameter. My plan now was to use these "shrub-dowels" to pin the handrail to the riser blocks where it had broken free, and then run a stainless screw through the middle of each "dowel" to expand them for a solid, tight bond, locked in by the resin.

I still needed to remove the paint and primer from around the cracks on the plank lands, and I set to the job with the cold chisel, scraper, and my sailing knife – first etching a line around the broken area with the blade and then scaring it with cross-hatching cuts. After, I came through with the cold chisel and dug out the paint chips right down to the wood. This was tedious work, but I knew from the building of *Cormorant* that if she was to regain her structural integrity, she needed to be rebonded on a structural level.

I only had enough material for one try at it, so I took the whole day to prep the plank lands and shape the dowels. On the following day, the third since the accident, I would put resin down and laminate the broken pieces together.

The next morning, after the men had launched the boats, I went to the camp to pay a visit to Don Jose while waiting for the temperature to rise to work with the resin. The old man was weaving a long driftnet with black nylon line strung between two vertical posts set about 50 feet apart. It was a cruel-looking piece of crochet work, and I thought of the clumps of the stuff I had seen on the beaches here and there in Baja, and of the seals and birds that got snared.

We chatted about how far the boys went out to sea, about what they were catching, and about my friend Aurelio (who Don Jose knew) up at the San Carlos camp. The boys had a small German shepherd puppy that scampered underfoot and bit at the hem of my woolen army pants.

Without ceremony I had taken the last of my Prozac that morning, encouraging myself vaguely, feeling that I had passed through a time of dependence. As I spoke with Don Jose, I saw one of the men down at the trailer near *Cormorant* come outside. Don Jose glanced toward him, and the man looked up the hill to where we stood, then turned and went back inside. The old man went back to his work with the line and said nothing about him or the trailer, and I thought it better not to ask. But later in the day, after I had repaired the handrails on my boat and tightened the C-clamps while the resin cured, I walked back towards my tent and again saw the man standing in front of the trailer.

I went over to say hello. *"Espero que mi trabajo no les moleste"* – I hope my work doesn't bother you – I said.

"*Esta bien,*" he said, looking at me with what seemed an emotionless expression. "*¿Quieres café?*" – do you want a coffee – he asked and motioned for me to come inside.

Like the fishermen in the other camp, this fellow was young. He wore a blue knit hat with the UCLA logo across it and a matching sweatshirt. Inside the trailer, the other man sat at a small booth table with a similar, hard-to-read look on his face. I introduced myself, and we shook hands. The men both called themselves Angel. Angel the younger put a kettle on a burner, and I sat down opposite the older man. They were waiting for their boss, they explained, the younger Angel speaking first, and the older one agreeing: "*Si, esperando por el jefe*" – yes, waiting.

I told them what had happened with *Cormorant*, and the younger said that he had watched it all through the window. I explained that my food was running out, and that I would be sailing down the coast, and that I hoped the fishermen from the other camp could help me get into town to resupply.

I felt that these two were probably on some narco-business out here, but I didn't feel threatened by them, and it didn't seem they had anything to do but wait, day after day. The younger Angel said that their supplies were running out too, and the older one jumped in and said that their boss was supposed to have come last week, which had them exchanging glances, as if perhaps he had said too much.

They came from Tijuana, the younger one said, pouring cups of hot water for the three of us and passing the Nescafé to me. He was cool, in both demeanor and style of dress – bringing something of a hip-hop gangster vibe to the remote fish camp trailer. I offered that I had read in the news that the federal police had moved into Tijuana and taken over from the local police force. While this was probably not the wisest topic of conversation, I got the sense that if I didn't ask too many questions about them specifically, and what they were doing, or observe out loud that it was strange that they had no fishing equipment, it would be OK to just talk. We were all out here waiting together, after all.

"*Nosotros no gustamos la policia*," the younger one said. And then, in English, "We can take care of the city ourselves."

———————▶

That night I went to the fishermen's camp again, and again I brought my tobacco, and again they fed me. Dinner was plain pasta. They were running low on food as well and had been unable to make the drive into town, first because of the weather and then because of the condition of the road. I had decided that I could make the fix with the materials that I had on hand, and asked the brothers to get supplies for me when they went in to shop for the food for their camp. I made a list of the things I wanted and gave them 600 pesos (about 60 dollars); I also asked the McLeishes to buy a case of beer for the boys at camp in addition to the supplies they would get for me. Pedro said he hoped they could go tomorrow or the day after and that they usually spent three days in town.

There were still the plank lands to repair, and then the reinstallation of the side benches and reorganizing my gear to do, so the timing looked pretty good. This being Baja however, I knew that I had to let the following days unfold as they would. The main thing for me now was to get resupplied. Eating plain pasta in the back of the delivery truck was a little alarming, because with the fishermen running out of food the situation seemed that much more dire – even if there was an ocean full of fish and mussels to eat.

In the morning I watched both pangas launch, disappointed that the McLeish brothers were not driving to town. Don Jose said, "*¿Posible mañana, quién sabe?*" – possibly tomorrow, who knows. Fatalistic and powerless – that one statement contained the breadth of the cultural difference that lay between us.

I set to finishing the repair on *Cormorant*, rolling back the canvas and cutting the bottom-third off a beer can to mix the resin in. I first painted the raw wood of the plank lands with straight resin, and then mixed another resin batch and added thickener, laying that in like spackle with the edge of the scraper and removing the seagull quills I had used as spacers as I worked forward along the cracks, so that the planks laid together.

Last, I drove drywall screws through the edge of the inside planks, one approximately every four inches, and drew the wood tight. The thickened resin squished out like cream filling.

Working quickly, before the resin hardened, I cut the fiberglass rope to length, saturated it, and laid it into the seam. It turned out that I had brought just enough rope, right down to the inch, to reinforce the areas that had broken apart. The resin, too, I used up entirely.

The afternoon had turned cold and grey, and as the tide pulled out the surf began working off the boulders about halfway in from the point, and I decided to have a go. I brought my fishing rod along, as it was just far enough from the middle of the beach where *Cormorant* and my camp lay to not want to make the trip twice. The surf was small, but clean and breaking fast like it had been when the campers were here, and I took the 8'2" *Californio*, anticipating the fast glide and the high line across the steep pockets.

When I waded in, the water felt cold and severe. Paddling over the shoulders of the sculpted peelers, spray lifting off the top like sequins all silvered against the sun in the muted sky, I imagined another truck coming over the rise. This time it would be a load of surfer girls.

No one came of course, and I considered how far removed I was, how many miles were between this place and the place I had started from. I had covered those miles in a boat of my own making. I was in the desert wilderness, and I had sailed here, and though I had marveled at this before, the lonely afternoon made the reality of it all very present.

The surfing was the same sustained meditation that surfing alone in neat little waves always is – the same hovering glide, the same joy. The displacement hull, with its convex belly, long and slightly curving outline, and thinly foiled rails that cleave into the face of the wave, made the ride something other than "regular" surfing across the surface; it was actually surfing down into the surface, along a slick swale of one's own furrowing.

I went in after awhile, put the *Californio* on the rocks with the fin up, and took up the fishing rod. Wading back in up to my knees by the boulders where the little waves started their speed run across the shallow sandbar, I made a cast with the light sinker and feather I had rigged up. The feather was just small with a silver head and white tail, and I flicked the weight out with the lure trailing behind and reeled it back under the tumbling whitewater. I got a powerful strike almost immediately, and a flashing, silvery form darted through the face of a wave, zipping downwards and up again, and then straight in towards me before curving back out in a swift tugging arc.

It was a surfperch, perhaps a pound or a pound-and-a-half, and when I pulled it to the surface its silver body, pure white underneath with black bars along its side, seemed the perfect representation of this area of interface between clear sea and clean desert – a vivid bit of the life of the planet. A few more casts brought two more fish, and getting cold now standing in my wet wetsuit, I took my catch and my board and rod and made my way back to the tent.

Once there, I laid the fish on a flat rock outside, peeled my wetsuit off and changed, and then put lentils on to boil. Walking down to the beach in front of camp, I gutted the three perch and then rolled up my trousers and walked to the water's edge to wash them and clean the knife.

Back at the tent, I set the lentils aside and fried the perch in a skillet with a thin coat of oil. The fish fit perfectly in the pan, and when they were done I laid them over a plate of the lentils, pulling the meat off the bones with the edge of my fork, the skin nice and crispy. The meal was surprisingly satisfying and flavorful, and I felt a little better about the prospects for harvesting protein. I only wished that I had more rice, beans, and lentils.

After my early dinner, I walked with the fish bones in the skillet off into the desert and tossed them. The sky was still grey but infused with light so that the hills and the ocean gleamed, and as I came over the rise, back to my tent, I saw the two pangas returning from the day's fishing. Later that evening, after dark, and as I lay reading Muir by headlamp, I heard the pickup rumble by on the coast track and thought it must be the boys heading in, so I got up and walked over to the kitchen truck to see what was going on.

The fellows had already eaten, and one of them, Pepe, was washing the big pot, which looked to have bits of ramen stuck to the sides. They asked me if I had eaten, and I thanked them and told them that I had, and that I had a cup of beans left – not knowing the word for lentils. Don Jose said I should come tomorrow, they still had rice, and again I thanked him.

The McLeish brothers had, in fact, gone to town, the others told me.

"¿Tabaco?" Pepe asked, and I fished the pouch out from a jacket pocket, but only a thin line of crumbs lined the bottom. Still, I handed it to him with the papers, and he rolled a very meager cigarette.

It was three days of waiting then. The boat was repaired, and I replaced the side benches the afternoon after the McLeish brothers had gone – but not before washing down the interior of *Cormorant* with many buckets of seawater

and scrubbing the mud and bits of soaked trail mix away.
There were even some remaining bees from their takeover at
Colonet, three weeks previous.

With the weather indeterminate, and the surf conditions
wrecked by a wind out of the west, the three days passed
slowly. Food was my main concern, I caught fish and pulled
mussels from the rocks, but the energy this took seemed more
than the harvest supplied. Each night the fishermen gave me
a plate of rice – once with a scrambled egg, and once with
squash chopped finely. It surprised me how quickly lethargy
set in, and I spent much of the time in my tent reading John
Muir:

> "*Now came the solemn, silent evening. Long, blue, spiky
> shadows crept out across the snowfields, while a rosy glow,
> at first scarce discernible, gradually deepened and suffused
> every mountaintop, flushing the glaciers and the harsh
> crags above them. This was the alpenglow, to me one of the
> most impressive of all the terrestrial manifestations of
> God. At the touch of this divine light, the mountains
> seemed to kindle to rapt, religious consciousness, and
> stood hushed and waiting like devout worshipers.*"

Yes and yes and yes! I thought.

———————

When the brothers returned late in the afternoon of the third
day, the supplies they brought were disappointingly slim. The

beers that I had asked them to buy for the rest of the crew were also missing, but I didn't feel up to making a fuss about it, nor apparently, did any of the others. I should have said something though, because not only did they short-change me, they stiffed their companions.

The whole thing stunk of opportunism, but the chance to gain fifty pesos would probably have been taken by any of the men, and perhaps they understood this and so did not demand the beers I had offered to buy on their behalf. Whatever the dynamic between them, I took the small box of food back to my tent, looking it over and trying to determine how many days' worth it all amounted to.

I had worked *Cormorant* up and over the berm earlier, swiveling the bow and then the stern around before repacking her. The fishermen had plenty of water in 55-gallon drums, and they let me fill up my two five-gallon bottles, the two-and-a-half gallon collapsible jug, and the three liter-sized bottles I had. These I staged by the boat. It had been a full week since the accident. I had gotten the boat back together and onto the beach again and was eager to resume my journey, but I would wait for morning to have the whole next day to travel.

Unhappy about the supplies, I stayed in my tent that last night in camp and did not go hang out with the boys. Was it their job to see I was taken care of? Of course not, and I was probably being overly sensitive, probably making things up, but that's how I felt. I had already forgotten that the fishermen had fed me for most of the nights over the past week. But five potatoes, a bag of rice, a bag of beans, a small can of Nescafé, some cassava, a bag of sugar, and a packet of Bimbo cakes was not going to get me very far. It also did not occur to me to go over there and hang out and ask for some more supplies out of their stores – at least a bag of pasta or something.

In the morning the boys launched their boats early to get back to fishing, and I waved to them from the berm, and then broke camp to load the last of my gear in dry bags. Don Jose came over as I walked *Cormorant* down to the water, helping to push the bow and the stern around with each turn of the boat. The Angels stood in front of their trailer; I waved and they gave their subtle nods and low waves in response. The surf was still small, and I pulled *Cormorant* over a little line of white water and pushed off the bottom, leaping aboard and taking up the oars. Another wave broke before us, lifting the bow sharply, and I pulled with the oars and was beyond the surfline with two or three strokes. Don Jose waved from the beach. I waved back to him, and then readied my boat to sail.

The mainsail went up smoothly, ballooning out full, and *Cormorant* cut across the bay. I looked at the handrails and the bow section where I had repaired the strakes, half expecting to see water pouring in through the side, but none poured in. The fixes appeared solid, and *Cormorant* was like her old self, heeling with the wind and carrying on confidently. Out past the short headland on the south side of the cove, she began picking up steep swells and surfing forward, and what had seemed like a steady wind was now a proper blow.

Whitecaps were up all around, and I sailed further offshore to give myself plenty of sea room from the cliffs that guarded the coast here. But "whitecaps" is not adequate to describe the condition of the ocean, which was strewn with slurries of rolling foam, and pitted by deep gullies of water that seemed to collapse in on themselves.

I soon let out the mainsail and rounded up to put the reefs in. The mizzen performed wonderfully with the tiller lashed down, holding *Cormorant* in place as she climbed into the wind and dipped heavily in the waves that stood up in a confused but generally southward running sea. With the sail shortened, I unlashed the tiller, and she swung around before the wind, rushing along amid the billows. A particularly large swell rolled up alongside *Cormorant* with another coming into it at right angles, the two swells then broke together and a heavy wash of foam rolled over the rail, smothering the entire boat.

Checked for a moment in her progress, *Cormorant* wallowed with only the tips of her bow and stern poking out of the water, and I thought the next wave would finish us. But she rose with the following crest and continued on as if shaking the water from her wings. Swamped to the tops of the benches I sailed on, bailing with the plastic jug I had. It took 30 minutes to get the water down to the floorboards, and although the sea was as wooly as ever, I seemed to have found its rhythm and rolled along with it even as great rushes of whitewater broke all around. Running dead before the wind I could manage these conditions, but if I had been trying to tack broadside to it all, the swells and the blow would have driven *Cormorant* under.

By midafternoon I was passing the crumbling volcano cone where I had anchored through the night the year before, but from that experience I knew to continue on for another

half-mile and round the end of the natural jetty into
the wide bay. I dropped anchor well off the beach,
resisting the urge to nest in too close in an attempt to
get out of the wind.

It was a smooth sand bottom, and I ran the anchor
line all the way out and so had a good long angle
for a firm grip. There were about six pangas resting
side-by-side on the beach in front of the clustered
shacks of another fish camp. The wind blew harder,
and the sky went dun-colored with dust and sand. I
put the boat tent up and felt farther away than ever
in the bleak afternoon. I wrote in my journal about
the desolation of the bay I was in, the cold and lonely
wind, and the fatigue I was beginning to feel. The
light seemed to dim late in the day, and then faded
out altogether with no hint of color in the sunset.

I boiled the rice and potatoes. I read, I ate.

And at dark, having already had dinner, I
scrunched down in my bag into the sleep of oblivion.

Morning came with a hail from the fishermen heading out in
their pangas. I lifted the edge of the boat tent and waved, and
one of them called out with some comment, or a question, but
I didn't care what he was saying and I waved again, and lay
back down. It was a cold morning with a brisk, cutting breeze
running down the slope of the hills behind the bay and out
over the surface of the water, biting into any exposed skin

it could find – my face, my ears, my neck, my hands. Sitting upright in my bag, I heated water for coffee and reheated the rice from the night before, spooning sugar onto it for a breakfast mush.

Around the next headland lay my favorite point from the previous year's run – the place that felt remotest of all, that had the pure, trackless beach and the arroyo with lion prints in the sand. This was the place where the second, inner-point waves sizzled as they broke, so sleek and fast in the clear, clear water. I packed my sleeping bag away, and scrubbed the pots over the side, watching the coffee oils spread in rainbow rings over the water. Stowing the tent canvas and sail battens that I used for tent hoops, I then hung the rudder and tiller, placed the daggerboard in its slot, and pulled anchor. Mainsail up, *Cormorant* glided on south by southwest, diagonally across the bay towards the dark rocks about a mile-and-a-half on.

The little outer point, with its slanting rock shelves that stepped down into the sea, and the sweep of its cove beach around to the second, inner point where the desert plants came right down to the rocky shore – all of it was just as I remembered. I rounded up and dropped anchor in the second cove, very close to where I had stayed before. It didn't seem to have taken more than an hour-and-a-half to get here, and I watched the surf and looked over the rolling hills of the desert, and debated whether or not to go surfing. The waves were very small, perhaps one foot, and the water was clear and icy, and the wind cold. I didn't feel like I had shaken the sleep from my head, and this was probably reason enough to go surfing, but I chose to have another cup of coffee and sit and wait.

I did not go surfing, but swam to shore naked with my clothes in a dry pack, and changed on the hard sand where the tide had pulled out. Walking the curve of the beach around the inner point, and then along the next little beach out towards the first point, I was soon climbing the tide pool rocks and making my way to the very end of the outer point. I found a rock to sit on and looked at Isla Cedros far across the water

– a light silhouette whose craggy outline seemed to emerge from beyond the horizon.

There was something inscrutable in the jagged shape of the island out there 55 miles away. The sea was smooth for as far as I could see, but much more of it lay between here and the island that was not visible. By now I knew full well that the sea rarely just laid there; it heaved and rolled, tumbled and hissed, its winds turning the mood from bight blue and playful one moment to grey and howling the next. But there was logic to its movements as well, and going with the energy, never opposing it, I hoped to continue my run across its broad, undulating back.

I had brought my compass and binoculars to shore, and I alternated between them now, gauging the course that I estimated I could sail with the wind direction, and then peering out across the depths, trying to see if there might be a hint of what the water was like farther, ever farther, outside.

After watching until I had thought everything through and could gather no more information, I headed back toward *Cormorant* on a path into the desert, seeking the top of the arroyo that led down to the second cove where I had anchored. The cut of the arroyo was visible from a distance, and the ground sloped towards it like a broad, funneling pan from a half-mile out. Following the incline down towards the cut, I guessed that the path I had left connected to the fish camp in the bay I had anchored in the night before. The cut led down, its sides eroded with fissures draining from the desert plain above, and flat sandstones like pyramid rocks sat exposed, forming an almost perfect stairway.

Stands of willows grew here and there in the bottom of the arroyo, which ran about 15 or 20 feet below the level of the desert. I strolled along, mindful of the tracks I had seen the year before, particularly when I walked below a couple sections of sandstone platforms where it seemed a lion might rest. But there wasn't a feeling of predatory danger, not like the feeling of great whites while surfing some of the reefs and river mouths in Northern California. I was soon on the beach again looking at *Cormorant* at anchor, the waves even smaller now with the lower tide but reeling perfectly at only six inches.

I found a sheltered spot from the wind in front of two boulders where the sun shone down on the pure white sand, and I lay down, curled on my side in my jacket and woolen trousers, soaking up the heat in anticipation of swimming back to the boat. I was so alone here, a feeling of exile building with these days father south and ever more remote. The wind had come up as it usually did in the afternoon, but not with the intensity of yesterday's blow. I tried to read the character of the sky, perhaps by catching something in the quality of light, I might learn what the weather was setting up for. But there was nothing to go on really, and I could not decide just then what the best move would be.

I wouldn't be going anywhere today, regardless. My plan for the moment was only to get back to *Cormorant* (a very short but cold swim), cook some rice and cassava, and see if the surf improved in the evening, or by the following morning. But the surf stayed tiny, and even though the hours stretched before me with little to fill them, I was content to read, to write in my journal, and to write some letters as well.

I was awoken the next morning by a squawking roar, and lifted the boat tent to see thousands of sea birds converging on my little cove – pelicans, terns, and cormorants, coming in low over the water like endless bomber squadrons. Birds wheeled and dove out of the sky, others ducked under and swam – all of them gulping down anchovies with each sortie.

The feeding went on for more than an hour, a kind of avian bacchanal. The water was alight with chattering splashes from the baitfish and the birds all in a frenzy. And then, almost imperceptibly, the crowd of them thinned little by little, until the rush dwindled to a few pelicans sitting calmly on the water.

Afterwards, it was a time of waiting, trying to find a sign for what to do. I had no way to get a weather forecast and had to rely purely on my observations. By evening the sky had gone grey again, and the wind fell off and the air got very cold. Looking at the tide chart, I saw that in two more days there would be little difference between the high and low, and remembered that Aurelio suggested this for the best time to cross. I resolved to wait until then, watching carefully. In those two days the sky remained grey, the wind remained calm, and the surf remained virtually flat.

I thought a lot about being alone – not only alone on this trip, but about the idea that I had organized my life in such a way that I would be alone after the trip as well. I had a strange dream about the girl up north who had hurt me so much, and in the dream – so vivid it was like a visitation – I told her that

I understood what had happened between us, and when I woke up I felt as though I had made peace with her.

Valentine's Day was the day I thought to make the crossing.

I had no place to go, other than to sail onward and see what berth I might eventually find for myself. My old California family – my mother's great-grandparents arriving from Denmark and Ireland respectively in the 19th century, and my dad's dad from New Zealand in 1932 – through alcoholism, madness, and divorce, no longer had any property, no place to call a home that wasn't rented.

Despite my worry and isolation, I knew that viewed another way, this just meant that I had the opportunity to make a new foundation.

And I laughed at one point, laughed until tears streamed down my face, remembering all the family drama that we had gone through, the screaming fights with my mother, the anxiety about the fate of my father – that all of it had been utterly unnecessary, that it had not been such a big deal then, or now, or ever.

I realized that in the most essential and eternal sense, we are not alone and that there was a place where all would be set to rights. The days crept by – so grey, so still – and in this self-imposed exile, I came to some place in myself I had always known was there, but that I had been distracted from in the daily business of living.

God whispers over the water.

John Muir knew that.

Having made my decision for Cedros, I sat through the
following two days as if waiting for a sentence to be carried
out. Why I thought that a crossing of 55 miles for supplies was
a better option than a two-hour sail to the top of the Seven
Sisters series of point breaks, where there were sure to be
fellow surfers I might know and could barter with or beg from,
I cannot explain.

Not only would I be far safer sticking to the mainland, I
would have more surfing opportunities as well. My mental
argument in favor of crossing to Cedros was, ostensibly, the
problem of rounding Punta Eugenia, the big fishhook on the
west coast of Baja, about halfway down the peninsula. If I
continued following the coast, I would then have to work back
against the wind and current to gain the point. But I could
still have crossed the bay from Punta Morro, some 40 miles
south, and reached for the big point from there.

It must have been the prospect of dealing with surfers
that I wished to avoid. That, or perhaps I *was* trying for a
disappearing act at sea, as my friend wondered before I set out
on this journey. But I had also been thinking about a Cedros
crossing for months, wanting the challenge of putting all that
water under the hull, in addition to wanting to avoid the more
heavily traveled places.

So I watched the weather, counting on intuition to judge
the right time to go. When the right day came (however long
that might take, given my supplies held out), I would depart
late in the morning, with the idea that if the wind came on

too strong later in the afternoon, I could come about and run back in to the coast and shelter in one of the many coves that marked the next 40 miles.

On the third day a light breeze came up at about 11 in the morning under a broad, gray sky. The outline of Cedros stood visible on the horizon, which at least provided the comfort of a destination that I could see. I had boiled the beans the previous afternoon, and I mixed those with the last of the cassava and another pot of rice. My supplies were again down to a cup of rice, a cup of lentils, and four Bimbo cakes, but I still had tea, and I boiled three pots full and poured these in the big thermos with a good bit of sugar.

Setting sail, I glided out from my beautiful cove anchorage and passed the headland as close in as I dared as I headed out to sea, wanting to keep as far upwind as I could on the crossing. Outside the point, the breeze was about eight knots, and my best guess was that *Cormorant* was making two to three knots, a moderate walking pace – walking to Cedros, overnight.

I always took solace in moving along, however slowly, by equating this form of travel to backpacking. It was certainly camp-based, with full exposure to the elements, but I carried far more gear and equipment than I could have on foot, and, like backpacking, I used not one drop of gas.

The day wore on, the mainland fading steadily back into silhouette like the island ahead. Towards evening, the sky held green swaths on its underbelly, reflecting on the great face of the grey sea like a giant watercolor painting. The land was now even farther back off the stern, and I estimated that I was 20 miles offshore. The wind had come up too, not dangerously, but enough for me to have rounded up and put a reef in for safety. Spray flew back off the tops of the larger swells when *Cormorant* crested over.

I wore my rain pants over the woolen army trousers, wool socks and hiking shoes, a wool sweatshirt, wool sweater, foul weather jacket, wool scarf and hat, with the life jacket as my top layer. I secured a line from the stainless steel loop on my belt to the handrail as well.

Sipping from the thermos of tea regularly as the hours passed, and eating the Bimbo cakes one by one, I kept warm. Sitting on the cushion on the aft thwart hour after hour made for a stiff back and sore knees. Without much physical movement once the sails were set – other than the slight adjustments on the tiller – I eventually got chilled. I stood up from time to time as if I was surfing *Cormorant*, as the angle of heel felt like a giant board rising up and riding back down on the swells. Fortunately, the wind kept on through nightfall, steady at perhaps 12 knots, which increased our speed to about four knots.

Cedros was still visible after dark, its hulking shape a dense mass on the horizon outlined by the million stars in the night sky around it. Bright Venus shined out from the others. I checked my compass bearing in my headlamp beam and saw that when I had the star over my right shoulder I was on the right course for the island. Darkness now – a real 30-plus miles

out to sea kind of darkness – and I sailed on through the stars
with everything suspended in the night. A calm was coming
down now so that it was hard to tell where the sea ended and
the night sky began, floating as I was between the firmament
above and the depths below. Very late, the wind seemed to let
out a final sigh, and the ocean lay oily smooth all around and
even in such darkness I felt its vastness and depth.

———————————•——————————

In such stillness there was little to do but rest. I had sailed
for 12 hours or more, and I might have done better to go to
oars and make more progress in the easy rowing conditions,
but I pulled my sleeping bag and the boat tent canvas over
me like blankets and laid on the stuffed dry bags I had stored
amidships.

Morning broke soon after it seemed, with the very air
infused with a blue light that seemed to emanate from the
incredible, deep and clear blue of the ocean. At best I was only
40 miles or so into the 55-mile crossing, but Cedros looked
closer than 15 miles away. A massive ridgeline ran across,
with steep rock chutes and canyons, and sheer cliffs plunging
downward from overhanging precipices. Through binoculars
I saw pines and solitary, drifting clouds on the peaks, a
thousand feet above the sea.

A fishing trawler chugged by a little later in the morning,
the crew a rough-looking bunch of men who called out, asking
if I was OK and if I needed water. I thanked them and said
I was fine. I asked where the village was on the island, and

they all waved and pointed down to the southern-most tip, shouting over one another. I couldn't understand exactly what they said but got the idea that I had to make it all the way to the end of the island to find the village. The men remained on the rail of the trawler as they motored away, watching me as if not quite believing what they had seen.

From my charts, I knew the village was at the far end of Isla Cedros, but with the actual mass of the island before me, I realized the grave error I had made in my estimation. Cedros was indeed "only" 55 miles from the mainland, but I failed to account for the fact that once safely across I would still have to sail, or row, 30 or 35 miles down the inside coast to make the port and town.

Now the desolate island lay before me, and the stupid realization of how far I actually had to go to reach safety and resupply hit me – hard. The sun shone down full and warm as the morning progressed, breaking the previous days of grey like some new beginning. But there was no wind, just the wide placid sea before me, and the island still a long way off.

A very light wind came up from the southeast, and I sailed as close to it as I could, making for the furthest point on the island to the south. Because I had set the main for the northwest wind of the day before, the yard from which the sail hung was balanced on the port side of the mast, which made an inefficient crease down its center in the light air. I took the time to drop the sail, unhook the tack and dip the yard around the mast so that the sail billowed out freely on the starboard side with the southerly breeze. Then I set the cushion on the floorboards of the boat and slouched down, leaning back on

the aft thwart, using my life-vest as a backrest, and sailed at
an achingly slow pace on an oblique angle to the shore in the
glare of the progressing day.

————————➤

Accepting the slow pace of this mode of travel had been fine
to this point, but after 30 hours at sea – the past five or six of
those with the island coastline not seeming to get any nearer
and with no landmark passing to mark our progress – I began
to get frustrated. I realized that not only would I not make the
village today, at this rate, I would not even make the island
before nightfall. My lips were cracked and dry, my hair so
greasy that my scalp ached. The whiskers of my mustache and
multi-weeks' growth on my cheeks itched painfully in the
deepening sunburn on my face, and water hurt to drink as it
met my parched throat.

The breeze picked up a little more from the south, and I
altered my course, steering straight in for the island to close
the distance, vaguely aware that this south wind meant that
I would have to tack my way against it to get down the coast
to the village. But no matter… *Cormorant* was moving again,
blessed movement. And then nothing; the wind fell away
like a cruel joke and left us rocking on the sparkling and once
more calm face of the sea. The island still lay too far off to pick
out any but the broadest details of the shore – a cliff face or
the lower ground of a rocky beach.

Then, about a mile to the south, I saw a heavy line of torn
water rushing towards me, driven by a heavy wind. I might

have had time to drop the main but not to tie in a reef, so I decided to risk it and leave the sail up to catch the gust and reach farther in for shore.

Cormorant heeled hard over when the wind hit and plowed forward, and I sat on the port rail with as much of my weight outboard as I could, my gaze intent on the island that was still too far away. I wondered about the wind continuing and whether or not I could drive the boat so hard, or rather, wondered how long I could drive the boat so hard before she went over. But the wind fell off again.

Afterwards it came in williwaws – crazed blasts whirling up from the south in furious, whipping lines of driven spray. If I could keep upright I would reach the island, but the sea was cut now with short, steep chops and *Cormorant* smashed through the rough water.

Then the wind fell off again, but the island was now just a tantalizing mile or so away.

I went to oars, but the wavelets were like speed bumps, and my boat tossed over them at sharp angles, flinging me back and forth on the midships thwart as I tried to keep myself steady enough to set the oars in the locks. Rowing was impossible; the oar blades popped out of the agitated water and the shafts jumped free of the locks with each attempted stroke. The sail wrapped and buffeted my head like an antagonizing bully.

The wind came on again, but this time from the north, exactly opposite the other gusts, but I managed to use it to cut in farther. A little closer now, the island loomed like some imposing fortress of fractured rock – inhospitable,

indifferent, and hateful to me in its aspect. As I struggled to
reach the shore, I realized that a strong current was pulling
me northward, as promontory after cove slipped by while I
wallowed in that reasonless sea.

A hot wind came down now, straight offshore out of the
canyons, trying to blow us back out into the open ocean. I
took this as a personal affront and got furious at that mute and
tortured piece of rock that called itself an island, that horrible
shore with its mystery current dragging me northward
towards a substantial headland, around which I assumed was
the killing north side that I had been warned from. But this
place would not kill me – I was too enraged to die. I would not
succumb to these ridiculous forces, and I hated it all then, and
screamed and cried in anguish. I pulled at the oars and did
not care when they broke free of the water, because I stabbed
them in again. I would not stop until I ran my little craft right
up on the godforsaken coast of this island.

The water stayed the same inky blue of the open ocean as I
approached the shoreline. The plunging heights of the island
continued straight down into the sea. I was within 150 yards
now, and tried to pull the daggerboard up but it had gotten
wedged in its case and would not budge. The current pulled
more swiftly here, and the next stretch north was nothing
but sheer cliff. Here at least, directly before me, was a rock-
strewn beach that I might be able to drag my boat upon – my
last hope. But I could not land with the daggerboard down,
and unwilling to lose more ground to the sweeping current, I
went to oars again and pulled hard, another 75 arm-burning,

back-searing yards. And there, a stone's throw off the horrible island shore, I threw the anchor.

The anchor line pulled all the way to its very end, 150 feet, and finally seemed to grab something down there. *Cormorant* held steady even though the angle of the line ran down too sharply, almost straight down off the bow, and did not inspire much confidence for the prospect of a solid hold. But I was here. I could rest a minute anyway, and look at the broken rock cove and formulate a plan.

First, in my exhaustion, I knew I needed to eat. The next effort of bringing the boat in, and potentially swimming underneath to work the daggerboard loose, would be the last push I could muster.

I dug out the stove and poured the rice and the lentils in a pot and boiled these. The boat bucked awfully and I crouched over the stove, holding the pot steady with a T-shirt doubled over in my fingers.

Numb and spent, I felt pitiful and stupid in my little boat: at the way I had cried and raged at the wind and the current that were defeating me; at my dumb mustache, all snotted-up; at this sunburned man-baby alone on his big, silly adventure.

As the rice and lentils boiled down and were near ready to eat, I took the last of my olive oil and sugar and poured those in for whatever added calories they would provide, and took the pot off the burner and wedged it with the T-shirt under the neck of the water bottle in the cockpit area, and let it steam-cook for a while longer.

The day was coming to a close, and I knew I would have to act soon before the light was gone, but I could not bring myself to move.

Just a few bites of food, I thought, and then I would try.

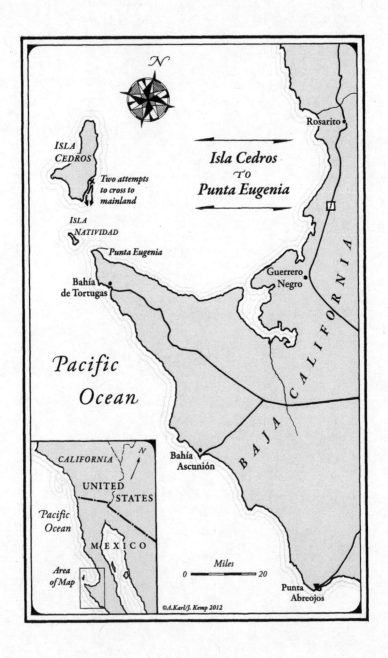

N

ISLA
CEDROS

Two attempts
to cross to
mainland

Isla Cedros
TO
Punta Eugenia

Rosarito

ISLA
NATIVIDAD

Punta Eugenia

Guerrero
Negro

Bahía
de Tortugas

BAJA CALIFORNIA

Pacific
Ocean

Bahía
Ascunión

N

CALIFORNIA

UNITED
STATES

Pacific
Ocean

MEXICO

Area
of Map

Miles

0   20

Punta
Abreojos

©A.Karl/J. Kemp 2012

CHAPTER NINE

ISLAND DAYS

The rice and lentil mixture was nearly ready, and the wind was coming on hard again from the southeast, putting an ugly, short chop across the water. As I sat there, trying to decide whether to eat or to work the boat ashore, a panga with two men on board appeared from around the next headland, a few hundred yards to the north. The helmsman brought the boat alongside and glanced at the gear I had stowed in *Cormorant*, and then at me and said, *"Jale su ancla,"* motioning for me to pull the anchor line in.

He then held out his hand for the bow line, and I passed it to him and he tied that off to the stern of his vessel. Once I got the anchor and line and chain aboard, the older man told me to get on his boat. This was not an offer of assistance but a command. Once aboard the panga, I turned and introduced myself to the men and explained that I was just getting ready to row ashore. The older man looked at his companion, shook his head, and told me to sit down on the forward thwart.

"*Es muy peligroso aquí,*" – it's very dangerous here – he said to me, "*no bueno* for you."

Another blast of wind started in from the south, and the panga bucked over the chop, spray shooting out from the bows. I looked back at *Cormorant* swinging wildly from side-to-side in the churning wake. Cumulous clouds were boiling up in the sky, tinged orange and majestic in the evening light as we motored along the rocky coast. The realization of how exhausted and vulnerable I had become in the face of this ocean vastness, and the incredible fortune of these men having come along to help me, brought tears to my eyes.

It was 45 minutes before the village came into view, night coming on steadily, and we motored into a small harbor in the darkness with the lights of the town twinkling across the hillsides like a Mediterranean village. The man in the ball cap tied the panga off to a buoy can, and the older man told me to bring *Cormorant* alongside and tie off to their boat. A stone quay, built on a jetty, curved around the harbor, and a woman with a toddler stood waiting beside a van parked in front of where the panga was moored.

The older man pulled on an algae-strewn rope and drew the panga and *Cormorant* in close to the rocks and held the boats there while his mate and I scrambled from the bow. We then held the boats steady for the skipper to climb off as well.

Once we let go of the bow, the line drew the panga out with *Cormorant* tied alongside. The noise of the engine and the wind had kept us from talking on the trip in, and now the men climbed the rocks and got into the van, and I followed without a word – the young woman sitting down to drive with the boy in her lap, glancing at me but not saying anything either. From the back, sitting on an upturned bucket, I saw the broken down hulks of warehouses and a derelict wharf.

A few streetlights dimly illuminated a dirt road with shops and a few people standing around here and there. Small houses rose up from the harbor in terraced lines. The dirt track we drove followed a beach with the dark ocean beyond and swung up into the neighborhood; dogs ran out from darker corners to bark in the headlights. Soon, we pulled up to a cinderblock house. The young woman parked the van and got out carrying her son, and the men and I followed her.

———————————

"Look what we caught in the nets today," the older man said as we entered the house, though I only understood the words "*las redes*" and "*hoy*"– the nets and today. An old woman was in the kitchen, and the smell of cooking meat and tortillas almost made me faint. She hobbled out and shook my hand, and said in a murmur, "*mi hijo*" – my boy. Her name was Angelita and it

couldn't have suited her better. The older man and his fishing
mate, Esteban, sat down at a table and he motioned for me to
join them. His name was Catarino Burjez, the old woman, his
wife, Angelita, and the young woman, their daughter, Paula.
The boy was named Diego, after his dad, who was out.

The little house had a linoleum floor in the kitchen and
small dining area. A circular table was covered in a plastic
tablecloth, and the front door swung loose in its frame and
was held closed by a nail bent over. A single bulb, like the
light at Aurelio's place back at Punta San Carlos, hung from
the ceiling. Angelita set a platter full of *carne asada* on the
table and a dish stacked high with tortillas and covered by a
cloth napkin. She placed a large bowl of beans, and another
of pico de gallo down next, and then went to sit with Paula
and Dieguito in the living room, leaving me and the two
fishermen in the dining room.

The food was the most essential and nourishing food I
could have eaten. I could not thank them, nor praise their
home, nor their hospitality, enough.

Catarino, with his serious demeanor, looked at me,
shaking his head like he had when they first found me that
afternoon, and told me that he would never – emphasizing the
word "*nunca*" – go to sea in a boat like mine. He ate hovering
over his plate, his thick arm curled in front of it on the table,
lips curled back to suck down the beans.

Where had I come from, anyway, Sr. Burjez asked? I had
sailed from San Diego about six weeks earlier, I told him.
Then I told about crossing from the mainland the day before,

and that I was trying to avoid having to sail back up and around Punta Eugenia from further down the coast.

Sr. Burjez again shook his head in disbelief, as if to say, "What would possess a man?"

After dinner, Angelita brought us coffees, and when we had finished our cups, Sr. Burjez stood and motioned for me to follow him. We walked outside and down a dark embankment to another cinderblock building below the house. The wind was blowing hard now and a pepper tree swayed in the light of a streetlamp, casting shifting shadows. Sr. Burjez fumbled with some keys and undid a padlock on an iron gate, which swung open with a funerary squeal. He turned on a single lightbulb in a storeroom where fishing gear was stacked in the back and three cots stood on end. He brought one of them down and pointed to a sleeping bag that was rolled up and stowed with some others on a shelf.

"*¿Está bien?*" he asked.

I told him thank you very much, and he nodded gruffly, turned, and walked out.

The wind buffeted the windows as I lay on the cot in the slightly mildewed bag, and I thought about still being out there on the north end of the island. Even if I had been able to get the boat on shore, it seemed a pretty good storm was brewing. An amber beam of light slanted in from the streetlamp. I had been surprised by how comforting the little town with electric light seemed as we approached the harbor that evening at dark.

I soon fell asleep.

It was late in the morning when I awoke. The storm blew through in the night, the road out front all puddles in bright sunlight and the storage room floor wet as well where the roof had leaked. But I had slept deeply, unaware of anything, my fatigue like an illness that was still upon me. I walked up to the house and found Angelita in the kitchen, and Paula and little Diego on her lap at the table. Paula told me Sr. Burjez was with Esteban and Paula's husband, Diego, down at the harbor, working on the catch from the day before.

Paula looked vaguely like a girlfriend I once had – a slender, athletic body, sandy-colored hair, fair skin. Seeing her there with her baby was like a glimpse of the life not lived, the path not taken.

Angelita brought me a cup of coffee and made eggs and heated tortillas and beans, and placed these on the table before me. What could I say, when I was brought so completely into a family and cared for so well? If I wanted to see the men, Paula suggested, it was a short walk along the road in front of the house to the harbor.

I thanked them. I ate, and drank the coffee. I thanked them again, feeling guilty that I had thrust myself into their lives by my desperate journey.

Down at the harbor I found Sr. Burjez and the others hauling the catch from their panga onto the afterdeck of a trawler that was tied off at the wharf. They had brought their boat over from where they had moored the night before, leaving *Cormorant* side-tied to the panga, and I made my way out onto the wharf, stepping carefully to avoid the planks that had rotted through. The warehouses I had seen from the van the evening before were the ruins of a cannery – rusted conveyor belts and elevated runs, the skeleton of a once thriving operation now all broken concrete, partially demolished walls, and jagged pieces of machinery not useable for anything more.

The men waved, and Sr. Burjez ordered me to come down to the deck of the trawler to help with the catch. A third man was there, a swarthy fellow with a black beard, smiling broadly and wearing a tank top, with a faded tattoo of a dragon on one arm. I extended my hand and asked if he was Diego, father of the younger Diego, he told me he was, and shook my hand and said let's get these fish.

I was grateful for the work, to at least feel as though I could help a little after everything these men had done for me. The catch was mainly sharks, small, four-foot sand sharks with a few blue sharks too – perhaps 150 or 200 of them, piled like bodies in a massacre – twisted in the folds of a black nylon net.

They also had an enormous black sea bass that weighed many hundreds of pounds and took the four of us, Catarino and Esteban on the panga, and Diego and me on the trawler above, to haul up. It was a beautiful, wise-looking old fish and should not have been killed. The men were happy with their catch, of course, and even joked that I must have brought them luck, but I didn't like thinking that old reef dweller, who had so many seasons as king of his domain, was now laid out on the deck of a trawler and would soon be carved into pieces of meat.

Cormorant was a jumble of sails, lines, and scattered gear. The pot of lentils and rice with oil and sugar still lay wedged below the water bottles. Diego suggested I bring my equipment back to the house, making a gesture with two fingers under his eyes, as if someone were creeping around the harbor late at night looking to steal my things. So I triced up the main sail to the mast, furled the mizzen, and heaved the dry bags, cooking equipment, and fishing gear on to the deck of the trawler. Diego took two armfuls, and I managed the rest, and we climbed back up to the wharf and then walked back to the house together.

Angelita made us coffee at the house, and Diego sat with little Dieguito on his knee in the living room. Paula and Angelita looked on, admiring the little one. Big Diego made a descending trill of baby talk to his son, the boy giggling wildly and wife and grandma so happy too, and it was all "*ito, chito, concito*" after every little thing the brawny fisherman said. It made me feel warm in my heart too.

My plan was to rest up, resupply, and continue the journey. There was the Port Captain's office I needed to check in with, and some letters to post that I had written in my three-days' wait on the mainland before the crossing. But over all of this was a deep-boned weariness that I had to shake – a weariness that no amount of sleep seemed sufficient to repair. The long hours that lay ahead on my journey, alone in my little boat, seemed too hard even to think about just then.

The sidewalk rose three feet above the street level on a solid concrete footing, and I passed some shops selling brooms and general household supplies, and a *mini-mercado* with Cokes and bags of chips on racks, and a meat counter with flies buzzing around. The concrete church, with white spackle and maroon-painted borders, stood facing the little harbor and would have had a view of the water if the decrepit hulk of the cannery were not blocking it. Two cupola towers rose over the thick, wooden doors of the entrance, and *La Virgin* with a flowing crimson robe and the infant Jesus in her arms perched between these. Inside, the beams of the church were hand-hewn, and the ceiling was painted with gold and silver stars like a nursery. A suffering Jesus was on the cross, and the pews were polished by years and years of sitting and standing and sitting again through masses. I bowed and made the sign of the cross, and then sat in a pew and lowered my head, feeling the mystery of this religion that was not mine but that connected to the one and same God.

Afterwards, into the light of day, I stopped for a Coke and then continued through town, up a steep winding hill to where a man told me the Port Captain's office was located. The news of my arrival, or of Sr. Burjez having found me on the north end of the island, apparently had circulated around town, as when I asked directions the man had said to me, "*Si, llegaste anoche*" – you arrived last night – as if it was high time I checked in with the Port Captain.

At the Port Captain's office, a nice young lady with full and rosy cheeks, her hair pulled back in a business-like ponytail, looked over my embarkation papers, stamped, and signed them. The office was orderly, with a polished floor and two desks on which computer terminals were set. A weather radio crackled from atop a metal stand, and framed pictures of the *Capitan* at official gatherings and aerial photos of the island and various fishing boats hung from the walls. The woman asked how long I would be on the island and where I was heading. I told her that I thought I would be on Cedros for a week, then cross to Isla Natividad, a small island about three miles on, and then cross back to the mainland from there – another short hop comparatively.

Were there marine forecasts available? I asked. Yes, of course, she told me, updated daily. I was welcome, she added, to come and read them on the computer in the next room and to use their email if I wanted. The captain himself emerged from the back office in a khaki uniform. He was a smiling gray-haired fellow with an air of naval efficiency about him, and I stood when he approached and offered my hand and we exchanged pleasantries. It all felt very diplomatic and formal, and with a final *"bienvenidos,"* he turned and went back into his office.

Coming back down the steep road, I went on to the post office, which they had told me at the Port Captain's was at the police station. The town was nestled in a bowl beneath the high ridgeline of the island interior, which was all ochre-yellow and dark brown like burnt lava, the sea beyond a deep blue. The post office amounted to a single room with one wall taken up by rows of four-inch square wood letterboxes. A neatly dressed man sat behind a desk with ledgers, inkpads, and stamps arranged before him. I handed him the envelopes with the letters I had written days and days before at my secret cove anchorage on the mainland and paid the postage. Despite the orderliness of the small office, I had a feeling of sending messages in bottles, so distant did this port feel from home.

An empty playground stood across from the police station/post office. It consisted of a walled concrete pad for fast-paced soccer and white-washed stones marking walking paths of dirt, winding through a wider area of dirt with a few stick trees; nothing there invited a person to visit. It was not quite prison-yard ugly but seemed designed in the same spirit. On the adjacent hillside stood a naval outpost with sandbags piled up for machine gun nests, concertina wire around a trailer that looked to be the headquarters building, and a tall radio antenna. An enormous panga sat on the dirt next to the HQ with a placard describing how the marines had discovered it adrift some miles off Cedros. The boat was painted grey, and though the placard did not mention it, one could easily imagine the hundreds of bales of contraband that could be stacked in such a high-sided hull.

The neighborhood houses started up again just on the other side of the park, and I took a path back to the Burjezes' that wound between them. The children playing on the dirt streets stopped to watch me as I passed, the youngest of them smiling broadly and the older ones looking on shy and curious. The boys called out "Hey you!" and ran off to hide

when I turned to look. An older, scarred and muscled dog –
mostly pit bull by the looks of him – lay in the driveway of
one of the houses, watching me as well. After I passed he came
charging after me silently and I spun around just as he nipped
at my ankle, just missing getting a hold of me, and I yelled at
him and picked up a rock. The dog slunk back but came close
again each time I turned to walk on, and I walked the rest of
the block backwards with the rock in my hand, ready.

Paula was hanging laundry when I reached the house.
She asked me how I liked their church. She was a pretty girl,
plain and sincere, and I liked her way. I liked that she and her
husband could live with her parents and make it work. Her
dad, the old fisherman Catarino, emerged from the house and
seemed to survey the hanging of the laundry and the two lazy
dogs lounging at the end of their long ropes.

"*Se llama* Obama," he said of the bigger, black dog –
amused by what he seemed to think was a clever and timely
nickname with the recent U.S. inauguration. I smiled a pained
smile; I didn't like the joke.

That night at dinner I told the family more about my
journey over the previous couple of months, and Sr. Burjez
again looked at me and shook his head as if to say "what a
pity," and then looked down at his plate. He took a bite, and
then looked up and told me that I was very lucky that he and
Esteban had picked me up the night before.

"*Sí,*" I replied, "*mucha suerte,*" and checked myself from
thanking him again, because at that point all I had were my
words, and I seemed to be spending these too quickly. But he
said "*No,*" wanting to clarify what he meant. He explained

that they never fish on the side of the island where they found me – it was only because of the south wind that they had been up there.

"*Es muy malo, allá*," – it's very bad there – he said.

I told him that I didn't expect that current that pulled from the south, and he just shook his head, looking at me like I had no comprehension of the forces I was dealing with.

"*Nunca*," he said once more, would he go to sea in a boat like mine.

Paula asked me if I had any children, and Angelita asked about my mother. As I told them about my family – that my mother lived alone and that I had never been married and had no children – I felt like a barren man.

Again I slept so deeply that it was as if I had been obliterated, and I awoke numb and disoriented. There was a toilet and shower in the storeroom, and I bathed and then went up to the house. Again coffee, and Angelita or Paula had been to the *panadería* and bought sugar breads, which they brought to me on a platter. Diego and Catarino had long since left to deal with the catch, and Dieguito was already down for a morning nap. I asked if there was a bank on the island, and the ladies told me that there was a *telegrafo* office where they kept their money, and finishing my coffee, I told them I was heading out and asked if I could get anything for the house.

No, nothing, they said, "*Que te vaya bien, Christián*," – go well – as if there were spirits afoot that needed warding off. Perhaps the island was getting to me.

By the downtown streets I ducked through a hole in the fence at the abandoned cannery, following a path through rubble and past broken block walls, and then up another slanting path to a concrete patio where offices used to look over the pretty little harbor. The pathways were clear enough to see–well-worn routes that traversed the harbor front below the main street of downtown like hobo trails through vacant lots and down to the train tracks at home in Alta California.

Rounding the corner of the demolished offices, I encountered three bearded men sitting on a makeshift bench, smoking a joint. A palm stood on one side of the patio, shrouding the area with fronds that reached over, and a remaining wall of the building blocked the view of the other side of the patio from the rest of the community. They were middle-aged, with deeply lined faces and curly masses of black hair like gypsies, but their clothing was once-elegant enough to suggest that they used to have jobs. With leather dress shoes breaking apart from wear, and each of them in a button-down shirt under a ragged sweater, it seems they could have even worked here, at the cannery, in better days.

With casual nods, as if they saw me here everyday, the men said good morning. One of them offered the joint, but I just thanked him and held up my hand. I could see *Cormorant* down there at the harbor, still side-tied to Catarino's panga. Catarino had said they were going to finish filleting the sharks today, and I saw he and Esteban on the far side of the harbor, out by the end of the stone quay, loading plastic crates into the back of the van. I wished the men a good day, and kept on, ducking the palm fronds where the path continued past the other side of the building, back up to downtown.

The row of shops was interesting, as the town was not built strictly in concrete and block like many other places I had seen in Baja. Most of the structures here were of wood, with balconies over the ground-level shops. One of the places above was empty, with windows all around, and I imagined setting up an office there, a place with a view of the sheltered little harbor and the craggy rocks of the island. But I realized, as soon as that thought had come, that the impulse came more because I wanted a place of my own in the world than because I wanted to stay in *this* place in the world.

The day was not as far along as I had supposed. The Port Captain's office was still closed, and when I arrived at the *telegrafo*, the kids at the school next door were just doing their morning flag salute, standing in ranks with military caps on and marching in goosestep as the national anthem of Mexico droned out from speakers on the flagpole. Standing in line at the *telegrafo* behind a bent and gnarled old ranchero, I waited my turn. The young women working the counter were heavily made up, their luxuriant hairstyles spilling over their shoulders in what looked like heavily lacquered curls, their long fingernails clacking on the plastic keys of their machines. The old man seemed to come to them from another era, perhaps seeking trade with a sack of maize.

I handed one of the women my credit card and asked if I could get cash with it. She seemed unsure, and after some consultation with her colleague, agreed to give it a try, and to my surprise, I was able to get a couple of hundred dollars in pesos. Walking back down the steep hill I came into town on the opposite end, passing the fishing *cooperativo* office where about 25 men milled around in the driveway. I remembered what Diego had told me the other afternoon – that he and his father-in-law, Catarino, and Esteban, worked independently – "*independiente*," he said with pride.

I guessed the population of the town was about 2,000. The houses, painted in oranges and yellows and a few in pink, stood ramshackle on the hillsides overlooking the little downtown shops and the little harbor around which the town was built. There seemed a self-sufficient pride to this place that had been carved out of the side of an otherwise forbidding hunk of rock in the wind-scoured sea, and many of the cars and trucks on the island had stickers on them that read "*Nativo* – Isla Cedros."

I stopped at the *mercado* and bought a few pounds of *carne asada* and a two-liter bottle of Coke to bring back to the house. Across the street I noticed the *panadería,* and a *tortillería* just down from there, and decided that I would stop at those places too. A toddler stood grasping the top bar of a crib in the corner of the *panadería*, just inside the screen door. A glass case held *bolillos* and custard-filled pastries and large sugar cookies, some with rainbow sprinkles on them. A TV with a fuzzy picture was mounted high on a shelf above the crib, opposite the glass case. The baby and I looked at each other, both unsure, it seemed, of what to do.

But a cheerful woman emerged from the back and asked what
I wanted and then disappeared into the back again to get fresh
bolillos, she told me, just out of the oven. I bought a dozen of
those, and six rainbow-sprinkle cookies, four sugar donuts,
and two custard-filled pastries as well.

   With my double plastic bag of *carne asada*, the big bottle
of Coke, and now these items in another doubled plastic bag, I

was over-laden with goods and wrapping and clearly back into modern life.

"*Estoy aquí con el barquito, allá, en el puerto,*" – I'm here on a little boat down in the harbor – I told the woman as I paid, feeling the need to explain my presence somehow.

"*Muy bien,*" she said, nodding approvingly, "*bienvenidos.*"

A few doors down, at the *tortillería*, I bought a dozen flour tortillas and a dozen corn tortillas, and the lady behind the counter, with thick glasses that magnified her eyes enormously, asked if I was *el marinero*. I told her that I was, and she made the sign of the cross and said, "*Que te vaya bien,*" and again I imagined an unseen realm – a battle of spirit forces.

———————▶

I lifted the latch on the kitchen door, and put the Coke and *carne asada* in the refrigerator, which seemed only slightly cool but hummed as if some motor were working down in its guts. The baked goods and tortillas I left on the counter and, as I had at Aurelio's, helped myself to the kettle and lit a burner to make another, late morning cup of coffee.

As the water heated, I went down to the storeroom (Catarino had given me a key), and got my next book to start reading – Seamus Heaney's translation of *Beowulf.* Catarino and Esteban had plastic crates filled with the previous day's filleting and packages of rock salt stacked alongside. They laid the pearl-colored fillets like flat pasta in a lasagna, salting each layer and then stacking the next until the crate was full.

Catarino said, *"muy bien,"* nodding his head and gesturing to the size of the catch.

"Si," I told him, *"mucho pescado."*

"Pescado, no, tiburón" – shark.

"Si, tiburón," I said and asked if it was good to eat.

"Muy sabroso," – delicious – Catarino said.

Standing there with my book in my hand, the men working productively on something that might do someone some good, I felt again the uneasy feeling that had been with me from my first morning here. I stood there a moment longer, but Catarino and Esteban were fully engaged in the layering and salting, so I turned and went back up to the kitchen for my coffee.

I took a chair from the dinning room and set it in the yard under the pepper tree with a view of the small beach and the wide sweep of the water, and ate one of the custard pastries. As I ate the last bite, I went back inside to get one of the donuts and a cookie too. When I sat down again, Obama came and begged a piece of cookie and then curled at my feet.

Beowulf was part of the reading list I had put together because I thought its element of the hero's journey would be appropriate to my undertaking. But there was nothing that I was trying to accomplish necessarily on this "quest," except to get a sense of the coast. I was certainly gaining that, but here, so far offshore with so far still to go, I could not shake the exhaustion that dogged me. I felt unequal to the task at hand. Heaney's heroes would have nothing to do with the likes of me:

"... *Shield Sheafson, scourge of many tribes,*
A wrecker of mead-benches, rampaging among foes.
This terror of the hall-troops had come far.
A foundling to start with, he would flourish later on
As his powers waxed and his worth was proved.
In the end each clan on the outlying coasts
Beyond the whale-road had to yield to him
And begin to pay tribute. That was one good king."

I, on the other hand, just wanted another pastry.

The men's work shamed me finally into doing something, and so I went back down to the storeroom to retrieve my sketchbook. I stopped to ask them if I could help, well knowing that they had their system down and that I wouldn't be needed. I walked back downtown, which was closing now for siesta, and looked for an angle from which to compose a sketch of the small cathedral. On the far end of the block, I passed one of the wood buildings that I liked, and across the narrow street on the opposite corner, I found my angle and sat on the sidewalk and began drawing.

A small boy appeared by my side, watching my progress intently. "*¿Tú eres artista?*" Are you an artist, he asked, and I allowed that I was, just for the sake of conversation. But he grew tired of watching me draw and erase the lines, trying to get the scale right, and left after a few minutes.

A police car cruised up and stopped in front of me. I turned my notebook to face the officers, and inspired by my little visitor, I explained that I was an "*artista.*" I then mentioned that I was staying with the Burjez family, which seemed to be good enough, and the fellows nodded gravely and continued on, driving very slowly down the empty street.

It took a while to get the row of shops and the two towers of the cathedral, with the ridgeline in back and the houses terracing up the slope, in the right proportion. But when I had the basic sketch, I decided I would make a watercolor as a small gift for the Burjez family.

There was a store in the row of shops with record albums, movie posters, and knick-knacks, and it was the only place still open through the middle part of the day. When I entered, the fellow behind the counter smoothed the sides of his well-oiled hair, leaving the tight curls on top untouched. He wore cream-colored slacks and a polyester shirt, unbuttoned to his sternum, with a great flaring collar. The gold chain around his neck held a unicorn in the nest of his chest hair.

I asked him if he had a frame that would fit the sketch I had done and held my drawing up for size.

"*Es muy beuno, su trabajo,*" – your work is good – he said approvingly. "*¿De dónde eres?*" – where are you from – he asked, leaving the question of the frame aside for the moment.

"San Clemente," I said, "California."

He knew San Clemente; he had family near there, in Santa Ana. His face had a grey pallor, which put his black-dyed mustache and goatee in stark relief under a sharp and hooked nose. He was perhaps 45 or 50 years old.

I told him that I had arrived a few days before in my boat. He said yes, he thought that I was "*el marinero,*" adding that I looked like a *marinero,* in the same approving tone he used for my sketch.

He then searched around the shop, looking under the glass cases with cheap jewelry, and into a back room, emerging finally with a large, dust-covered frame that would have suited the picture of a family patriarch but would not serve for my little sketch.

As diplomatically as I could, since he seemed so eager to please, I said that I thought it was a little too big, and that I could find a frame elsewhere. He said no, I would not find anything in this town, with a disapproving tone. *"No hay artistas aquí, como usted"* – there are no artists here like you.

The combination of his coiffed hair and the almost breathless way he spoke – he seemed to tremble slightly – made me wonder how lonely this place of tough fishermen might be. He urged me to come back the next day, or, if I would prefer, I could come to his house that evening; either way, he said, he had something that would be perfect.

I thanked him for his help and explained that I had dinner plans with the Burjez family but that I could stop by the shop the following day to see if the frame he said he had would work.

A group of schoolgirls walked by just then, and seeing me in the shop, let out squeals of delight, taunting *"¡Ooooh, Arturo!"* and making kissing motions to us.

It was a festive mood back at the Burjez residence that night – both Angelita and Paula in the kitchen chopping and cooking away, Catarino and Diego sitting at the dinning room table, watching little Diego pushing a toy truck across the floor. I had slept through the later part of the afternoon, after returning from downtown, and then unpacked my bags in the storeroom to take stock of my possessions. I took the dogs down to the beach in front of the house at dusk and threw a stick for them, and when I entered the main house on the hill, the family greeted me warmly, chatting away about what a surprise it was to find the *carne asada* in the fridge. Diego lifted a glass of Coke in a toast, and I was glad I had gotten those things.

When we sat down to eat – again just the men at the table, the women and the toddler in the living room – I understood Angelita say to Catarino, "You should catch gringos in your nets more often," as she put a platter full of sizzling asada on the table. Again the fresh pico de gallo, and a great stack of corn tortillas covered with a napkin in a basket, and a steaming bowl of pinto beans, and another of steamed zucchini.

As we served out spoonfuls of meat and beans and vegetables, Catarino told me that they had a small farm up above the town, "*en el arroyo.*"

I was hungry, unable to satiate my desire for calories, and I tried to eat with some restraint, but I ate steadily, tearing pieces of tortilla and filling them with the meat and a dollop of pico de gallo and of beans. Catrino and Diego ate as heartily as I did, and we didn't talk at first, except for me to express how good everything was between rapid bites. But when I had eaten three tortillas or so and many chopped pieces of asada, I asked about the little farm, not knowing the word for "spring," but asking if the site had water.

"*Sí, todo el año,*" – all year – Catarino said, and then explained that Angelita's father had bought the land 70 years before and told me about the trees – kumquats, avocado, mango – they had up there. *"Muchos vegetales,"* he continued, with obvious pleasure, indicating that the zucchinis had come from there by jutting his chin at the bowl as he spoke. *"Y cilantro, y cebollas también"* – cilantro and onions as well.

It sounded so good to me – an ideal really – family land, passed from generation to generation, rooting them to their place, sustaining them. Seafaring gave me the feeling of the old ways, but a garden plot would work the same way – both activities connecting with the most elemental practices.

Diego asked where I had gone in the afternoon, and I told him about looking around downtown to do some pencil sketching and that I had stopped at the curio store and met the fellow with the slacks and gold chain. Angelita and Paula were clearing our plates from the table, and Diego asked me what I thought of the man.

Feigning oblivion, I said that he had been *"muy simpático"* – very nice. Paula turned to me, very earnest and concerned, and asked if I knew what he was. I replied that yes, I knew he was a very friendly man and then, really laying on the naiveté, I added that he had even invited me over to his place.

Diego laughed out loud and Catarino chuckled, but Paula seemed worried. Her mom shook her head disapprovingly at our boys' antics, while little Dieguito on the floor shrieked with delight at our laughs.

The women ate as they brought us coffee, putting together plates of food for themselves while organizing the cups, sugar, and milk. As we drank the coffee and ate some of the cookies I had brought, they sat down beside their men at the table. They would not hear of me offering to do the dishes, and the clean-up seemed to happen as seamlessly as the cooking and the coffees had. We then moved to the living room and watched TV together: two *telenovelas* that ran back to back, with lots of furious yelling between ex-lovers and glowering oaths from handsome men in business suits. I loved it – loved being with them that night, safe in a house, watching TV.

And I didn't feel out of place – at least not for the moment.

Morning came on clear with a smooth sea stretching out, and I went up to the house just as the men were sitting down to breakfast. Angelita and Paula worked their usual choreography of coffee, eggs, tortillas, and refried beans so that each of us had a full plate set before us at the same time. Catarino curled his forearm before his plate, and ate huge forks-full of eggs and beans, much of which landed on his chin, and he grunted towards me to pass the basket of tortillas.

I asked Diego what he planned to do that day, and he looked at me blankly for a moment and then asked, "*¿Necesitas ayuda?*"

No, I didn't need any help, I replied. Not knowing how to say that I was just making conversation, I went on to tell him that I was heading down to the harbor to check on my boat and then to the Port Captain's office to get the forecast and plan for when I might sail onward.

Where are you trying to go? Catarino asked me in his way of talking that went too fast for me to follow. After a couple

of tries, I understood him and replied that I was heading for
Bahía Magdalena.

"You want to go to Bahía Magdalena?" he asked, but it
wasn't a question. "Here's what you do: Leave your boat here,
catch the ferry to Guerrero Negro, and then get the bus the
rest of the way."

I nodded, and then asked him in a slightly joking tone,
"*¿Nunca, va usted al mar en un barco como mi barco?*" – never,
would you go to sea in a boat like mine?

But he just stared at me, shaking his head, not seeing any
humor: "*¡Nunca!*"

He had captained large and small fishing boats on the
island, working these waters for the past 40 years. So,
although I found him a bit gruff and overly dramatic, I
couldn't ignore his opinions out of hand.

After breakfast, I grabbed my knapsack with my
sketchbook and watercolors, and walked down to the harbor
to check on my good girl, *Cormorant*. Still side-tied to the
Burjez panga, with the marine canvas pulled over, nothing
looked to have been disturbed in the past day and night. One
of the "gypsies" I had seen the other day on the patio in the
cannery ruins stood on the wharf, about 50 feet across the
water, and we waved to one another.

I pulled the boats to me by the thick rope and stepped
aboard the panga as the slack tightened and drew us back
out to the mooring can. Rolling back the canvas, I found
everything as I had left it: The lines were in disarray on the
floorboards, the sails crunched up and shoved under the yard,
and the halyard a tangled mess as well.

Slowly, with the morning sun on my shoulders, I put the lines to rights, folded the mainsail to the yard more neatly, and then triced the works vertically to the main mast to clear the interior space. When I had made everything neater, I pulled the water bottles out from their spot alongside the daggerboard case where I held them tight with bicycle inner tubes, and set these in the panga. I brought the canvas back over, tucking it in tight around the sternpost, and tied the cover down around the base of the main mast.

I carried the water bottles, both half-empty, back to the storeroom with my other gear. Catarino and the family were just getting into the van when I arrived, and he motioned for me to come. They were off to the farm, and he asked if I wanted to go with them. With my knapsack still on, I got in the van and we drove off, all together, the family and their odd visitor. In my few days there, I already knew the layout of the little town: the *panaderia*, the *cooperativo*, the old fellow who sat on a straight-backed wooden chair on the sidewalk at the corner, a cane between his knobby knees, with his hands resting on top, and a continuous, languid gaze as if he were in a realm of his own visions.

Dirt streets cut perpendicularly from the strip of asphalt that wound upward from the basin where the town sat and continued on as a highway on top of a plateau. Smaller tracks cut away from the road on either side, up parched and trash-strewn arroyos. We passed the park that looked like a prison-yard and the school surrounded in chain link with a similar aesthetic. Soon we came to another nondescript cut out in the road and turned onto a dirt track with more refuse dumped in the sharp, dry cactus brush on either side.

The walls of a sandstone canyon came right down to the track now, and after a long curve, the path widened again to another arroyo with a fenced-off area of tin sheeting nailed to posts. Once inside the gate the dryness of the desert was replaced by a small grove of trees, not particularly tall, but coming on with budding new growth. The avocado and mango trees held bigger leaves and made a shady nook in the corner of the property. Diego beckoned me to follow him a couple of hundred yards up the sloping ground to the spigot. The fencing contained the whole plot with a solid perimeter, eight-feet high, which Diego said kept the deer out, although I could not imagine deer on such dry ground. As if reading my thoughts, he said, *"Más arriba, en las montañas"* – higher up in the mountains.

He lifted a sheet of plywood laid over a pit and reached in to turn a spigot, and water, clear and strong, gushed from a hose and ran down the slope in a sheet like a mini flash flood, soaking beds of carrots, onions, and cilantro. Letting the water run, Diego walked down to where Paula and the boy stood near a pomegranate tree. Angelita bent to weed a section of the bed, and Catarino stood under the cumquat tree.

He reached up and grabbed a piece of fruit. *"¡Eh!"* he grunted at me, held it up, and took a bite, juice running down his chin.

I asked if they could drop me at the Port Captain's on the way back into town, and there I checked the weather on the Internet, only to find light winds forecast for two days out, then gaining strength after that to gale force. Thanking the woman who worked there, I left to walk back to town along the steep trails that led down from the cemetery nearby.

Back on the street with the shops now, I turned to a café that I had noticed the day before. Here, two ladies talked behind a counter in an otherwise empty place. There were about 10 plastic tables, set with vinyl tablecloths and chairs on each side as if waiting for a rush of customers that did not seem likely to come. The place was especially clean; a waxed floor gleamed, and a tropical mural covered the walls. Cakes and a sandwich menu stood behind the counter. Ordering a coffee and a piece of the pineapple cake under a glass cover, I pulled my sketchbook and paints out of my knapsack to ask if I could sit awhile and work on my watercolor. The lady who owned the place said no problem and, happily, I sat down, ate my cake, and then got water in a bottle for the watercolors and started in on the painting.

By the time I had the sky and the buildings all painted in, the lady was closing for siesta but told me I could come back later if I liked, so I packed my supplies and made my way back to the Burjez house, not having the energy for the curio shop and the frame that may or may not have fit the painting. Crossing the main street, a fat man in a blue uniform pursued me, wanting my passport. I didn't have it with me, I told him.

I was a guest of the Burjez family, I added, as if I were under their protection. I had also checked in with the port captain's I pointed out. None of this seemed to matter to him – officious with patches sewn on the shoulders of his shirt and tinted sunglasses to complete his outfit.

A few teenagers watched this exchange impassively from the sidewalk. He needed to see the passport, he said again, and I repeated that I did not have it, but he was unwilling to walk the quarter-mile to the Burjez place and told me that I should have it next time I came into town.

Walking on, I passed the kids on the sidewalk, but they took no more interest in me and were already back to their own conversations. A mural on a wall just a little farther on urged the youth of the island to turn away from drug use. *La Virgin* looked over wasted forms sticking needles in their arms.

Catarino, Esteban, and Diego were hanging the fillets they had salted the previous day. Using clothes pins, they attached the pieces like socks on lines stretched across the yard to dry in the sun. The fillets would cure on the line for three days, before they stacked the dried pieces in boxes to sell around the neighborhood. Word had clearly gotten out, because a steady stream of people began showing up at their place, negotiating a few pieces here and there. Sr. Burjez also packed a box for a particular family, and it seemed I was getting a glimpse of the political alliances that ran through the small community.

As I sat writing in my journal that afternoon, Paula asked me if I was OK. The question made me uncomfortable, because I was most certainly not OK. I felt worn out and stupid, and constantly wanted to apologize for making myself so dependent upon the Burjez family. And although this was supposed to be a wilderness surfing adventure, I was whiling away the days eating pastries and drinking Nescafé, too exhausted to continue. And the fact that it seemed outwardly noticeable that I was not OK worried me too. I told her that I was fine, of course, and excused myself to find seclusion in the storehouse below.

But, no, I was definitely not OK. I was worried – worried about foisting myself upon the Burjez family, worried about how far I still had to go and the long stretches of open beach on the coast south of Punta Abreojos with no sheltered coves to land in, worried about keeping myself supplied, and worried about how weak and listless I felt.

On Sunday I went to mass with Catarino and Angelita, and afterwards, standing in the courtyard, Catarino introduced me to the priest, telling him of my sailing journey. The priest made the sign of the cross before me and said, "*Cuidado,*" – careful – and I felt guilty again just for being there. Catarino, now that he had the priest in front of him, said that he and Angelita had been married for 35 years. She nodded in sagely agreement, and Catarino then asked the priest if it was not true what he said.

The priest said, "*Por supuesto,*" – of course – with what seemed a slightly pained smile, and looked over his shoulder as if seeking somewhere else to be. He turned back to Catarino, and said, "*OK, me voy,*" and turned again to talk to another parishioner. We had sweet champurrado drinks in the vestry, and I couldn't take my eyes off the young woman who served them, she was so beautiful. For a moment I thought that she might be my destiny. I tried to talk with her, but she only smiled and looked down, the others there looking at me like I was a villain.

Catarino informed me afterward that she was becoming a nun.

———————————◆———————————

The next day, Monday, I returned to the café and finished the watercolor, and then went back to the curio shop for the frame. Arturo stood up when I entered his shop and walked over to the counter where I stood and asked me what had happened, why had I not come the next day like I said I would? He looked flustered and a little hurt. I told him that I was helping the Burjez family, but he waved his hand as if shooing flies and told me that he had the frame, turning to walk back to his desk with exaggerated movements in each step.

I brought the painting out and he took it from me, fitting it into the frame and taping the back in place. It was gold-colored and fit perfectly. It was just the thing, and I told him so, and asked him how much, but he would not take any money.

I thanked him, and noticed a fine sheen of sweat across his brow and that he was trembling again, like he had before. I told him that I was leaving the next day, as I planned to get supplies that afternoon, and he nodded his head seriously. I offered my hand and he took it, and we shook. And then he gave me a business card with his phone number, for when I come back to Cedros, he told me. I thanked him again for the frame and went to get supplies at the Super-mini Mercado down the street.

At the store I bought the supplies I thought would carry me – more rice, yams, onions, beans, Nescafé, and bullion cubes. I refilled the water at a purified tap the community used in the neighborhood, and staged my gear down in the storeroom by the side of my cot. Beowulf had slain the dragon and was a renowned king, and I still had *Moby Dick* to wade into, and the Fagles's translation of *The Odyssey* as well. I wrapped the framed watercolor in a paper sack and taped the flaps in place with duct tape that I had in my repair kit, and went up to the house to present this to the Burjez clan as some small token. They were immensely pleased and put it in a cabinet alongside the pictures from Paula and Diego's wedding.

I thanked them for everything and told them that I was setting off again in the morning.

CHAPTER TEN

INFLUENCED BY REASON

A breeze wafted down from the bleak hills. I had spent the morning loading *Cormorant* and organizing my gear, and the Burjez family came down to the quay to see me off. Now I stood with the tiller in my hand waving goodbye to them, the sky grey and the ocean blue-grey before me as I ghosted south from the harbor. Nondescript bluffs stood behind cobblestone beaches – the bleak island slipping by.

About three miles down the coast I passed the large, industrial salt facility and from there reached for the end of the island. The breeze picked up and I readied myself for sailing out into the deep, open water once again. *Cormorant* heeled in the wind and should have been drawing forward, but she seemed held back, as if snagged by kelp or a line. I leaned over the rail to inspect the rudder and then far over the starboard side to look down at the tip of the daggerboard but saw nothing there. About a quarter-mile offshore, I should have been well into the breeze, but *Cormorant* held fast as if treading water.

I tried to fall off – that is, let the boat turn away from the breeze in the hopes of gaining momentum downwind before coming around again to reach for the open water. But I only ended up a several hundred yards farther offshore, still in line with the rocks at the bottom of the island. The breeze lightened up slightly, and I began loosing ground – the rocks that I had been using as my markers moving away from me as I drifted backwards. I wallowed here for an hour or so, steadily pulled back, and realized that I could not shake the island. Finally, the day getting late, I turned back for the harbor, carried swiftly on the north-running current.

Tying *Cormorant* to the mooring buoy, I walked back to the Burjez home. They welcomed me of course and didn't seem surprised to see me. Catarino handed me the keys to the storeroom, and I walked down to set up the cot again. Angelita said she would have dinner ready in an hour or so. I turned the light on and spread the chart out before me on the floor next to my cot, the grey evening darkening early. The crossing to Natividad should only take a few hours, but the current that had given me such trouble when I first reached the island still held me.

Cormorant was a sprung shell, a mere leaf on the water, and though she was nimble in the surf and on the high seas, she could not generate enough forward drive to counter any sort of head-on resistance, which was precisely why I had thought to come out here in the first place.

Natividad would have waves, and I was missing surfing, but I was also tired – still so tired. From there, on the chart and in the sailing guides, I saw Bahía de Tortugas – only another half-day's sail on from Natividad by the looks of it – where I could resupply. The coast there looked to be steep cliffs with coves where I imagined I could anchor. Next would come the town of Bahía Asunción, with some off-lying islands and a long sweep of open beach before the notoriously wind-ravaged point at Abreojos.

South of there would be San Ignacio, one of the whale-birthing inlets. But with these strange currents off Cedros, where the bottom shoaled up between here and Natividad, I could only imagine the force of the water running in and out of the bay at San Ignacio during the shifts of the tide. And from Abreojos it was a long haul, potentially three days at the rate *Cormorant* sometimes moved, before the points at Scorpion Bay. Three days along open desert beach, and after the state I had gotten myself to in crossing to Cedros, I was inclined to be more cautious about long-distance runs.

It was time to head up for dinner, but I kept turning it over in my mind – the sheer distances and the hours of exposure between points of shelter.

I tried again to depart the next day, and again I met that sweeping current and was turned back. The boat hit a line in the sea it seemed, which swung the bow over hard, and even with the stronger breeze for this second attempt, *Cormorant* could only lift and dive, but not make any forward progress. And falling off to run with the current only put us on a course for the mainland and, I feared, well inside the hook at Punta Eugenia, which would have defeated the point of making the harrowing crossing to get out here. Again I hung it up after a few hours on the water, the boat simply not finding any bite in the water, no way to slip into the line to take me where I wanted to go.

Catarino and Angelita were heading down to the salt works co-op market on the south end of the island the next day, and they invited me to accompany them. We drove to an overlook on the southern-most tip of Cedros, with Isla Natividad and the point at Punta Eugenia visible out across the water, and what I saw there stopped me completely. A massive current churned at the bottom of the island – huge swaths of water sweeping in slow-moving whirlpools with weird lines across the surface, as if the ocean were being sucked in upon itself.

The charts show the bottom shoaling up to 70 fathoms between Cedros and Natividad from the virtual chasm of open ocean beyond, and it seemed the entire Pacific was funneling through here, and it looked like it would swallow a vessel whole. On top of that, a hard northwesterly drove whitecaps tearing over the sea. It was the first week of March, and I remembered what Yvon Chouinard had said to me when I told him the timeframe for my trip: He pointed out that the winds on this part of the coast get really bad in the spring. This seemed to be the first real clearing blow of the season. To put *Cormorant* on that water would be to throw her to the fate of forces beyond her capabilities.

The voice came to me then, the same quiet-but-insistent voice that first told me that I could do this trip, the voice that had said, *build the boat*, and the voice that said, *do this expedition*.

I heard it again now, and this time it was saying, *enough*.

I was depleted – physically, emotionally, and spiritually. With the powerful currents and the winds and isolation ahead, I had lost the will to push on, alone, across this desert sea. Was I defeated? I suppose in the sense that I would not continue on to Mag Bay, not make Abreojos and Scorpion Bay – which were two places I was particularly looking forward to – I was defeated, yes. But better to be defeated safely on dry land than to press my luck in the driving gales of spring. Exhausted as I had become, I had little in the way of reserve energy to see me through any prolonged trials.

———————————————➤

Walking through town that afternoon, wondering what I was going to do now that I had effectively called a halt to my journey, I stopped in at the café where the ladies sold a cup of Nescafé for six pesos. As I doctored my cup, a fellow with a cell phone on his belt and a gold bracelet and a thick mustache was also having coffee. We said *buenas tardes* to one another and stepped out onto the sidewalk with our Styrofoam cups. I mentioned that I had been to the bottom of the island and that the currents there looked bad.

"*Si*," the man said, "*el mar aquí es muy peligroso*" – the ocean here is very dangerous. He asked, "*¿Está su barquito, allá en el puerto?*" – it is your little boat there in the harbor? Although like everyone else in the village, he must have known that the "little boat" was mine.

"*Sí, soy el hombre con el barco*," I told him, and then added that with the spring gales coming on, I thought I would haul my boat to the Burjez family yard. Then I would come back in early summer to continue my journey to Bahía Magdalena – at least that was the plan I was starting to formulate.

The *Marie Carmen* was coming in from Ensenada in a few days, the man said. Why didn't I just put my boat on board when she went back? She was a supply ship, after all, he told me. I thanked him for his advice, and asked how I could arrange it. Go down to the *cooperativo* office, he told me, and ask to speak with the *jefe* – tell them Tony sent me. We shook hands and I thanked him again, finished my coffee in a gulp, and threw the cup in the trash.

At the *cooperativo* I walked through the group of young men who hung around in front, nodding and saying hello to them, and into a lobby with a marble floor and mirrored wall behind a black, shiny counter. A heavily made-up secretary listened to me try and explain my situation – that I wanted to speak with the boss and that Tony had sent me – and finally held up her hand and nodded. *"Bueno,"* she said, *"siéntate,"* and motioned for me to take a seat in the lobby.

While not gleaming like an executive office in downtown Los Angeles, compared to the dirt street out front or the bakery across the street with the filthy old dog asleep by the door, this place exuded a kind of professional air, despite the thick dust on the plastic plants and the wadded-up papers discarded on the marble floor. A few of the hangers-on slouched in the lobby chairs, and like many people on the island, they seemed to have been waiting for a long time.

With lightning efficiency compared to what I was anticipating, the receptionist called for me to go upstairs after about 10 minutes, and there I sat down with the big boss and explained my situation. Within another 10 minutes it was all arranged. I was shaking hands and thanking him just as Tony walked in.

Although the exact date and time of the ship's arrival remained unknown, what was sure was that the ship was coming within the next few days. And within a few days after that, it would be on its way again back to Ensenada. *Cormorant* would have a place on the afterdeck, hoisted from the harbor with the ship's loading crane. The shipping fee would be forty dollars, payable when I retrieved my vessel from the *cooperativo* warehouse in Ensenada.

Next I went to the island air service office and booked a flight to Ensenada for a few days hence.

My money was all gone after I bought the plane ticket. Not that I had had a bundle of it to start with, but now I was down to twenty-three dollars to my name. I thought of continuing to camp aboard *Cormorant* once I returned – lurking from harbor to harbor and anchoring in various coves along the Southern California coast. But *Cormorant* is only a lifeboat in design, and I thought about the physical and mental shape that Shackleton and his men were in after their ordeal. My Baja trip was nothing like the extraordinary events of the *Endurance* expedition, except that the challenge of sea travel by small, open boat comes down to being able to counter the factors of perpetual damp, exposure to the elements, and carrying sufficient food and water.

This was the crucial split, the line I reached in this mode of adventuring. I could not continue alone. I could not live outside with only a thin sheet of canvas over my head. I needed a roof, I needed to write and shape surfboards. I needed to return to life in a community.

But I got what I had come for: solitude, wilderness surfing, full nature immersion. It came at the cost of succumbing, ultimately, to the effects of prolonged exposure – the relentless sun, the parching salt air, and the problem of getting proper nutrition and rest. I found my limit, physically and emotionally, in this mode of travel. Once back, after retrieving *Cormorant* in Ensenada and finding another studio apartment in San Clemente (paying for it from a line of credit and setting up another cycle of indebtedness), I spent weeks recovering.

Listless back in San Clemente, I slept late into the morning and napped again in the afternoon. I had weaned myself off the Prozac and though I felt the old mental fog threatening, I could not bring myself to get back on the medication; it wasn't as if everything was sparkling and nice when I was on the pills anyway. It runs deep, whatever this demon is in our minds. Mark Twain said that the Irish have ghosts on their shoulders, and I guess he was right. But I also recognized that I was just really, really tired, and mainly what I needed was to rest.

Looking back, I think had I truly wanted to continue, I could have slid around the corner of the island close in, under oars – possibly running with a falling tide – and worked my way up the coast a couple of miles. From there, on the outside, or the west coast of Isla Cedros, I could have then jumped into the current from "farther up-stream," and made my way across the channel, even if I was swept eastward for a time. But in view of my exhaustion, I made the prudent choice.

My concerns about the effect of the digitized age were not assuaged by two months on the open coast, nor did I tap into "blood memory" in the way I thought that I would. The electric whirring and fuel-driven roar of this new world that we have been born into – seductive in its immediacy – still pushes me to seek repose in the quiet of the wind and surf breaking upon forgotten shores. And when I remember *Cormorant* pulling to a breeze, the angle of the hull rolled over to the blow, I think that perhaps I had been tapping "blood memory" all along – ever since that first evening sail in San Clemente. Navigating and anticipating, all of this running with the sea, stretched back to Odysseus and the psalmist, too, who wrote: "They that

go down to the sea in ships, that do business in great waters;
These see the works of the Lord, and his wonders in the deep."

Once I had physically recovered in the spring, I picked up
where I had left off in my surfboard shaping, experimenting
with keel fin designs that my friend, Richard Kenvin (a
formidable presence from the notorious surfing grounds of
La Jolla), had resurrected from Bob Simmons' work of the
late 1940s to early 1950s. Kenvin had proven the dual-keeled,
"modified displacement hull" boards' validity in serious reef
surf, and most intriguing to me was the idea of incorporating
the convex bottom of the *Californio* (the "modified
displacement hull") into a shorter board, with keels set out
by the edges of a wide tail-section that would provide a lot of
planing surface.

   I shaped a 6'2" with this concept in mind, and hand-foiled
a set of fins out of scrap marine ply left over from building
Cormorant. The finished craft came out with something of the
Bob Simmons original in its low-tech/high-concept design
aesthetic, and on good, clean waves at Trestles, I discovered
that the board had all of the qualities I was seeking – quick
acceleration while holding momentum down the line, and,
most gratifyingly, a solid, driving arc through tight turns in
the pocket.

Those few weeks of rest and one new surfboard set me on a
better track. I got some writing work at *Surfer* and *The Journal*
and got my cash flow up again. Dad and I got together at our
favorite Mexican place in San Pedro, where he lives, and over
a couple of beers and enchilada plates, he asked me what I was
going to do next. "I'm really glad you're back," he added, "that
Mexico gives me a bad feeling."

I nodded, and told him that I knew it gave him a bad
feeling – not bothering to remind him, yet again, how
singularly wonderful the fishermen and their families had
been to me all the way along.

Tired of living alone, and now that I wasn't in an office
all day, I wanted a dog. Dad, of course, thought that was a
questionable move, he being a man who refuses to get an
answering machine for the complication it might bring to
his life.

I ended up with more dog than I bargained for in the
young German Wirehaired Pointer named Rio. He was a
rescue, found wandering in Concord, near Berkeley, and the
Wirehaired Pointer Club had him up for adoption on their
website. Although he is a sweetheart, he also runs like a
racehorse (and needs to, twice a day), swims like a seal, and
kills chickens any chance he gets.

When I drove up to get Rio in Santa Rosa, I arranged
to stay with a friend for a few days in Bolinas. I also towed
Cormorant up and made repairs and reblacked the hull, and
in those days I awoke at dawn with my new friend and we
ran the endless beach north of town. With the repairs and the
painting done, we went sailing on Tomales Bay.

Rio, it turns out, is a field dog, not a boat dog. He stands as high as he can get on the forward partner beam with his paws on the rail, leaning outboard and falling off so regularly that I now tether him when we sail together. Still, I chose his breed because of their supposed versatility and intelligence. While the latter quality is debatable in Rio's case, he is capable of long hours in arduous conditions, which he has proven many times over. And, truth-be-told, he is actually pretty smart: Recently, on a long hike to surf a remote point, we got separated and I continued on, hoping to find him later. I tied my sweaty T-shirt to a piece of driftwood and propped this with beach-stones in front of where I left my gear, with the hope the wind would take my scent down the beach towards where I had last seen him. I went surfing and stayed in the water until sunset, and when I came in, there was my good friend, waiting for me on the sand.

I still wanted to see Mag Bay, explore the mangroves, and surf the point on the outside, so I invited my old friend Kristen Anthony to join Rio and I, and we hit the road. We drove 800 miles, sailed across the inner bay and spent a week surfing the point, and then came home just as the desert dirt, the saltwater crust, and the burning sun began to get the best of us. This, I realized, was the highest and best use of my craft: trailer to the cruising grounds and take advantage of the lightweight yet seaworthy vessel to get to distant shores and camp, fish, and ride waves. It was so easy, not another life, just a fun getaway.

Next, not yet satisfied that I had met *Cormorant*'s potential, I set my sights on Vancouver Island in September. But the trip was a fiasco, which I should have seen coming when I violated one of my earliest operating credos by building an outboard well and utilizing an engine to travel the 25 miles down an inlet to reach the open coast, rather than row or sail, as the boat was designed to do. Traveling with my friend, Eli Andersen, who is a big man, Rio, the motor, fuel for the motor, and all of our gear had the boat dangerously overloaded.

We managed all right, since the water was mostly smooth for the trip. But leaving *Cormorant* at anchor one night, just at the gateway to the region we had come to surf, the motor got hung up in kelp and the action of the tide was enough to tear the well apart, exposing a 12 by 14-inch hole in the hull. We spent the following days patching the bottom with a tarp, surf wax, and the floorboards – which we unscrewed and shaped to fit the curving strakes from the inside. We were stranded on a pretty little islet until we could get a tow to a lighthouse nearby, where the keeper and his wife gave us plywood for covering planks and roofing tar to smear over the works and get ourselves out of there.

I eventually sold the outboard motor and learned what a great medium wood is for boats, as I was able to fix the torn-open bottom by scarfing-in new planks for a repair that made *Cormorant* look freshly built. Another friend, Dillon Joyce, accompanied me on a return to the Channel Islands the following July, in 2010. We launched from Gaviota, 30 miles north of Santa Barbara, and crossed to the northeast corner of Santa Rosa on a lucky summer day of steady, 12-knot winds. We spent the next week surfing the beautiful reefs and sailing and rowing our way down the backside of the islands, jumping off finally for the harbor in Oxnard, where my mother met us with the wagon and the trailer.

These trips, the ones with a friend to share the experience, have been the best ones. Ultimately, I think the perfect use of a boat like *Cormorant* would be to build another just like her and assemble a crew of four like-minded sailor-surfers and pursue a series of wilderness surfing expeditions. With four people, there would be help in difficult situations and good times around the campfire.

We'll do this, my future shipmates and I, and continue, by sail and oar, to seek the magic of the natural world.

Back on Isla Cedros, a little more than a year earlier, I told the Burjez family that I had made my plans and offered to get some supplies for them, as I would have to cross the border to get my car and trailer in San Diego before returning to Ensenada for *Cormorant*. I had stored my rig behind the workshop of sailor-surfer-shaper-green technology innovator, Ned McMahon, who I met just briefly as I was preparing for my journey and who offered the space for my vehicle and trailer as a favor to me in support of the trip. Catarino wanted tree fertilizer in spikes and various fruit and vegetable seed packs for the garden, and Paula needed diapers for little Diego.

When I went to pick up *Cormorant*, I sent a box on the next ship back to the island with the supplies and some money in an envelope for little Diego's second birthday cake, because

Paula had been saving up for that by collecting cans whenever she went out. I think about the Burjez family, and Aurelio, the Rudys, and the boys at the camps farther south, and how generous and gracious that have all been to me. Catarino Burjez's son, who lives in California, called to wish me a happy New Year on behalf of his family. Arturo, from the curio shop, also calls every now and then to wish me well.

My friends at Punta San Carlos and Isla Cedros were such important connections, as they appeared, as if by fate, to help me on my journey – the larger journey of my life, it seems to me now. Can I do more than thank them? Perhaps the best I can do *is* only to thank them and take note of their graciousness towards a stranger washed up on their shore – take note, and act as they have acted.

The flight out from Isla Cedros was on a small, twin-prop plane that bounced and rumbled its way into the air just as the runway ran out at a cliff edge over the sea. Circling and climbing over the village, I saw all the little houses below, the downtown area and the church, and the way that the coast made a natural indentation there to provide some toehold from the wind and the brutal rock of the rest of the island. The plane reached altitude and began the slog north to Ensenada, with strong winds buffeting the fuselage and the plane making stomach-turning drops. The jagged peaks of Isla Cedros were only a thousand feet below us, the surface of the ocean much farther down, and secret little meadows and valleys, high up between twisted crags, stood with a lonely few trees and patches of grass where perhaps some spring bubbled to the surface.

Off to the northwest, the ocean was an endless series of whitecaps in the spring wind, the backside of the island gnashed at ceaselessly by the gale-driven waves. The open water reached far across to the mainland, which from this high up looked like it had been laid down on a chart. I could see the point and cove from where I had started the crossing, and I was astounded to see how far I had come. The distance was so vast that the coast, although clear in its main features of points and bays, was made up of mere shapes and shades for the hills and mountains and the contours of the land.

With all that water between, I could not picture a boat as small as *Cormorant* making the trip, and if I had seen this before I would never, *nunca*, have attempted it. The scale of the crossing, along with a sense of how vulnerable I had made myself, came to me like a realization of some moral shortcoming. There was enough ocean out there to disappear in completely, and never a trace be found.

I had made it, of course, as if guided the whole way. My grand experiment – my vision – showed me the limits, but more important, the great possibility of a small boat and the vast and changeable sea.

ACKNOWLEDGMENTS

I would like to thank the staff of the Mountain and Wilderness Writing Residency at The Banff Centre, particularly Marni Jackson and Tony Whittome, for their long hours of help as I developed the manuscript. Also Debbee and Steve Pezman of The Surfer's Journal for their generous support of my pursuits, as well as John Dutton at Patagonia for sitting shoulder-to-shoulder and going line-by-line with me on the final drafts. Thanks also to Professor Margaret Cohen for her feedback and encouragement, and to Sue Jett and Scott Hender for readings and comments. Thanks to my parents, Mary Jo Reilly and Bob Beamish, who have always understood my particular form of wanderlust. Finally, this book is for my wife, Natasha Elliott, and our daughter, Josephine Elliott-Beamish.